TO KEN.

CHRISTMAS 1999

FROM

IRENE

In the Shadow of the Hun

Edited by
Philip W. Steel

This book is dedicated to my mother

'Mrs Penny'

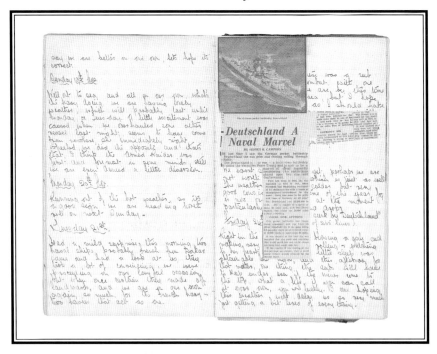

*Original pages of diaries, which includes news paper clippings of relivent Allies
and Nazi reported activities.
Four volumes, with a page size of 13" x 8"*

Copyright © 1999 Philip W. Steel

First Published in 1999
by Paul Cave Publications Ltd.

British library cataloguing in publication data.

Steel, Philip W.

In the Shadow of the Hun

ISBN 0 86146 093 6

Typeset & Printed by The Graphic Direct Group
Century House
Priestley Road
Basingstoke
Hampshire RG24 9RA

CONTENTS

Royal Tournament, 1923.   Royal Marine Artillery

Winners of Royal Marine and Inter Serveces Tug - of - War, 130 Stone

Gnr. A. Le Gassick   Gnr. H. Ballard   Gnr. D. C. Pinninger   Gnr. C. F. Dale   Gnr. W. George   Gnr. J. Brennan

Gnr. R. W. C. Durrant   Cpl. A. G. Crowther   Col. Comdt. Picton Phillips   Sgt. Major Charles Ellis   Bt. Major R. A. D. Brooks   Cpl. E. Philpott   Sgt. S. G. Tilley

Gnr. L. F. Penny

FORWARD
by Philip W. Steel

My fascination with the sea, and Union Castle Line in particular, goes back to my earliest childhood. My late father, Bert Whettingsteel worked for Harland and Wolff at Southampton, and was therefore involved with many of the Castle Boats. I recall vividly the nights when he used to come home and announce that he had a 'special pass' to show me a ship. The first one I remember was the 'Pendennis Castle,' which was the last Union Castle Ship built by Harland & Wolff (Belfast) in 1958. In 1960 'The Windsor Castle' came to Southampton for the first time, which of course was another treat, and in between times there were the older ships the 'Pretoria,' 'Carnarvon,' 'Athlone,' 'Edinburgh' and more besides, which were to me equally as fascinating.

My father died in 1975. The following year my mother met a widower Leslie Penny. Together they commiserated, and helped each other come to terms with their respective grief and eventually they fell in love and were married.

When I learnt that Leslie had worked for the Union Castle Line for 38 years we immediately had a rapport, and over the next 20 years spent many hours talking about his maritime experiences, not only with the Union Castle, but also as a Royal Marine during the Great War and as a crew member on a three masted Barquentine that sailed on a scientific expedition to the South Sea Islands in 1923.

In spite of spending nearly 50 years at sea he always considered himself to be a 'landlubber,' which is reflected in his journals. When at sea, he referred to his own ship's business as 'on the home front,' he also declined to ever use the 24-hour clock!

To keep such concise journals as he did, under the most difficult conditions and constraints of War, was indeed a work of art, not least of all for a man who left school at the age of fourteen and was expected to follow in father's footsteps on the farm without question. It became his ambition in later years to have his journals published, so that others who had similar Wartime experiences could identify and enjoy reading them.

From an editing point of view it has been an enormous task trying to decide what to leave or take out. The text is virtually unchanged, but unfortunately it has not been possible to include the numerous newspaper cuttings and telegraph reports that were to be found throughout the journals. I have included many photographs that he took in the first few years of the War and were found in his own album in my brother's loft! In the latter part of the War he found it impossible to get hold of photographic material, but through my own research I have been able to include some of the Union Castle Line ships of the time.

I hope I have done justice to the journals and that people will enjoy reading them.

Philip W. Steel

GOING ASHORE?

Be careful to whom you talk and what you say. On no account discuss the movements of ships, crews or cargoes. You are in a position of trust. The safety of men's lives—perhaps your own—may depend on how well you can keep what you know to yourself

ΕΧΕΤΕ ΑΔΕΙΑΝ ΕΞΟΔΟΥ;

Προσέξατε σὲ ποιὸν ὁμιλεῖτε καὶ τὶ τοῦ λέγετε. Ποτὲ μὴ συζητεῖτε τὰς κινήσεις πλοίων, πληρωμάτων ἤ φορτίων. Κατέχετε θέσεις ἐμπιστευτικὰς. Ἡ ἀσφάλεια τῆς ζωῆς πολλῶν—ἴσως καὶ τῆς ἰδικῆς σας ἀκόμη—ἐξαρτᾶται ἀπὸ τὸν τρόπον κατὰ τὸν ὁποῖον κρατᾶτε μυστικὰ ὅσα ξέρετε.

GAAT GE AAN LAND?

Wees voorzichtig met wat ge zegt en met wie ge praat. Spreek in geen geval over de beweging van schepen, bemanningen en vrachten. Ge bekleedt een positie van vertrouwen. De veiligheid van menschenlevens wellicht uw eigen—kan afhangen van de bewaring van de geheimen die ge kent.

LANDLOV?

Vær forsiktig med hvem du snakker til og med hva du sier. Snak ikke under noen omstendighet om skipsfart, mannskap eller last. Husk på at du har en betrodd stilling. Husk også på at mange menneskers velferd—kanskje din egen—kan bero på at du holder tett med hva du vet.

VOUS DESCENDEZ A TERRE?

Prenez garde à qui vous parlez et à ce que vous dites. Sous aucun prétexte, ne discutez les mouvements des navires, des équipages ou des cargaisons. Vous êtes à un poste de confiance. La sécurité des hommes, leur vie—la vôtre peut-être—peuvent dépendre de la manière dont vous gardez pour vous ce que vous pouvez savoir.

PRINTED FOR H.M. STATIONERY OFFICE BY FOSH & CROSS LTD., LONDON   (51-8591)

PREFACE

Leslie Fred Penny was born on a bleak December morning at Shipton Bellinger, Hampshire in the year 1898. He was one of a family of nine children, his mother kept house, and his father was a 'Carter' driving a team of heavy horses on the farm where they lived and worked. He left school at the age of thirteen and joined his father and elder brother working on the farm. In 1914, his elder brother was away on camp training with the territorials, when the First World War broke out, as a result of which he was unable to come home, unable to bid farewell to his family. He was sent straight to France to help reinforce the regular army and didn't actually return home until five years later. Consequently this enabled Leslie to be 'promoted', into the position left vacant by his brother to 'Senior Hand' behind his father!

Sadly, when he was only fifteen years old, his mother died, so his elder sisters took over the role between them of running the house and helping to bring up the family. After a couple of years Leslie decided that farmwork was not for him, so in complete contrast, took an office clerk's job in nearby Andover. This too, proved to be rather more mundane than Leslie desired, what he wanted was some excitement in his life, he often thought of his brother away fighting in the war. So when he was approaching his eighteenth birthday he decided to join the Army. By mistake he went into the Navy recruiting office and ended up joining the Royal Marines!
When he arrived at Eastney Barracks Southsea to start his training, it was the first time in his life, that he cast his eyes upon the sea. When he finished his training he was posted to 'H.M.S. Malaya,' as a gunner. Of the many assignments given to the Malaya probably the most satisfying was forming part of the escort that took the remainder of the surrendered German fleet into Scapa Flow. He stayed on the Malaya for a further two years after the end of the war, and was then drafted back to Eastney Barracks.

After only a few weeks of menial duties, he was invited to join the Marines tug of war team and ended up the No.1 in the team for three and a half years, winning at the Royal Tournament at Earls Court and receiving his winners medal from King George V. During those years, they pulled against the Army, Navy, Air Force, Police and many civilian teams, and to their credit, never lost a single pull! However, Leslie's life was about to change, he met a young lass from Portsmouth and fell in love. He had been thinking for a while that it was time to move on from the Marines, and this prompted him to make his mind up, so he bought his discharge on 6th September 1923 for the sum of £24.00, which he thought would enable him to spend more time with his beloved, whose father owned a confectionery shop in Fratton, Portsmouth.

His first civvy-street job was working for his future father-in-law, which was certainly a change from the regimented life he had been used to! After working in the shop for only a few weeks, a relative of the family called at the premises. His purpose was to enquire as to whether or not Leslie would be interested in joining the crew of a 1,000 ton square rigged sailing ship the 'St George' which was being made ready in Plymouth to set sail on an expedition to the South Sea Islands, taking both passengers and scientists. As he was already missing the sea, Leslie decided to go for an interview and being an ex-Royal Marine, had no problem in getting the job, and subsequently set sail from Plymouth for the South Seas on 9th April 1924. He was taken on initially as a Steward, but in fact ended up as Jack of all trades, and in the course of the voyage acted as a relief, for all the other crew members including the navigating officers.

For much of the trip he kept a daily diary to record the progress of the expedition, which now gives a fascinating insight into the daily life of expeditionary travellers, and how they coped with various adversities in the early part of the century, compared with the mod-cons and modern communications such a force would set out with today!

The voyage was supposed to be of a twelve - month duration, but ended up lasting almost double that time! After the expedition Leslie joined the Metropolitan Police for a short period but that didn't suit him, so he joined up with the Union Castle Line at Southampton as a Steward. Thirty Eight years later he retired as Chief of Shore Staff! As soon as he went back to sea after the Met, he took up again the writing of his daily journal, and through the war years he kept a journal not only of his own exploit's, but of the progression of the war. Reading the journals today, one can only just begin to appreciate what a Merchant Navy man's war was like, sailing in the constant shadow of the enemy aircraft and submarines. Diaries and accounts from the war are numerous, in connection with the three main services, Army, Navy, and Air-Force. To have such a story from this particular view-point is indeed rare.

Leslie Penny was decorated nine times whilst serving King and Country, firstly as a Royal Marine, and latterly as a Merchantman, he died peacefully on the night of 13th December 1993, two days after his ninety fifth birthday.

From the time he was on the 'St George' right through the war years, and until he finally came ashore in 1951, he was given occasionally to writing poetry, usually with a tendency to highlight the virtues of the all too often, under-rated merchantmen, an example of which can be perceived in the following few verses:-

"Lest we Forget"

Our soldiers are doing a wonderful job
our sailors are right on the scene
but some of our praise
In these "war troubled" days
must go to the Merchant Marines.

For our forces must have ammunition and food
so they won't become lean
but all of these things
don't reach them on wings
they're brought by the Merchant Marines

So here's to our boys in the Army
and our sailors on waters so green
but in drinking our toast
don't forget we must boast
of our men in the Merchant Marines

Twin screw steamer 'Norman' 7537 Tons
The first Union Castle vessel on which Leslie Penny served

Chapter One

RMS Windsor Castle

Friday 1st September 1939

Prepared for homeward voyage from South Africa

Hostilities commenced at 5.45am.

German forces attack Poland, all along Silesian border. Several towns bombed, including the capital of Poland - Warsaw. The holding of Danzig by the Poles instituted by the Versailles Treaty, is the cause of dissension. Several days of negotiations between Germany, Great Britain, Poland, and France eased the situation for a while, then the final demand by Germany of Poland's rights were turned down by Poland, and Germany decided to get by force, what they could not, and would not have got by their impossible terms. There were fourteen points, the most important being the return to the Reich of Danzig unconditionally, and a plebiscite to be held for the corridor.

Britain and France send a note to Herr Hitler to say they will stand by their obligations to Poland to suppress the aggressor - Germany. General mobilisation in Great Britain and France is the result. All merchant ships taken over by the Admiralty.

'Windsor Castle' now proceeding to Port Elizabeth as per company arrangement.

Ship darkened down as per Admiralty instructions.

Leslie Penny Aged 41 on board RMS Windsor Castle 1939

Saturday 2nd September

Docked at Port Elizabeth

Still under company's normal conditions

Mr Chamberlain denounces Germany's aggressive action towards Poland - declaration of war likely. Free city of Danzig returned to the Reich, but not as yet recognised by the other powers. All the smaller European states decide to remain neutral. Italy, after an emergency cabinet meeting, decides to remain neutral.

President Roosevelt asks the powers to refrain from bombing the open towns - answers to this to be sent immediately. Britain, France, and Poland all ready replied in the affirmative. Ultimatum to Germany by Chamberlain to stop any further aggression of Poland, the answer to this awaited hourly, no time limit - this the final and last effort for peace. Hostilities by Britain and France to start tomorrow, held as certain by the majority.

Due to have left port at 5.30pm but now will not sail until 6.00am tomorrow, in port with us also the 'Capetown Castle' and 'Dunvegan Castle.'

Sunday 3rd September

Left port at 6.00am.

Whilst proceeding to Cape Town, the news came through that a state of war existed between Britain and Germany. Given out at 12.45pm local time, a great shock for all concerned although we were expecting it.

'Windsor Castle' was sailing from Port Elizabeth to Cape Town when war was declared

'Athenia' sunk 200 miles west of Hebrides with 1400 passengers on board. 128 lives lost

Monday 4th September

Arrived at Cape Town 7.30am.

Heard the news that the 'Athenia' of the Donaldson Line had been torpedoed with 1,400 people on board, it sank 200 miles West of the Hebrides with loss of 128 lives.

Uproar in the South African cabinet. Followers of Hertzog - for neutrality. Followers of Smuts - for, to assist against aggression.

State of war in Australia as from Sunday midday.

The King's speech to his people last night appeared in print today as did Mr. Chamberlain's.

Tuesday 5th September

Still in Cape Town Dock

All sailors busy painting the ship from the usual colours to naval grey. Funnels that were Red with Black tops are also to be painted out. Sand bags are being filled and placed in position around the bridge. Plenty of general provisions being put on board. The 'Dunvegan Castle' which was at East London Dock, South Africa on her way home via the East Coast has been recalled, and arrived here this morning. South African cabinet, split over supposed neutrality by General Hertzog, finally put to the vote, and Hertzog forced to resign and General Smuts now the Prime Minister of South Africa for the second time.

Greek steamer sunk by a mine in the Baltic

British planes bomb two German ports, Wilhelmshaven and Cuxhaven

German communiqué states twelve planes took part in the raid, and five were brought down

Chamberlain broadcasts to the German people with reference as to why we were at war with them - not the German people, but the Nazi leaders

Neutrality act about to be passed in the USA.

Over six million copies of a note were dropped in Northern and Western Germany by RAF planes.

Have received copy of the King's message to the British Merchant Navy and British Fishing Fleets it reads as follows:-

In these anxious days, I would like to express to all Officers and Men in the British Merchant Navy and British Fishing Fleets my confidence in their unflinching determination to play their vital part in defence. To each one I would say; Yours is a task no less essential to my people's existence than that allotted to the Navy, Army, and Air-Force. Upon you the nation depends for much of it's foodstuffs and raw materials, and for the transport of it's troops overseas.You have a long and glorious history, and I am proud to bear the title;Master of the Merchant Navy and Fishing Fleets.I know that you will carry out your duties with resolution and fortitude and that the high, chivalrous traditions of your calling are safe in your hands ....God keep you and prosper you in your great task.

Wednesday 6th September

Cape Town Dock

Still busy loading ship with general cargo.

Painting continuing with full blast.

Rejoicing in Cape Town over the cabinet split. General Smuts is very popular, and has a decided leaning towards Britain. War continuing with zest on the Eastern Front. Poles making a great stand.

No operations commenced on the Western Front to date, but expected daily. More British planes fly over Southern Germany, and drop leaflets amongst the population. Not engaged and all returned safely.

Report of first enemy air raid on England.

Thursday 7th September

Cape Town Dock

South Africa declares war on Germany.

Germans push well into the Polish territory

Enemy aircraft appeared for the first time over the South of England at 6.30am yesterday morning - no bombs dropped.

Adderley Street, Cape Town

Still busy loading and painting ship.

Marked activity on the Western Front in the form of artillery duels between the Seigfried and Maginot Lines.

Survivors of the Cunard freighter 'Bosnia' which was torpedoed and sunk off the Portuguese coast landed at Lisbon - thirty three saved.

Friday 8th September

Cape Town Dock

Still busy painting and loading

'Carnarvon Castle' arrives from England with full compliment of passengers. Immediately taken over by Admiralty. Stripped right out and sailing for Simonstown, due to arrive next Monday morning. We get ready to sail, all stores finally aboard we leave at 5.00pm. We all wonder, will we get through safely and to what port are we bound? May it be Southampton. The first night at sea passed comfortably, ship steady and completely darkened down.

The offensive on the Western Front gathering strength.

Battle raging between the two lines, all private wireless sets had to be dismantled today.

Saturday 9th September

At sea

Everything so far proceeding to schedule, and at times it's hard to realise there is a war on!

Sunday 10th September

Usual routine on the ship.

Steaming 20 knots to some unknown destination.

Monday 11th September

Everything very peaceful, and usual happenings taking place.

Sports, pictures and dancing at night are stopped owing to darkening of ship.

We have just heard that we are proceeding to Freetown, Sierra-Leone, to either pick up a convoy, or our escort - both I expect.

Gas masks issued to crew.

Thursday 12th September

Usual routine

Definite statement by Captain that we are proceeding to Freetown.

Poles making a stand before Warsaw, there were fourteen raids on the town in one day.

French very active on Western Front.

British troops land in France and also the RAF.

Duke and Duchess of Windsor return to England on a British Destroyer, their first return since his abdication 11th December 1936.

Gas masks issued to passengers.

Wednesday 13th September

Very little to report apart from the usual routine.

ARP drill 11.00am.

Thursday 14th September

Getting near to Freetown in Sierra-Leone, and according to the extra precautions taken, we are near also to the danger zone. Volunteers requested from amongst the passengers to keep submarine watches. Over fifty volunteered and even ladies wanted to assist the males!

They have now taken up their allotted stations, four in a watch of one hour each. We started a zigzag course from daybreak this morning, one more indication of danger. All water tight doors being kept closed as an extra precaution. We all wonder what will happen on our arrival at Freetown, and whether or not we are the last one in, thus completing the convoy before going home, or are we the first one to arrive and then have to await for other ships? May the former prove to be nearer the mark!

Friday 15th September

We are now full steam ahead on a zigzag course for Freetown, we hope to arrive there sometime during the late afternoon. Everything is going well on board, the one major exception being that the ship is darkened at night with the necessary closing of all ports, and being in the tropical zone this adds still greater discomfort to our well being in so much as it is terribly hot, and the evenings seem very long once dinner is finished, there being no amusement of any description.

Arrived off Freetown at 4.00pm, had to find our own way in, to the disadvantage of some of the Mark buoys, and possibly to our screw! No one seemed very interested in our arrival, apart from giving us the anchorage billet.

There are fifteen other ships of various colours already here, all cargo boats with the exception of an Elder Dempster passenger liner. She has been camouflaged, and looks anything but what she actually is, possibly it's the 'Accra'

The Navy is represented here by a light cruiser of the 'C' class.

three destroyers, a repair ship, a boom defence ship, and possibly two seaplanes.

This is apparently the rainy season, for it's raining now, and it looks as if it might rain for weeks. The ship has still to be darkened and battened down, and is terribly hot and uncomfortable.

No news as to where, or what we might do.

Saturday 16th September

Freetown

Fine for a little while this morning then more rain.

Three more ships came in this morning, so there is now eighteen in total. To date we hold the record for size and speed! We can get nothing definite as to when we might leave, I think we could be here for anything up to a week, or it may be for a year, or it may be forever! No chance to get a letter away with any degree of safety as to it reaching it's destination. Normally we should now be at Cape Verde or thereabouts. Very busy this afternoon transferring stores to the local food controller, more ships arrive, and one or two depart on their own.

Sunday 17th September

Freetown

Rained all during the night and still raining first thing this morning. More stores sent to the local store. Officers of several denominations come and go, but nothing seems to happen. I cannot find out why we came here yet, unless it was to entertain a few locals and for them to grab a few of our stores!

Passengers allowed to go on shore today.

We have just heard that Russia has marched into Poland, a move we fail to understand at the moment.

'HMS Courageous' sunk by a torpedo at 8.00pm. Loss of 515 lives.

Monday 18th September

Freetown

Everything much the same, and we are just waiting, but goodness knows what for! At the moment the Navy is very active, patrolling the port entrance. A good few passengers and some of the crew have been ashore. Various small craft come and go, but all to no purpose as far as we are concerned. We are, I understand, liable to leave this rotten hole tomorrow or Wednesday. I honestly think that of all the various ports I have visited this is definitely the worst. We receive very little War news, radio reception being very poor.

Tuesday 19th September

Freetown

Time for a change, 'HMS Neptune' arrived this morning at 6.00am, immediately oiled, and now standing by, we wonder if it is our escort. According to rumour we may sail sometime tomorrow. Leslie Henson gave a concert party to the Navy, consisting at the moment of HMS's 'Despatch,' 'Neptune,' 'Albatross,' 'Winchelsea,' 'Hunter,' and 'Bridgewater' plus a destroyer and a sloop. We are all very much tuned up at the moment also fed up, we want to be on our way. We hear very little War news, today we heard again that the Russians had marched into Poland, and several U boats had been sunk by a French Navy unit.

Wednesday 20th September

Freetown

A beautiful morning and very fitting to the occasion, we are leaving today, presumably sometime this afternoon. Ships still continue to arrive, and many appear to slip out during the night. If we leave today, we ought make home by October 1st.

The 'Dunvegan Castle' arrived today at 2.00pm.

At last! We are leaving for home. We are leaving Sierra Leone, and with us is a Clan Boat and the 'Sultan Star,' we are now only able to do 15 knots, which is the speed of the other two ships.

We left at 3.00pm with 'HMS Neptune' as our escort, with two seaplanes in attendance, scouting for possible submarines.

It is now 8.00pm we are all steaming a steady 15 knots. We are taking the 'Vanguard' with the Clan Boat on our starboard quarter, and the Star Boat on our port quarter. The 'Neptune' is watching generally - we hope!

The ship is battened down once more and it is as hot as hell, there are many sources from which we may succumb, and being battened down seems to be the most likely!

Thursday 21st September

Awakened this morning at 5.15am by the drone of the 'Neptune's' seaplane, it had been catapulted a few minutes before, and was starting out on patrol. This continued until 7.30am when it finally returned to the ship. The weather has been perfect, just the right sort of day to be torpedoed! This is the very hottest day this voyage, enough to roast one, possibly pick up a little breeze tomorrow.

Friday 22nd September

Have not the slightest idea as to our correct position, but by the breeze we must be somewhere in the region of Dakar, although possibly a good deal to the West.

The convoy is still intact and the 'Neptune' is still with us, we are I believe liable to lose her any moment, her plane is still very active, giving us an added sense of security. Tomorrow I feel sure we shall proceed on our own. By that I mean the convoy, less the 'Neptune'. Convoy will then consist of 'Windsor Castle', 'Sultan Star', and the 'Clan Forbes'. The total armaments between us being one 3"-7" gun mounted on the 'Clan Forbes.' We are all steadied up today, owing to the choppy sea. We still get very little War news.

Saturday 23rd September

We are now three days out from Sierra Leone, and we are I presume somewhere off Cape Verde Islands. Days are much the same with reference to routine, but everyone seems a little fed up, having passengers continually in ones' mind doesn't help things, although they are very good really, carrying on outwardly of course as if nothing had happened. But their innermost thoughts are no doubt mutual to ours in realising that we are every hour nearing the danger zone, and one naturally thinks of home and all that it means to us.

None of us say very much but I feel sure that the thoughts of us all are running in the same channels. With luck we hope to be home this time next week, without luck - well who knows! Our escort is still with us and continues to be very active, but unfortunately, I think she will leave us tonight. To the layman it seems strange that we are brought nearly a 1,000 miles nearer the danger zone, and then suddenly left to do battle on our own, just when we imagine we need protection most. We shall not complain but carry on and hope for the best, with St Christopher well in the foreground.!

Sunday 24th September

Well here we are all on our own, open to the first sub that comes along, our escort the 'Neptune' sailed away into the blue last evening, and wished us goodbye and good luck, we shall need the latter I think. We are steaming very slowly, owing to having the other two with us, we all feel that we ought to leave them, but that is not very nice from their point of view. I feel sure that if we are attacked, we shall be the tasty morsel, and my next Sunday's dinner is gone west, still who cares!

Monday 25th September

Still going strong and past Madeira, well away to the West. We are still without any visible help, the 'Silent Navy' is being ever watchful we hope.

Have just heard we may arrive Friday if all goes well.

Tuesday 26th September

Still above water, and making steady progress.

The weather is much cooler, and I presume we are somewhere off Lisbon.

We have I believe, to survive two more days if possible, before picking up an escort, and I presume we shall then be between 300 and 400 miles from home.

Everybody is getting tired of this uncertainty, on and on, not knowing where you are. Passengers seem to make things worse, more exacting than normal times seemingly.

Saw a ship yesterday away to the starboard in the same direction, but very slow, she has our sympathy. Everyone feels they should be doing something, but don't know quite what it should be. A day seems like a week, and to me it seems as if I've been away for years.

Wednesday 27th September

Very rough today and making poor headway. Our two partners are not doing at all well, we have to come back and find them almost. We hope to pick up with our escort tomorrow morning and join up with another convoy I presume. We hope to make Southampton by sometime on Friday, of course with our usual luck, and we have without doubt had plenty this voyage - so far anyway!

Thursday 28th September

Well here we are off Ushant or thereabouts.

It is blowing a gale and the sea is running high. Our two partners are very much slowed down, particularly the 'Sultan Star'. This morning we went back to find her, what we didn't say is not worth mentioning! Still I hope we shall all make landfall tomorrow and ease the tension. Murders could be committed with the slightest provocation at the moment. Our long looked for escort and convoy are conspicuous by their absence. If they do not come soon we shall not require them, but perhaps it's too rough for the Navy! This weather is keeping us back considerably and anything may happen, but so far as we are all concerned usual routine continues.

Left the other two ships at 6.30pm and proceeding alone at full speed, sighted the first light at about 9.00pm, going very well, and may it continue. We are still looking for the promised escort!

Friday 29th September

All is well, we are now opposite Swanage and making good headway. Arrived at The Needles at 8.30am. After waiting a while we came around to Spithead, picked up the pilot at noon, and proceeded on our course to the docks. Balloon barrage up, the first we have seen. Plenty of activity off the Island, with reference to small Naval craft, and flying machines. I wonder what is in store for us? A rest would be appreciated!

Arrived along side at about 2.00pm, and as far possible we carry out the usual routine.

Two other Union Castle boats are in, 'Pretoria' and 'Llanstephan.' The 'Pretoria' is to go to Belfast for Naval conversion and the Llanstephan is to be put on the Mail Run. The 'Durban Castle' is due in tomorrow.

Saturday 30th September - Wednesday 11th October

In Port

Thursday 12th October

Back on board 'Windsor Castle.'

Left Southampton at 4.00pm and proceeded seawards.

A large number of passengers are on board.

Two guns were fitted whilst we were in port - one a 4"-7" and one 3" anti aircraft gun, two naval ratings are in charge, and the balance of the gun crews are to be drawn from the Deck Department.

No news with regard to making up a convoy or as to an escort. Personally I don't think we will have an escort, we've heard that story before!

We came out the Spithead way, and then full speed for the open sea. We are on our own as I thought, not another boat in sight. The guns are not actually manned, but a continual watch is being kept. I wonder, shall we fire an angry shot? (I hope not) .

Friday 13th October

Sea rough, and a strong wind blowing, which is fortunate in a way as I believe that it keeps the subs under. That is much better than being calm and us being under! Getting a shake down now, and will I hope, soon be in the usual routine.

Saturday 14th October

Weather even worse today. Heard the news today that three U boats had been sunk. That's three less to worry us anyway!

The joy of hearing the U boat news was short lived, we have just heard of the loss of 'HMS Royal Oak,' with a loss of 810 lives, by torpedo presumably. It has dampened everyone's spirit a little, but I suppose having so many ships at sea, it's an easy matter for one to be singled out. It seems remarkable to the layman, or landlubber, that a ship of her type can be got at when so much protection is afforded. Either the ship is weak from a torpedoing point of view, or else the torpedo it'self must contain some unknown explosive, but whatever the reason it is very sad to think that so many young lives have been lost. This is the second big Naval disaster costing us 1,500 lives in total. What of the poor merchant seamen and their ships, if they can sink battleships so easy? Still where there is life there is hope - we hope!

Sunday 15th October

Things are a little better today as regards the weather, sea and wind down, and much warmer, normally we should have called at Madeira today, but we are I presume about in that sphere, and well to the Westward.

According to today's news, survivors from the 'Royal Oak' four hundred and fourteen.

We are still on our own and above water, thanks to the R.N. which we haven't seen yet, luck is our chief asset I should imagine.

Monday 16th October

We must be well South of Madeira by now, having run into warm weather, and are now in whites. The ship continues on a zigzag course so I presume we are still in the danger zone. Our guns look a bit more business like now, having had a very good clean (very much needed) and shell racks have been made just behind the gun and shells actually placed there! Smoke canisters are also placed in position, ready to drop over the side to act as a screen to help in our protection, should a raider pay us a visit.

The general ship routine is about the same, one day just a repetition of another.

We heard this evening that an air raid was carried out by the enemy over the Firth of Fourth, and near to Rosyth the Naval Dockyard - no details to hand, but we are led to believe some of our ships were bombed and hit.

Tuesday 17th October

Weather extremely pleasant but a trifle on the hot side.

The raid of yesterday on the Navy at Rosyth, and presumably the Forth Bridge, was carried out by about a dozen German bombers. They appeared in the first instance coming from the direction of May Island, they were intercepted by the RAF and some were shot down. They managed to hit the 'Southampton' (a Cruiser) on the fo'castle, doing I presume a fair amount of damage, although the main force of the bomb was misspent, having struck a glancing blow . Her barge and another boat sank, which were tied alongside. Two more ships suffered minor casualties through splinters.

This is the first raid carried out over British territory, no civilian damage was done, and no one was killed. According to a French report twenty two subs have been accounted for to date, which is definitely in our favour.

We have just heard that the 'Royal Oak' was sunk in Scapa Flow whilst at anchor. Words fail me in an endeavour to understand this. For a sub to be able to get past boom defensives, enter a harbour, fire four or five torpedoes, and sink a battleship and then presumably get out again, if it wasn't for the terrible toll of lives, it would be almost laughable. My Lords had better get together and do their job. I suppose some poor non-entity will carry the baby! If I were in power I would present the Captain of that U boat with the VC, it was a wonderful feat of seamanship and daring! If they can sink the Navy at anchor what hope do we stand, which reminds me we haven't seen a Navy boat, so far this voyage, so 'Bull Dog Churchill' wants to get busy!

Wednesday 18th October

Very little news on the home front today, doing our steady 10 knots, and with luck hope to make Cape Town on Saturday week. Personally I shall be very pleased about that, what with a double sitting full up in the second class, it is a case of a lot of work with no extra money. These dark nights get on ones nerve, and being battened down completes the issue. Heard today at 1.45pm that the sub that sank the 'Royal Oak' has got back to Germany safely, and has been awarded with the Iron Cross. They certainly deserve it, a wonderful feat of seamanship.

Gun practice carried out this morning and everything went well, six rounds each gun, the target was not hit, but it was good shooting, none the less!

Thursday 19th October

Things very much the same on board. The weather has been atrocious, nothing but rain, rain, and more rain, and this evening being blacked out, and boxed up, it is almost the last straw! I should imagine we are now somewhere off Cape Verde, that is if the weather is any indication. My one desire is to get rid of these passengers, then maybe we shall be able to do something. To date we shall be doing the normal run, but of course that is likely to be altered at any moment. So far we have not sighted a ship of any description, not that we expected to see a Navy boat, but we did expect to see something on the ocean besides ourselves!

Friday 20th October

Just a little cooler today thank goodness, and we also are out of the wet zone. Until today we have had news at 1.45pm and 6.15pm and 1.45am. News now discontinued, so I cannot say what the Navy has been doing.

Saturday 21st October

Usual hot weather, and very little news, apart from the fact that a sub was crippled having come in contact with an armed Merchantman, a general engagement over the North Sea, but no details to hand.

Sunday 22nd October

Very much like any other day, the only difference being that there is now a little more to do. The good news of this morning is that the commercial raider 'Schwabinland' has been sunk by a British cruiser, being as she was operating this way, we had an idea she might have caught up with us. The action over the North Sea between escort vessels, and enemy bombers is still vague, apart from the fact that three were shot down, and one forced to ditch. This to my mind was a good effort, the RAF seem to be doing very well so far.

Monday 23rd October

Another day has rolled away and nothing much has happened. Looking forward to Cape Town and to the getting rid of this crowd of passengers. We shall by all accounts arrive there Saturday, but if it's sooner then so much the better!

Tuesday 24th October

Weather changing considerably, and we are cooling down once more, we are back in blues this morning, it is still warm below decks though, but very nice on top deck for those able to take that advantage.
Yesterday, two subs were disabled and believed sunk by the RAF.

Wednesday 25th October

Things very much the same again today, heard definitely that we will arrive at Cape Town on Saturday morning at around 7.00am, also heard that we were to be on top line today, as the War Authorities at Simonstown had informed the ship that they had reason to believe that a sub was in this vicinity, so perhaps we shall not get to the Cape! My respect for the Navy diminishes daily, to think that the Pocket Battleship 'Deutschland' has been able to get out, and career around the ocean ad lib, perhaps it would be more appropriate for the 'Silent Navy' to be called the 'Sightless Navy'!

Thursday 26th October

Nothing to report.

Friday 27th October

Same as yesterday.

Saturday 28th October

Passed Robben Island at 6.00am, arrived at Cape Town docks and tied up by 7.00am. We have now steamed 6,000 miles, and not seen a single ship of any description, so much for the 'Convoy System'! There are only few ships here in port, which is most unusual as there is generally hardly a berth available. One Blue Star boat is unloading steel rails, and one unknown is loading at the other side of the Basin. The 'Athlone' has just arrived at 8.00am, she left Southampton a fortnight before us, but has by all accounts been all over the South Atlantic, and called at Gibraltar, Sierra Leone, and St Helena. It is rather nice having dispensed with the blackout for an evening, and being able to get a breath of fresh air. Cape Town is lit up as usual with the neon lights ablaze, so much for being out of the danger zone!
We are to continue our voyage coastwise, and presumably keeping to schedule as near as possible.

Sunday 29th October

Left Cape Town this morning at 6.30am for Port Elizabeth. Had a very good passage so far, there are very few people travelling with us this time. We have had no news today, so perhaps we shall hear good news tomorrow - here's hoping!

Monday 30th October

Arrived at Port Elizabeth at 9.00am, lying up at our usual berth.
Two other ships are here 'Rothesay Castle' loading fruit for home, and the 'Duneden Star' which is discharging. The weather is really lovely, and by the general run of things the War at the moment seems to be a secondary consideration. Every endeavour is being made to discharge our cargo, and we hope to move on to East London, sailing again by 10.00pm tonight, still trying to make up time.

'Rothesay Castle'

Tuesday 31st October

Arrived at East London at 8.30am, discharged cargo and proceeded on to Durban at 4.30pm.

Wednesday 1st November

Arrived in Durban 8.00am, things seem very much the same as a normal voyage. The War is a long way off as far as Durban is concerned. The 'Carnarvon' was here over the weekend, real Naval style, when tied up she had an armed sentry at the bottom of the gangway, and another rating at the top carrying a service revolver. In port with us are several Dutch boats, also 'Dundrum Castle', 'Rovuma', and the 'Gloucester Castle,' so we are well represented here. I received my first letter of this voyage today. Everyone is very busy particularly with cargo, and engine room, we carry on our usual routine, though to me it seems senseless; Still, even here there are people who need to justify their existence!

Thursday 2nd November

Yesterday was a beautiful day - my day out!
But today I've never seen anything like it, pouring with rain all day, and generally miserable. Working all night on the cargo, or at least should have been, had it not been for the rain!

Friday 3rd November

Well, we should have left today, but owing to the amount of cargo, and the amount of rain for that matter, we are delayed, and now we are due to leave tomorrow at 4.00pm. That in turn will make us late to the Cape, and again I'm afraid to Southampton, still we shall see!
A flying boat arrived today, so if there is a letter aboard for me, I sincerely hope it will be delivered before we leave. The news at home seems very bad to me, in so much as Russia is forcing the issue with Finland to the detriment of the Allies. In Holland there is Marshal Law and in Belgium there is general uneasiness, all adding to the confusion. Where it will all end, goodness only knows.

'*Rovuma*'   *A. Duncan*

'*Gloucester Castle*'

'Carnarvon Castle'

Saturday 4th November

Well, it's now past 4.00pm, and we are still here, now that's a day late to start with already. Now I hear we are to leave at 5.30pm. This rain is enough to get one down. The Durban letter was conspicuous by it's absence, so goodness knows what's happened to the mail, lack of space has been the trouble no doubt, still we continue to live in hope.

We have finally left at 6.30pm and we are going all out now to East London. We have very few people travelling with us this time, six first class, twenty second class and thirty third class, all for coast ports with three exceptions, so by the look of things I hope we are going to have a quiet run home! It is still raining.

Sunday 5th November

Arrived at East London 7.30am, considering we did not leave Durban until 6.30pm last night, we made a good fast passage. Distance two hundred and fifty three miles speed 21 knots.

It is actually fine today and that really is a treat. We hear that the lifting of the arms embargo has become law, having been signed by President Roosevelt. This is a good gesture on their part in favour of the Allies, although it is of extreme importance to USA.

We have only three people joining us today, a most unusual happening, cargo again is the main item, and rightly so one might say! Left East London at 6.45pm.

Monday 6th November

Arrived here at Port Elizabeth at 7.00am, a good smooth passage, and above all it is fine beautiful weather, as a matter of fact, out of the wet zone I presume! In port with us is the 'Capetown Castle' which is two days late, and also the armed cruiser 'Carnarvon Castle'. The latter looking very much the same, apart from her guns.

Had my second letter this morning, and glad to know everything is well. I think we shall arrive at Cape Town on Wednesday morning, and I only hope we shall leave on Friday, but in any case I think that our stay at home will be cut down by three or four days, a good weekend gone. Is this too much to hope, that this is my last voyage? I wish

'Durban Castle'

to goodness it were.

We left at 7.30pm this evening, and I believe we are making for Mossel Bay, where we shall anchor in the Roads, still representing the tasty morsel to the sub, let's hope my Lords know best.

Tuesday 7th November

Arrived at Mossel Bay at 7.00am.

This is the first time that I have been here for about two years, and it might as well have been yesterday for all the difference one sees, same old tugs and filthy barges. This place surely must be at the end of the world! This morning I heard that the French had brought down nine German Fighter Craft, a very credible performance, in spite of the great odds. I think there were twenty nine enemy planes, and nine French planes. For nine planes to shoot down nine, in other words one each, is quite remarkable.

Lots of buzzes are to hand, with reference to what we shall do on arrival at the Cape. I make no comment but just wait and see.

Left Mossel Bay at 8.30pm.

Wednesday 8th November

Arrived at Cape Town at 12.00noon, we have in Cape Town with us the armed cruiser 'Carnarvon Castle' and the 'Durban Castle' and several other ships of lesser importance (to us). Also arrived is 'HMS Sussex' a completely new arrival to this part of the world, her presence at this moment being unknown, unless it is to round up the German Raiders - but obviously not the Pocket Battleships!

The 'Durban Castle' has been here a week, having a final gun fitted, she had one Anti Aircraft Gun already fitted whilst at home. News as to our movements come in hourly, and we are at a loss as to know what our exact date of departure is to be. Sunday would suit us admirably! Today I received my third letter which came by Air Mail, a credible performance taking all things into consideration. According to latest figures we have very few passengers for home.

Thursday 9th November

Cape Town Docks

We are today busy generally, with cargo, ships stores, and oiling. Fuel to the extent of over 2,000 tons has already been taken in. The 'Dominion Monarch' has arrived from Australia, she seems very much up to date, well sand bagged, and with a formidable looking 6" gun, Anti Aircraft Gun and Rangefinder. The 'Carnarvon Castle' has left for an unknown destination, we think it is probably Sierra Leone. The 'Durban Castle' also has left for home, loaded to the plimsoll with cargo.

Let us hope they all make a safe landing.

Friday 10th November

Everyone is extremely busy in trying to get the ship away today.

We finally leave at 6.00pm.

We are full to the hatch tops with cargo so it will be a great pity if we get pipped! I hear now from an unreliable source that we may go straight home, if that is the case we ought to make it back to Southampton by Sunday 26th November.

We have very few passengers this time they number only four first class, eight second class, and thirty five tourist class, that is the least this ship has ever carried!

The 'Dominion Monarch' also left this morning for home, so including us there are three big ships homeward bound within a radius of a couple hundred of miles.

Saturday 11th November

We have now I suppose to settle down once more, and hope for the best. Owing to the small number of passengers, stewards are keeping submarine watches, and assisting the gun crews. We sincerely hope that both will be proficient by the time we reach the danger zone! The weather today is not at all desirable, a bit blowy with the sea running, and also raining, therefore poor visibility.

We hear today that 'HMS Northern Rover' is reported missing by the Admiralty presumed lost. This is the 4th Naval loss after 'HMS's 'Courageous', 'Oxley', and the 'Royal Oak'. We are battened down once more, and we dread those few tropical days.

Well for that matter we dread all of them!

Sunday 12th November

The weather has improved already, and apart from her rolling, (which makes it impossible to open ports on this deck) caused by copper ingots, and a following sea things are not too bad.

I went to Church today, the first time for many moons!

Monday 13th November

Weather still improving and things generally straightened out. Very little to do for the majority of us, really there is so much wasted time, but there is one consolation and that is we are getting nearer home, but unfortunately that means nearer to the danger zone as well! I am expecting every day to hear that we are to call at Sierra Leone, but I hope our luck will hold good and we will continue on our way.

Later

The bottom has fallen out of the ship, what I mean is the bottom has fallen out of the world, I have just been told we are going to Sierra Leone, blast!

Tuesday 14th November

So to Sierra Leone we go, well let's hope it's for three or four days, one day would be just sufficient to mess things up! The weather has improved and we are in whites once again.

There was a raid on the Shetland Islands yesterday, and the first bomb was dropped on British soil, apparently there was no damage done.

British destroyer sunk by mine.

Wednesday 15th November

Things much the same today, still steaming a steady 19 knots. Very little general news.

Everybody is playing a waiting game.

Thursday 16th November

Nothing to report.

Friday 17th November

The weather that has been so wonderful, suddenly came to an end last night, and things gradually got worse until 5.30am this morning. A severe thunder storm broke upon us, and it rained as if it had not done so for a 1,000 years. A final crack at about 6.40am actually shook the ship, I thought at that moment that a German Raider had caught up with us!

Saturday 18th November

Dutch liner 'Simon Bolivar' sunk.
It is 7.00am we are now making for Sierra Leone and I can just see land taking shape.
We have just passed two Navy boats of a doubtful denomination, and two Navy Drifters presumably mine sweepers sweeping for mines.
We finally anchor at 8.00am, there are a good many ships here, Navy as well as Merchantmen. For the Navy there is HMS's 'Ark Royal', 'Renown', 'Albatross', five Destroyers, one Submarine, one Oil Tanker, and 'Carnarvon Castle'. For the Merchantmen, 'Windsor Castle', 'Dominion Monarch', 'Australian Star', and many other lesser fry. The captured German freighter 'Uhenfels' is lying fairly close to us well down with cargo and flying the White Ensign. She was seen in the first instance by a plane from the 'Ark Royal', who in turn got a destroyer on the job, the crew by this time had abandoned ship and had left her in a sinking condition, they were forced back on board and ordered to sink with the ship or pump her out and take her to port - they chose the latter! Our old friend and escort of the last voyage the 'Neptune' came into port this morning.
After a stay of a few hours, we will get under way once more.
We finally get through the boom defence at 4.00pm. We are on our own at the moment, and personally I believe it will continue that way. I have come to consider the Navy a thing apart, some say we are better on are own, let us hope that is correct!

Sunday 19th November

Well out to sea, and all on our own, what's the Navy doing?
We are having lovely weather, which will probably last until Monday or Tuesday.
A little excitement was caused when we over hauled some other vessel last night, it seemed to come from nowhere, she immediately right wheeled, we did the opposite and that's that! I think the armed raider was first and foremost in some peoples' minds, but we are still denied even a little diversion.

Monday 20th November

Running out of the hot weather so it is a good sign we are heading North, roll on next Sunday!

Tuesday 21st November

Had a mild surprise this morning, two Naval ships probably French from Dakar came and had a look at us, they took a lot of convincing, we were proceeding on our lawful occasion, but when they were certain they made off landwards, and we are on our own once again, so much for the French Navy - two Navies that act as one!

Wednesday 22nd November

We heard last night there was a sub ahead, engaged in combat with one of our Merchantmen, we are by this time getting near that area, but I hope he has pushed off, as I should hate to have my afternoon nap spoilt, he can come this evening if he likes! Very little ship news apart from the submarine business.
Arrival at Southampton expected at 10.00am Sunday.

Thursday 23rd November

We haven't see the sub yet, perhaps we are not worth a torpedo which is just as well really! The weather is much colder but still good considering the time of the year. Fog is our chief worry, particularly if the wind drops, 'Raval Pinde' sunk by the 'Deutschland' with the loss of two hundred and sixty five lives.

'Deutschland' German pocket battleship

Friday 24th November

We are right in the middle of a bad storm, it's blowing a gale and making very bad weather, the ship is rolling and pitching to her heart's content! Very little sleep was obtainable last night, or this afternoon for that matter. One thing is for certain the subs will have to keep under, even if the mines come to the top, what a life, you can hardly call it your own! I am hoping that this weather will not delay us too much because I am getting a bit tired of everything.

Saturday 25th November

Our last day, if we are lucky! The weather has eased down and we have a following sea assisting us up the channel. Picked up the first light at about 9.00pm, so we might be off Spithead by about 8.00am in the morning.

Passed a convoy at about 1.00pm but it was too misty to see the actual ships, but I believe a cruiser and a destroyer were in attendance. Had an idea that firing was going on, but could not be certain.

So far we have seen nothing of the 'Durban Castle' and 'Dominion Monarch' which left Freetown just before us, let us hope they make a safe landing if they have not already done so.

Sunday 26th November

Still atrocious weather, but we are making good headway and are now opposite the Nab Tower.

Arrived at the defence boom at 10.30am, took on the Pilot and proceeded up Spithead, heard there wasn't a berth available and we drop anchor at 11.15am to await further instructions. It's still blowing and raining, just to add despair to our already frayed tempers. Goodness knows what time we shall get alongside now, I wonder if it will be today or if we shall lose another day. At 3.00pm it was decided that we should remain off Hamble River until tomorrow, what a waste of time!

Monday 27th November

8.00am; Still at anchor off the mouth of the Hamble, owing to the weather still blowing and raining.

1.15pm left our anchorage at last and proceeded up to the Docks. Arrived at 106 berth in the New Docks at 2.00pm and then the usual routine.

Tuesday 28th November

Usual Dock routine.
Paid off at 2.00pm.

Wednesday 29th November

On Leave
Three British War Ships enter a Norwegian port.

Thursday 30th November

On Leave
Russia marches on Finland.
Air raid on Helsinki one hundred and fifty believed dead.

1st - 6th December

On Leave
'Doric Star' sunk in the South Atlantic by gun fire from German Pocket Battleship, believed to be the 'Admiral Von Scheer'.
The King is crossing the channel in a destroyer on his way to France to visit the front line.
Later report confirms Pocket Battleship to be the 'Admiral Graf Spee' not the 'Von Scheer' as earlier report suggested.

Thursday 7th December

'Windsor Castle' voyage number 98 commencing.
Joined ship at 7.00am, then the usual routine, we should have left at 4.00pm, but owing to various rumours we are not leaving until tomorrow. We have about a dozen passengers in the first and second class, and about one hundred and ten in the tourist class.

Friday 8th December

We pulled away from the quay at 7.00am and when just clear, the main steam pipe burst and we had to tie up again! Workmen tried all day to repair the damage so we could get away before 4.00pm. They were unsuccessful so we had to stay another night, I went home for a few hours.

Saturday 9th December

Pulled away from the quay once more and finally got under way, passed the boom defence at 9.00am.
We saw two destroyers and a sub, and a bomber was also with us for a few minutes. We also saw the 'Pretoria Castle' at anchor, she is now armed as an auxiliary, also lying at anchor was the 'Queen of Bermuda'. She has been in Portsmouth Dockyard to fit out with guns and torpedo nets.
The weather is getting worse every minute, I wonder what the Bay of Biscay will be like when we get there!

Sunday 10th December

Making bad weather, otherwise things going very satisfactorily and we hope our luck will continue. Saw our new 6" gun today, well I would'nt say it was new from an armament point of view but it's new to us, it looks a very formidable weapon, but I hope we never have to use it, only for practice!

Monday 11th December

A general improvement this morning.
We hear that three ships are overdue from Australia. I should say that the Pocket Battleship the 'Admiral Scheer' has been busy, come on the Navy! My final opinion of the Navy is that it is over rated, and that it has got too much gold braid, still they might win the War with a little help from the Merchant service!

Tuesday 12th December

Today the 6" gun was tried out, four rounds practice shot with very good results apparently, at least it went off! We heard this morning that Russia has been given twenty four hours to come to terms with Finland - what then? German liner 'Bremen' reaches a German port.

Wednesday 13th December

Still proceeding on our course unmolested, due to what?
Warming up considerably, and I should imagine that we are somewhere a few miles South of the Canary Islands. 'Bremen' reported officially to be in the German port Bremerhaven.

Thursday 14th December

This morning we heard the good news that the three British cruisers 'Exeter', 'Ajax', and 'Achilles' contacted the 'Admiral Graf Spee' in the South Atlantic yesterday, and a running fight ensued, which lasted for several hours. The 'Graf Spee' was repeatedly hit, and the 'Exeter' through being hit also had to drop out of the fight and the chase was continued by the other two cruisers, and the 'Admiral Graf Spee' is believed to have made it to the River Plate. It will be interesting to see what happens next.

12 noon;   - It is reported that the 'Graf Spee' as well as the 'Exeter' have gone into Montevideo for repairs. Personally I think the three cruisers did well. It appears that the 'Ajax' was escorting a French liner when the 'Graf Spee' appeared, help was asked for and the other two appeared, so then the chase was on!

In command of squadron; Commodore Henry Harwood.

Captain Parry - 'Achilles'.

Captain Woodhouse - 'Ajax'.

Captain Bell - 'Exeter'

Captain Langsdorf - 'Graf Spee'.

From information to hand the German Navy at the moment consists of the following:-

2 - 26,000 ton Battleships 'Scharnhorst' and 'Gneisenau'

3 - 10,000 ton Pocket Battleships.

'Deutcshland' 1933 'Admiral Scheer' 1934 'Admiral Graf Spee' 1936

2 - Heavy Cruisers 'Bluecher' and 'Admiral Hipper' both capable of 32 knots.

6 - Light Cruisers

22 - Destroyers

65 - Submarines (minus those already sunk)

12 - Torpedo Boats

30 - Motor Torpedo Boats

Friday 15th December

Further news of the fight - German official news confirms that on the 'Graf Spee' there were thirty six killed and sixty wounded, British casualties not yet to hand. My personal opinion is that I think she will come out and scuttle herself.

Destroyer 'Duchess' sunk by collision.

British Naval losses to date;

'Courageous', 'Royal Oak', 'Oxley', 'Gipsy', 'Jersey', 'Blanche' and 'Duchess'.

Although we are in whites the wind is quite keen, and far from what we expected being a week out, but I suppose being afloat is the main thing!

Saturday 16th December

We hear more news concerning the Naval engagement. The 'Graf Spee' has been given until Sunday to come out and fight or to be interned for the duration. It's rather a hopeless proposition for her, as there are many Naval craft outside waiting. Namely, the French Battle Cruiser 'Dunkerque' and the British ships 'Renown', 'Ark Royal', 'Achillies', 'Ajax' and the 'Exeter'.

Two more German Merchantmen have been sunk, the 'Adolf Leonardt' and the 'Dusseldorf'.

Mr Chamberlain flew to France yesterday.

The last dying moments of the German Warship 'Graf Spee' after being engaged by British Warships including the 'Achilles'

Sunday 17th December

'Der Sag' for the 'Graf Spee' - she has to be out by 9.30pm GMT that's 6.17pm Montevideo time - or 8.17pm ships time, so let's hope for the best. Let's also hope that the 'Admiral Scheer' has gone to her assistance, and that will be another one out of the way! Saw another ship this morning away to the East'ard, well down, and on our side. All deck hands are busy painting the ship, all that was grey is slowly becoming Buff, and additional protection against Aircraft. Everyone seems a little easier with the Pocket Battleship bottled up, that was the main worry, particularly when we are well South.

The 'Exeter' caught it rather badly; five officers killed, sixty six ratings killed and twenty injured.

Heard at 11.00pm ship's time that the Pocket Battleship 'Graf Spee' had blown herself up and sunk. What an inglorious end!

Monday 18th December

The above news of the 'Graf Spee' was verified from home this morning. What a crowd they were! They spent all night attacking an armed merchant cruiser, but when it came to their turn to come out and fight they had no guts. I don't think you'd find a British ship behaving like that. I sincerely hope that the 'Admiral Scheer' will be the next for the big jump!

Picking up a little breeze today.

Tuesday 19th December

Naval news is well to the front these last few days. If they continue in this way I shall almost have occasion to change my mind about them!

On 14th December the submarine 'Ursula' sank a cruiser of the Kohn class, even though it was screened by six destroyers. The 'Ursula' was completed in 1929-30 weighs 6,000 tons and is capable of 32 knots, it is armed with 5 5" - 9" guns and 12 - 21" torpedo tubes.

Captain Bickford of the submarine 'Salmon' sighted the 'Bremen', one day later sighted the battle cruisers 'Scharnhorst' and 'Gneisenau', a Pocket Battleship and three light cruisers. The sub fired six torpedoes, one hit the light cruiser 'Leipsig' and two others found their mark also with one ship or more possibly sunk, no definite confirmation to hand as yet.

An air raid on Heligoland by the RAF was met with a strong fighter formation of twenty four Messerschmitts, a fierce battle ensued and twelve of the Messerschmitts were shot down, but unfortunately seven of our bombers are unaccounted for.

Ships news still the same, no unusual happenings, and looking forward to the Cape.

Wednesday 20th December

We fear that the German liner 'Columbus' (32,000 tons) has been scuttled off Virginia, to avoid capture after being intercepted by the Royal Navy.

The RAF has been generally busy over the North Sea.

Hoping to reach Cape Town Sunday morning and possibly off load same day.

Thursday 21st December

Reported suicide of Captain Lansdorf of the 'Graf Spee'.

Same routine, still waiting and wishing. We will definitely arrive in Cape Town on Sunday.

The German liner the 'Cafs Corte' has been intercepted and captured by the British Naval force and has now arrived in a British port. It was well laden!

The submarine 'Ursula' which sank the German cruiser has arrived safely in port, and was given an enthusiastic welcome.

Friday 22nd December

Captain of the 'Graf Spee' buried with full military honours.

Usual ships routine.

Saturday 23rd December

Usual routine again, very little news.

Sunday 24th December

Arrived at Cape Town at 6.15am and tied up.

It is a beautiful morning, but that's all that can be said at the moment, there was just someone to tug us in and then they left. There are no papers and no news until 1.15pm. After a shake up I hear that they are going to work cargo, so they are alive after all! They are going to work cargo until it's finished, so we hope to get away by 6.00am tomorrow morning, and what a Christmas it will be being at sea, but let us hope this is the last one.

Very little news from the Western Front, and no arrival activity.

Christmas Day - Monday 25th December 1939

Left Cape Town at 6.30am

Usual Christmas festivities, but very few passengers. We have received Christmas message from His Majesty King George which reads as follows:-

TO ALL BRITISH MERCHANT SHIPS, FROM HIS MAJESTY THE KING

It has not been possible for me to send a Christmas card to each member of the British Merchant Navy and Fishing Fleets as I have done to members of the fighting forces, because their ships are so widely scattered over the Seven Seas. Instead I send to each one of you this personal message of good will and good cheer. You are facing the special perils which in these days surround the seaman, with a coolness courage and fortitude which are the admiration of us all at home and I know that I speak not only for myself but for all my fellow countrymen when I wish you a Happy Christmas and a good landfall.

George R. I.

Tuesday 26th December

Arrived at Port Elizabeth

Plenty of activity today in getting out cargo, so that we can get away as soon as possible. We eventually leave at about 7.00pm, having done very well apparently.

Wednesday 27th December

Arrived at East London at 7.30am.

Left for Durban at 2.30pm.

Picked up some heavy weather just outside, but still hope to make port early tomorrow morning.

Thursday 28th December

Back in Durban once again, arrived about 7.00am, there is one other Castle Boat here, the 'Richmond', loading sugar for home. Terribly hot today, and not feeling a bit like work. But there is plenty of work going on, loading cargo out and in, and trying to finish painting the ship.

Finns are still going strong, and I sincerely hope they will get the help that they deserve.

Friday 29th December

Still busy and still very hot.

Usual boat stations and grace.

Submarine 35P came in this morning.

Saturday 30th December

Heard late last night that a British Battleship of the Q.E. class had been torpedoed but managed to reach port under her own steam. Three reported dead and one missing.

Still busy loading and may get away late tonight.

We have been very fortunate in a way, we left at 5.30pm but our good luck only lasted a short while, we ran into extremely heavy weather and had to ease down, several sailors were injured during the night, and we shall be late getting to East London now.

Sunday 31st December

Arrived at East London at 9.45am after a very rough passage, four sailors were landed to hospital.

Very little other news.

Chapter Two

New Year New Hope

'Richmond Castle'

Monday 1st January 1940

Arrived at Port Elizabeth and left again same day.

A start of another year and I wonder what it holds for us, at home may our wishes be realised, and afield our hopes materialise. There was good news today from Finland, and I hope they continue with their good work. The 'Tacoma', the supply ship to the 'Graf Spee' has, with her crew and with that of the battleship been interned at Montevideo for the duration. We hear officially that the 'Windhuck' which is well known to us on this run, is now at Santos in Brazil. The 'St Louis' has reached Germany from Momansk.

'Boxhill' is the first steamer to be reported sunk in the new year. The second contingent of Canadians arrive at a West Country port having been safely escorted across the Atlantic by the French Navy.

Tuesday 2nd January

Arrived at Mossel Bay and left again in the afternoon for Cape Town. The Finns still reported to be doing well and 'HMS Ajax' is visiting Montevideo and has been well received by the British community, owing to her success in the 'Graf Spee' engagement

Wednesday 3rd January

Busy painting ship, and loading cargo in an endeavour to get away tomorrow, if we are lucky! Fifty cabins have been stripped and used for general cargo, we are now just a super cargo steamer, more for the dole when we get home!

Thursday 4th January

Still busy and waiting.

Friday 5th January

Eventually got away at 8.00pm, full to the hatch tops with cargo. The 'Durban Castle' arrived from home and docked at 6.00am.

'Ajax' and 'Achilles' are reported to have left the River Plate.

Leslie Hoare-Belisha is reported to have given up his post as Minister for War, confirmed late this evening. All were very surprised as we felt he was a square peg in a square hole. Maybe there were things going on behind the scenes!

Saturday 6th January

Getting along very nicely, but the sea is a little swelly, hope to run out of it tomorrow. The ship is well down, necessitating in my port having to be closed, to the detriment of my stiff collar. All white tomorrow, thank goodness!

Sunday 7th January

Heard that Belisha had resigned.

Still getting along fine, nothing else to report

Monday 8th January

Heard the very good news today, that we are not calling at Sierra Leone, and that we were on a two hundred mile shorter course. We saw three ships this afternoon all homeward bound. One was the 'Japanese Prince' that had bunkered at Cape Town while we were there, and left twenty six hours before us, so I assume round about 14 knots - a safe landfall to all of them.

Tuesday 9th January

Leslie Hoare-Belisha hands in seals of office, and officially ceases to be our Secretary of State for War. To my mind with his passing, Britain loses a good man, and the army a good friend. Mr Oliver Stanley son of Lord Derby, and until a few days ago, President of the Board of Trade, succeeds him as our new minister.

Wednesday 10th January

More raids yesterday by the RAF over Germany, believed to be successful.

We hear the sad news that two Union Castle boats have been lost, namely the 'Dunbar Castle' by a mine and the 'Rothesay Castle' by torpedo, this has not been officially given out on board, and as much as we believe it's true, we sincerely hope that it isn't.

The above information has been confirmed. Apparently the 'Dunbar' was mined in the channel with the loss of her Captain and five other ratings and one passenger is missing.

Thursday 11th January

Several raids on East Coast ports, but no casualties.

'Windhuck' is unloading some of her cargo that was destined for Britain, she is still at Santos and is likely to remain there, as I believe a cruiser is waiting somewhere in the vicinity. The 'Ajax' called at Rio-de-Janeiro on a courtesy visit, and presumably to be near the 'Windhuck!'

Friday 12th January

We have made good headway so far, for we are according to reckoning, on a parallel with Freetown. Thank goodness we are not going there! The weather is somewhat cooler today, a good indication of being near the Verdes. We all wonder if the Leesen radio will be correct, in so much as we are due for Davy Jones Locker once we get in the bay, lets hope it's just more Goebbels Gob!

'Dunbar Castle'

Saturday 13th January

Very little news today. There is a concert in the 2nd class dining saloon, given by the tourist class passengers.

Sunday 14th January

This morning we saw a French torpedo boat on patrol, she apparently satisfied herself as to our identity and allowed us to proceed upon our lawful occasion. We heard tonight that Holland and Belgium had practically declared a general mobilisation, this is a bad sign in a way, for it makes one realise that the whole of Europe will be involved before it's all over.

Monday 15th January

Very little to report today apart from the fact we are back again in Blues and zig zagging, both an indication that we are nearing the danger zone, once more we had the usual A.R.P. this morning

Tuesday 16th January

Beautiful weather and making good headway. We should be there by noon on Saturday if we are left alone! We have just heard that the 'Highland Princess' has been torpedoed just three hours ago and about fifty miles from us, so there is a Hun about somewhere, anyway whatever happens it's a nice day, and you can't have it all ways! We will just go on hoping, it is one of the few things we are able to do.

Personally I think the submarine campaign will start in earnest very soon, their inactivity during the last few weeks may be perhaps the lull before the storm; I hope I am wrong.

Just received the news that the Dutch liner 'Oranjekerk' has been sunk, without warning in the Bay of Biscay. Things are warming up, here's to the next time!

 The beautiful weather has now changed to rain. One more indication of getting nearer home.

The Admiralty has just reported the loss of three British subs 'Undine' 500 tons 'Seahorse' 700 tons and 'Starfish' 700 tons. A very sad affair, but we are led to believe that most of the crews are safe.

Wednesday 17th January

Loss of British subs officially confirmed by the Admiralty. 'The Houston City' reported sunk according to rumour about 500 miles ahead of us. The weather has changed, and it is now raining. The moonlit nights are a constant terror to us, and we continue with our submarine watches until the moon has disappeared.

Naval losses to date;   HMS's 'Courageous' - 'Royal Oak' - 'Oxley' - 'Jersey' - 'Gypsy' - 'Blanch' - 'Duchess' - 'Undine' - 'Seahorse' - 'Starfish.'

Thursday 18th January

Passed Finistérre at about 4pm, but away to the Westward, weather fairly good considering the ship's position.

Friday 19th January

All news to ship suspended as from last night, owing to close watch for S.O.S

Atrocious weather conditions, raining, cold, and blowing pretty hard. In spite of the weather we are making good headway. We hope to make the Boom by 9.00am, we shall be at the docks at noon.

Saturday 20th January

Sighted the Island at about 6.30am, opposite St Catherines 7.30am. A convoy of nineteen ships passed us with the usual Naval escort. Extremely cold, but who cares!

Passed through the Boom at about 9.30am, and ships of every description are about; Navy craft are also in evidence. We were doing very well until we received news to anchor, what was said is almost unprintable, and I am afraid I assisted in this direction. The weather is terribly cold, and as a matter of fact I have never known the wind so keen, particularly in the shelter of the Island; We hope to be alongside by 2.00pm - home by 6.00pm.

We finally tied up at 2.30pm at berth 36. Usual routine to continue as far as we know.

Sunday 21st January

Enjoyed some of the deserved rest; but it is extremely cold, which tends to cramp one's style. Still it's an ill wind etc......

Monday 22nd January

Destroyer 'H.M.S. Grenville' sunk after striking a mine in the North Sea.

Tuesday 23rd January

I heard today that I am to leave the 'Windsor' to go on the shore staff for an indefinite period.

After my short period of leave, I remained on the shore staff until 15th April, and resumed my journal in the week prior to my new assignment.

Tuesday 9th April

We hear this morning that Germany has invaded Denmark and landed troops at several Norwegian ports. This was confirmed later, and according to the German version, was in answer to our laying mine fields off the Norwegian coast. We are giving immediate Naval assistance backed by the R.A.F.. A Naval engagement took place at Harvik. We lost two destroyers, the 'Hunter' and 'Hardy' . The Nazi's have lost to date two Cruisers, the 'Bleucher' and 'Karlsruhe,' other ships are reported sunk but not yet confirmed. The R.A.F. bombed the Nazis' fleet and inflicted damage. The crack Nazi liner 'Bremen' has been reported sunk.

Wednesday 10th April

Everyone is waiting news of the Naval action, but nothing confirmed as yet.

The Norwegian army is resisting, but news of this is also very scarce, owing to their broadcasting station at Oslo having fallen into Nazi hands.

Thursday 11th April

The War at sea has started in earnest.

Monday 15th April

My stay on the Staff is over, and in many ways all too soon. I join the 'Llanstephan' at noon. She has just finished a voyage as a cargo ship, and at the moment she is anything but a liner to look at. Still what is to be will be and I hope for the best. The vessel is lying at the Royal Albert Docks still discharging cargo.

Tuesday 16th April

Still finding my way around, and busily engaged in getting things to my way of liking, with reference to the office and cabin etc.

Wednesday 17th April

Proceeded on six days leave.

Friday 26th April

Usual ships routine the past few days, getting ready for sea.

Saturday 27th April

Had a shock today on being told I was to leave the 'Llanstephan Castle' and proceed on a long weekend prior to joining the 'HMS Cheshire' at Langdon docks in Liverpool.

Tuesday 30th April

I leave for London and Liverpool at 11.20am from Southampton Central, going via Euston.
I left Euston at 2.40pm and eventually arrived at Lime street Liverpool at 7.00pm. I got a taxi to the ship which was a distance of about five miles. After having a good look at her I went a board and she seemed to be a hopeless mess. The next day I looked over her thoroughly and came to the conclusion that this ship is no place for me!

Thursday 2nd May

I decide to see the paymaster and be returned to duty with the Castle company, and with this in view I pay off and leave Liverpool for London on the 10.00am train arriving at Euston at 2.15pm. I went to the office to explain my case and have now been told to report to our office at the Royal Albert Docks for duty.

Friday 3rd May

After working in the office all day, I am told to report back to Southampton. This was a pleasant surprise and I think it is for the 'Durban Castle'. I do hope so, as it would be really nice to settle down once again after the turmoil of this last week. I am weary of carrying baggage to and fro!

Monday 6th May

I have not been posted to the 'Durban Castle' after all, but as before I must assist on the shore staff until something comes along.

Monday 8th July

After having spent many weeks on the staff, I am at last appointed to the 'Athlone Castle.'

Tuesday 9th July

What a day! All the French sailors taken off and Men of War at Portsmouth come on board until other accommodation is found for them, over 2,000 in total, what a shambles!

Wednesday 10th July

We hear that the French sailors will be leaving tomorrow and that we have been taken over by the government to do a trooping voyage.

Thursday 11th July

The French sailors leave us, much to our sorrow (I don't think) and we get really busy in readiness for our troops.

Friday 12th July

The advance guard of troops join the boat and I understand that we are to sail tomorrow for Gibraltar, after having embarked the remainder of the troops. Hustle is the pass word at the moment!

Saturday 13th July

Left Southampton at 12.30pm with 1,500 troops on board bound for Gibraltar. After getting off Gosport we made circles adjusting our compass, whilst waiting for darkness, and finally slip through the Boom at 9.00pm. With us came the 'Strathaird', a three funnelled P & O Liner with passengers and troops on board for Australia. Once outside the defence we were picked up by two Destroyers which are to become our escort for the whole voyage. We steamed on into the night expecting at any moment for something to happen but nothing came and we sailed merrily on unmolested - for the time being that is!

Sunday 14th July

All well so far, and we are making to the Westward and down channel.   The most inspiring thing so far, is the mounting of sixteen Bren Guns at various points around the ship, to help repel an enemy air attack which we knew would almost certainly come as it was ideal weather and we were well within coastal range. We hadn't long to wait, for at about 1.00pm, three German aircraft launched an attack, and there was a terrific explosion just astern - one near miss! All guns then from all four ships put up a strong barrage and drove them skywards, but in spite of this they continued to drop more bombs, one of which dropped quite close to our starboard bow, exploding on striking the water and sending showers of spray on board, getting too close to be comfortable now, guns still rent the air and eventually they are beaten off, to our great relief I may say.   We were just sitting down, thinking it was all over, when one of our escort destroyers let go and the attack began once again.   All guns once more came into action and once more drove them off, finally this time! We had been under attack for over an hour. We continued on our way all ships at full speed, with the 'Strathaird' just off our starboard beam, and a Destroyer ahead and astern.   This formation continued well into the late evening until we were out of the attack range.

Monday 15th July

This morning at 4.00am we prepared for a dawn attack, but thank goodness it never materialised. At 6.00am on going on deck we were surprised to find that one Destroyer had left us. At 8.00am the 'Strathaird' left us, proceeding in a Southerly direction, whilst we turned South East with just a single Destroyer as escort.

We had many stand by calls during the day but nothing happened. At 7.00pm the Destroyer that appeared to have left us in the morning, reappeared, and came close alongside, and after rousing cheers, which were returned to the limit by the troops on board her she finally bade us goodbye and good luck and turned for home. The other Destroyer then left us, two more having appeared from ahead to continue the escort.   With one Destroyer on either side and feeling fairly secure we leave it to the Navy for once as we steam into the night, hoping that the Navy's watchful care will bring us ultimately to our destination.

Tuesday 16th July

Still steaming merrily along, the day passing without incident.

The Destroyers at times turned off, and went looking for trouble, and having found none returned to us and took up usual steaming positions. We hope to arrive at Gib tomorrow at around noon, in many ways we shall be pleased to get there, having had so much work to do being the chief reason!

Wednesday 17th July

Still going good and in sight of land, we gradually make port and The Rock is now in view. We get alongside at 2.00pm to be greeted by an air raid but nothing out of the ordinary happens. The Navy is well represented, consisting of the 'Ark Royal', 'Hood', 'Valiant', several Light Cruisers, Destroyers and Subs. We lose the army and settle down to clean the ship, which is an almost impossible task. We have two more air raids during the afternoon, but without result, as far as we're concerned. After all my labours I decide to turn in early and get a little rest, but was disturbed at 1.00pm by the ships air raid siren. I looked out of my port and saw the planes caught in a search light beam. All guns immediately went into action and after the dropping of several bombs, the planes were driven off. Several places on shore were hit, and a few people were killed, we still survive the ordeal. We hear that we are to take 1,672 evacuees from The Rock for home, another nightmare for a day or two. I tremble to think what will happen if we have to take to the boats, or even bombed, having as many as 800 children amongst them.

Thursday July 18th

Gibraltar

Much the same routine as yesterday, the army are still unloading the ship.
Another air raid.

Friday 19th July

Gibraltar

As for yesterday - but no air raid.

Saturday 20th July

Gibraltar

As for yesterday - with a raid.

Sunday 21st July

Gibraltar

A day of rest much appreciated - no raid - plenty of ship movement (Naval)

Monday 22nd July

Gibraltar

Finished cleaning ship and preparing to leave.

Tuesday 23rd July

Gibraltar

We hear we are leaving on Saturday with 2,000 evacuees, mostly women and children. We are now busy with the extra beds, stores, etc. We have moved into the inner harbour and anchored. The harbour is almost full of ships awaiting convoy. From where we are anchored we can see several Italian Oilers lying off the Spanish coast, in a scuttled condition.

Wednesday 24th July

Gibraltar

Had two more raids today, but nothing happened as far as we know, but plenty of gun fire. The 'Ark Royal' has left with an escort of four Destroyers and a light cruiser. We hear that some Naval Ratings are joining us tomorrow for guard duties etc.

Thursday 25th July

Gibraltar

We hear the evacuees are coming tomorrow, and we leave for somewhere, probably home. The exact number is 1,762 and amongst them there are 1,500 women and children. The Lord help us if anything happens. The Naval

Ratings joined this afternoon, so things look a bit more hopeful. Two more raids, and few bombs dropped, we're getting a bit used to them now.

Friday 26th July

Gibraltar

This morning at 1.30am, we had a rude awakening, all guns and search lights must have been in action. Five bombs exploded in quick succession, on Europa Point, quite near to us, and the blast almost blew us out of our bunks! The raid was over in a few minutes, there being little damage done to property, and none at all to shipping, although there are dozens in the harbour, apart from Naval craft.

The evacuees joined us today and what a mob. Women and children streaming aboard all day long. We finally get them settled in after a long struggle, and we get under way at 8.00pm. At the moment I cannot say if we have an escort or not, but I think we have. From what I can gather we are taking them home, and if all goes well we should make port by about next Tuesday, at the moment we're doing fine - may it continue!

Saturday 27th July

At the moment we are steaming 20 knots and doing fine, up to a point. This crowd is enough to drive one mad, thank goodness it's only for a day or two. Our escort Destroyer left us at noon today, so now we have the ocean to ourselves (we hope) we will possible pick up another escort nearing the channel.

Sunday 28th July

A day of rest, but unfortunately it doesn't apply to us, we have had our usual day of hell, so roll on Wednesday morning!

Monday 29th July

Much the same as yesterday, steaming well, working well, and .... well!

Tuesday 30th July

A little choppy today but doing very well, passed a convoy in the distance steaming North. Hope to be somewhere near port by this time tomorrow, what a blessing it will be to get rid of this crowd. We are at the moment steaming North East, which means we are lying off the North of Ireland heading for distant Scotland.

Wednesday 31st July

Sighted land this morning at about 8.00am, a very welcome sight, we should be at safe anchorage inside the Boom at 9.00pm. Saw a couple of Mine Sweepers, and a Cumberland Flying Boat, the latter we hope will be keeping an eye to Subs.

Thursday 1st August

Liverpool

Arrived alongside landing stage at 11.00am, and proceeded to get rid of the crowd. Had order to prepare and sail again on Monday. This was cancelled later in the day, then we had more orders to stand by for trooping again in nine days time. This was also cancelled later, now it's possible we may go back on the Mail Run. Stayed alongside landing stage until 10.00pm, then anchored out in stream, we are hoping to go alongside to pay off. We are all in a turmoil wondering what will happen, more muddle!

Friday 2nd August

Still waiting news as to what we might do, but so far the wait has been in vain. Still cleaning ship and waiting to pay off. Had an air raid last night, but nothing happened to us.

Saturday 3rd August

Still no news and getting a bit restless, were we alongside it wouldn't be so bad, being anchored in the stream and no connection with shore is hopeless, isolated, and apparently forgotten. The 'Otranto' moves out into the steam with troops for East Africa.

RMS 'Otranto' Orient Line

Sunday 4th August

Had a rotten night having to turn out twice for air raids, but as far as we know no bombs were dropped. I think they must be trying to drop mines at the river entrance. We are still in the stream and waiting to pay off.

Thursday 8th August

The "Luftwaffe" launches it's first heavy daylight attack - one hundred and thirty planes attack our convoys off Bournemouth.

Saturday 10th August

At last we leave our anchorage after ten days and proceed to Langdon Dock. We eventually get inside the basin after a struggle with wind, currents, etc. and tie up at about 4.00pm. Not paying off until Monday.

Sunday 11th August

Had a quiet day for a change, went over the River Mersey by steamer and returned by the Tunnel Route, which by the way was very interesting.

Monday 12th August

One hundred and fifty planes attacked Portsmouth and the Isle of Wight.
Usual Dock routine.

Tuesday 13th August

'Warwick Castle' comes into port from South Africa.

Wednesday 14th August

Heard for certain that I may proceed on leave on Friday.

Thursday 15th August

Still waiting - this time for leave!

Friday 16th August

Proceeded on leave for six days, left Liverpool at 10.00am and arrived at Southampton Central at 6.00pm in the middle of a raid. Saw the cold storage depot still burning.

Saturday 17th August

Went to Fareham and the pictures.

Sunday 18th August

Day of complete rest!

Monday 19th August

Went to S.M.B.

Tuesday 20th August

Toured Southampton.

Wednesday 21st August

Returned form leave, leaving Southampton at 11.20 for Liverpool via Euston.   Arrived at Lime Street 7.00pm aboard by 8.00pm.

Thursday 22nd August

Awaiting orders.

Friday 23rd August

Heard I am to leave the ship, much to my regret.

Sunday 25th August

Portsmouth and Southampton attacked by enemy aircraft at about 4.00pm, but no serious damage was done. I shall now be working on the shore staff for the next few weeks.

Thursday 5th September

Finally leave the 'Athlone' and go into digs at 77, Bailey Drive, Gorell, Liverpool 20, still continuing on shore staff duties.

Sunday 15th September

One hundred and eighty five enemy aircraft destroyed - Our Greatest Day! Went to the pictures, came home in a raid.

Saturday 21st September

Went to the pictures again, and owing to raids, decide to stay home in future. Heard today that I may go to the 'Roxburgh Castle'.

Sunday 22nd September

Decide to give up the digs, and remain on board the 'Roxburgh Castle.'

Monday 23rd September

Standing by ship

Tuesday 24th September

Possibly going on leave on Friday.

Thursday 26th September

In view of my leave starting tomorrow, I leave the ship at 7.00pm so as to get to the station before the raids start. I hope to travel through the night, to save time. On arriving at Lime Street Station, the siren sounded and the fun started. I went to Hunts Hotel shelter where I remained for nearly four hours, the raid still being on at midnight. I managed to get to the station and eventually into the train, the journey to Southampton took eighteen hours, normally it would take seven to eight hours, the delay again was owing to various raids. Eventually arrived at Southampton Central at 5.30pm tired, and fed up.

Friday 27th September

After a good nights sleep all is well once again.

Wednesday 2nd October

Returned from leave, leaving Southampton at 8.25am for Lime Street. Arrived at Liverpool at 7.30pm a little better run than going down! Arrived on board at 8.00pm finding everything in order.

Tuesday 8th October

Signed Articles - Still loading, heard we may not leave until Saturday.

Wednesday 9th October

Not sailing until Friday, loading general cargo.

Friday 11th October

Finished loading and waiting to sail. Had a terrific air raid, worst so far, but fortunately there was no damage to the docks or ships.

Saturday 12th October

Made ready to leave Canada Dock Liverpool for an anchorage in the stream to await convoy escort, left our berth at 2.00pm and after passing through several locks and gates we finally go into the river and make for the safe anchorage, where we dropped anchor at 6.25pm. Many other ships are here awaiting orders to sail, which no doubt will be early morning. Our crew consists of fifty seven various ratings, from Master to Cooks Boy, a motley crowd, but what matters, if we bring home the bacon, which is our direct aim!

Chapter Three

'Roxburgh Castle'

Sunday 13th October   -   1st Day Out

Our last day at anchor and we prepare to sail, leaving our anchorage at 7.00pm. There are six ships in the convoy consisting of : 'Roxburgh Castle', 'Duchess of Atholl,' 'Australian Star,' 'Port Townsville,' 'Glenartney,' and a Belgian ship; We have two destroyers for escort the H44 and H88.

At the moment everything is peaceful and we are steaming very well. Went to Boat Stations today, the first time on a Sunday during my whole sea career, the boats were turned outboard and lowered to rail, then bought in and provisioned and watered in case of emergency.

We steam in the following order:

"Glenartney"

"Belgian"

"Roxburgh Castle"

"Port Townsville"

"Duchess of Atholl"

"Australian Star"

'Roxburgh Castle'   *B & A Feilden*

36

Monday 14th October - **2nd Day Out**

Blew up a bit rough last night, and things were not too good, a little better today, rolling slightly with a following sea. We have now six Destroyers with us, giving us a feeling of comparative safety. It is an unusual number for an escort, I should think they were meeting some big convoy, and thus killing two birds with one stone. The Belgian left us this morning, and proceeded to Glasgow, and two more joined with us so now we are seven, now sailing in the following formation:

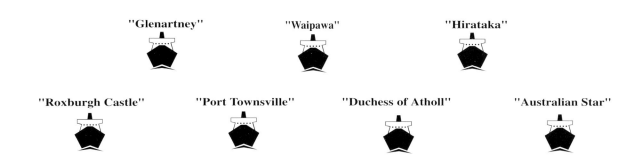

"Glenartney"   "Waipawa"   "Hirataka"

"Roxburgh Castle"   "Port Townsville"   "Duchess of Atholl"   "Australian Star"

We have two Destroyers ahead, two to port, and two to starboard, and have increased speed to about 14 knots, earlier we had only been steaming at 12 knots. Everyone is settling down and looking forward to a peaceful time, once out of the danger zone. Several bombers flew around this morning, on the look out for subs no doubt. It is now 10.00pm and at the moment all is quiet.

Tuesday 15th October - **3rd Day Out**

Everything so far still satisfactory, and all ships are present and correct. Early this morning one of our Destroyers left us. This afternoon at 5.00pm, two more returned, so we continue on with the three remaining Destroyers, probably until tomorrow when no doubt we will be left entirely on our own. Clock put back one hour.

Wednesday 16th October - **4th Day Out**

Had a mild surprise this morning when I looked out, we were entirely on our own and speeding South. I learned later that we departed from the convoy at 5.00am, and each ship proceeded singularly, the Destroyers will take up convoy duty on our return journey. It is pretty rough today, a very strong wind blowing, half gale I should imagine, the ship is pitching heavily at times but not too bad I suppose considering she is fairly light, with only about 3,500 tons of general cargo. Clock put back another hour.

Thursday 17th October - **5th Day Out**

Had a terrible night last night, ship rolling so much that it was almost an impossibility to stay in the bunk, much less to sleep! Continued very rough all day but the rolling has eased slightly. We are now roughly off Lands End, but well to the Westward, about 1,800 West of Greenwich. We are all looking forward to the Tropics when we shall be in a comparatively safe zone and have some decent weather, but there are a few more days to go yet unfortunately.

Friday 18th October - **6th Day Out**

Things generally a little better, gradually getting warmer and not quite as much rolling. At the moment it's quite good, if only it will last.

Saturday 19th October - **7th Day Out**

Everything going along nicely, and running into some decent weather, although I expect in a day or two it will be too hot. Getting things sorted out, and now more or less settled down. A lovely moonlit night, I only hope things are as peaceful at home.

'Empress of Britain' sunk by enemy aircraft

Monday 28th October - **16th Day Out**

Heard that the 'Empress of Britain,' has been sunk by enemy aircraft, possibly last Saturday. Also that Italy had declared War on Greece. Just beginning to wonder what will happen next.

Tuesday 29th October - **17th Day Out**

Heard that the Greeks and Italians are at it, but very little definite news. We are out of the tropics and getting well South, much cooler.

Friday 1st November - **20th Day Out**

Turned to the Eastward today, so getting quite near to Cape Town, we hope to arrive tomorrow morning sometime. Passed a ship this afternoon, it is the first thing we have seen for over a fortnight! Everything OK and I am looking forward to a change of scenery.
Message received from the War Ministry.

THE BATTLE OF BRITAIN

8th August to 31st October 1940

"The gratitude of every home in our Island, in our Empire, and indeed throughout the World, except in the abodes of the guilty, goes out to the British airmen, who, undaunted by odds, unwearied in their constant challenge and mortal danger, are turning the tide of World War by their prowess and by their devotion. Never in the field of human conflict was so much owed by so many to so few."

THE PRIME MINISTER

Mr. Winston Churchill
THEIR GREATEST DAY. 15th SEPTEMBER 1940
The enemy lost 185 aircraft.

Saturday 2nd November - Cape Town   -   **21 Days Out**

At last we are at port after a very pleasant but thankfully uneventful journey. We arrived this morning about 5.00pm, steamed slowly into the bay and dropped anchor. Around us there are twenty seven other ships of various sizes and nationalities. The 'Glenartney' is here, this is one of the new fast cargo ships which was in our convoy on leaving Liverpool, being as she is anchored in the bay, she can't have been here long, so we haven't done so badly! The 'Capetown Castle' is in alongside, and the 'Durban' has just arrived also. The 'Neptune' has come back into dock looking a very different sight from when I last saw her, she is now in her war paint and camouflaged.

Later

'Capetown Castle' has now left for home, and the 'Durban' and us are going alongside to start discharging right away and shall probably leave for the coast on Monday.

Sunday 3rd November   -   **22nd Day Out**

Had a more or less perfect day, no running to shelters etc. Hope to get away tomorrow.

Monday 4th November   -   **23rd Day Out**

Got our letters away, and now stowing ship in readiness for the coast.

Tuesday 5th November   -   **24th Day Out**

'HMS Jervis Bay' sunk by gunfire from a German raider, whilst protecting a British convoy. We are now coastwise to Port Elizabeth, having left Cape Town yesterday at about 5.00pm. Weather not too warm, a steady swell. We are well out to sea and have just sighted two more vessels also steaming East.

Wednesday 6th November   -   **25th Day Out**

Arrived at Port Elizabeth at 8.00am, and proceeded to discharge cargo. We hear the 'Winchester Castle' left here last night for Cape Town and home. Lovely summer weather here and everything seems quiet as usual.

Thursday 7th November   -   **26th Day Out**

Arrived East London 8.30am, and left at 1.30pm for Durban.

Friday 8th November   -   **27th Day Out**

Arrived at Durban at 8.00am and went alongside the Mail Berth. The 'Llangibby' is in, loading for home, after having been trooping from here to Mombassa.   Very busy off loading, hope to finish tonight then start loading for home. We should be able to get away sometime on Sunday.

Saturday 9th November   -   **28th Day Out**

What a day, nothing but rain! Stored ship, and possibly leave tomorrow at noon.

Sunday 10th November   -   **29th Day Out**

Weather a little better today, and everything possible is being done in an effort to get us away.
We finally leave at 5.00pm and once passed the Bluff we run into heavy weather. We are not calling at East London, we are going to Port Elizabeth direct.
We have just heard of the death of Mr Chamberlain.

Monday 11th November   -   **30th Day Out**

Had a good shake up last night, what with the weather and rolling etc! However we survived the ordeal and made the harbour at 3.30pm. The 'Arundel' was alongside outward from the Cape. We will have a quiet night and prepare for loading in the morning.

The 'Jervis Bay' (Aberdeen & Commonwealth Line)
Sunk by enemy gunfire after helping 38 convoy ships to escape

Tuesday 12th November - **31st Day Out**

Busy all day loading oranges for home, and we finally get away at 6.30pm for Cape Town where we hope to arrive on Thursday morning, possibly a two day stay then off again.

Wednesday 13th November - **32nd Day Out**

Have just heard that one of our convoys was attacked by a Pocket Battleship early last week. It appears that out of the whole convoy nine ships have been sunk including the 'Jervis Bay,' who made a good fight against the raider for over two hours, thus giving twenty nine other ships time to escape. A jolly good feat against such tremendous odds, and mostly by men of the Merchant Service.

Have also just heard that Mussolini has had a set back with his navy. By all accounts they have been bombed whilst in port and several ships have been sunk or partially sunk and put out of action; Now to chase the raider!

Thursday 14th November - **33rd Day Out**

Arrived off Cape Town 6.15am, and anchored in the bay awaiting the pilot.
We go alongside at 7.30am, and get busy right away. Expected to get some mail but we were disappointed!

Friday 15th November - **34th Day Out**

Still loading and expect to get away tomorrow.

Saturday 16th November - **35th Day Out**

We finish loading and finally get away at just after 1.00pm. Full up with cargo, mostly fruit, meat, and copper. We also have stores for the NAAFI at Freetown, that will mean another couple of days extra sailing. She has started rolling already, empty or loaded doesn't seem to make much difference to this wagon!

Sunday 17th November - **36th Day Out**

Getting well out to sea and going along nicely apart from rolling!

Monday 18th November - **37th Day Out**

Getting away from the Cape Rollers and running into warmer weather. Saw another ship away on the horizon.

Tuesday 19th November - **38th Day Out**

Heard today there is a Raider about, but so far we are still afloat.

Wednesday 20th November - **39th Day Out**

Still afloat. Boat stations.

Friday 22nd November - **40th Day Out**

Heard the good news today that the Greeks had taken Coritza and turned the Italians out, great rejoicing in Athens.

Saturday 23rd November - **41st Day Out**

Crossed the line today and started zigzagging getting into some new danger zone I should imagine. By all accounts we should arrive at Freetown either Monday night or Tuesday morning.

Sunday 24th November - **42nd Day Out**

It has been very warm today, but with plenty of rain. Getting near to Freetown and Paravanes are put out, in case of mines. Passed a Portuguese ship last night all lit up, quite a rare sight! Heard that the German Raider has been shelling ports of the West Indies. Although it's bad news in a way, it means good news for us because we know that she is away in that part of the globe. Hope to arrive tomorrow morning at 7.00am, and hope also that our stay will be short!

Monday 25th November - **43rd Day Out**

Stood off Freetown at 7.00am. We saw an aircraft carrier with a Cruiser and two Destroyers making for port, they have possibly been out looking for the Raider. The Pilot came on board at 8.40am and took us alongside the 'City of Dieppe' to discharge our stores for the NAAFI.

There are plenty of ships here, over thirty in number I should think, representing the Navy. 'HMS Resolution' is being fitted up after her affair at Dakar, there are two Aircraft Carriers, three Light Cruisers, two Destroyers, and one heavy cruiser of the Arethiusa class. For the Merchant Navy there are just too many to mention. There are two Vichy French ships here loaded with troops just eating their heads off, won't fight just want to go back to France! Extremely hot here today, let's hope we soon get away. The old 'Edinburgh Castle' is here doing duty as Naval depot ship; A nice square number!

Tuesday 26th November - **44th Day Out**

Still busy offloading, hope to get away later today or at the very latest by tonight.

Later

Have just heard that we shall not be getting away today, but we will be spending a few more hours in this rotten hole.

Wednesday 27th November - **45th Day Out**

Heard this morning that the 'Dunnottar Castle' which is an armed Merchant cruiser has been sunk by enemy action, but so far this has not been confirmed.   We finally leave Freetown at 2.00pm and make for sea, thank goodness we shall then pick up a bit of breeze; Hopefully we don't pick up anything else!

Good news; 'Dunnottar Castle' report proves to be false!

Thursday 28th November - **46th Day Out**

Still on top and going well to the West'ard getting a little cooler thank goodness.

Saturday 30th November - **47th Day Out**

Have heard that Southampton has had it's biggest air raid of the War.

Nothing else to report, just steaming along and hoping for the best. Weather a bit on the heavy side considering where we are.

'Edinburgh Castle'

'Dunnottar Castle'

'Carnarvon Castle' in Montevideo Harbour after fight with German raider

Sunday 1st December - **48th Day Out**

Yet another air raid on Southampton

Monday 2nd December - **49th Day Out**

Picking up cooler weather, we are now almost opposite Gibraltar, but off course West'ard. We have heard that a British Destroyer has run aground and been lost off the Scottish coast.
We have also heard tonight that to date 376 people have so far been killed in the Southampton air raids.

Tuesday 3rd December - **50th Day Out**

Boat stations and picking up bad weather.

Wednesday 4th December - **51st Day Out**

Weather continues to get worse, and I think we are in for a bad time; One thing though, it will keep the Subs away!

Thursday 5th December - **52nd Day Out**

Weather about as bad as it could be, and we are going through our paces, trying to get meals is almost out of the question, but still we battle on and as usual hope for the best.

Friday 6th December - **53rd Day Out**

Weather even worse today if that's possible! We have just heard that 'HMS Carnarvon Castle' has been in action with a German Raider 700 hundred miles NE of Montevideo, this action I presume took place yesterday.

Saturday 7th December - **54th Day Out**

Owing to having been in action, the 'Carnarvon Castle' has been allowed to put in to Montevideo for repairs.

Sunday 8th December   -   55th Day Out

Struck another bad patch during the night. Getting well to the North and in the danger area. Heard that an enemy plane is attacking a ship one hundred and ten miles to the North, that is as near as we want it!

Monday 9th December   -   56th Day Out

May possibly anchor in the Roads tonight with a bit of luck.

Off the Mull of Kintyre about noon and making good headway, bad weather and locality left behind. Table fiddles taken off for the first time for nearly a week. Passed a small convoy with two Destroyers as escort.

Tuesday 10th December

Arrived Alexandra Dock - England

Anchored this morning at 4.00am and now await further instructions. In the bay are several ships including the 'Athlone' and 'Llangibby Castle'. Moved into the harbour at 10.00am arriving off the Alexandra dock at 12.30pm.

Red Cross train bringing in patients at Alexandria
View through the Porthole

Wednesday 11th December

Heard I have to leave the 'Roxburgh Castle' and join the 'Llandovery Castle' at Southampton, it is now being converted into a hospital ship.

Thursday 12th December

Busy getting things a bit tidy prior to handing over to the other Chief Steward.

Friday 13th December

Finally leave the ship and proceed to office for final instructions; Issued with free railway voucher, and leave Lime Street at 3.00pm for Euston.

Arrived at 10.00pm, which was three hours late, and therefore missed the Waterloo connection to Southampton and had to wait just over seven hours. I finally got away from Waterloo at 5.30am. and arrived at Southampton Central at 8.00am, and home by 10.00am.

Monday 16th December

Joined the 'Llandovery Castle' at the new docks 104 berth, she's been converted to a hospital ship and will sail in the new year, possibly to the Middle East.

Tuesday 17th December

Usual ships routine

Wednesday 25th December

Christmas day at home; One day off only, due to the War effort.

Chapter Four

H.M.H.S. Llandovery Castle 1941

'Llandovery Castle'

Wednesday 1st January 1941

Expecting great things generally, particularly from the East.

Thursday 2nd January

General Wavell gets ready

Sunday 5th January

Bandai fell to the Australians after thirty hours combined blasting by the Navy, Army, and RAF.

Monday 6th January

All troops in the Western Desert pushing on to Tobruk.

Friday 10th January

Mediterranean Fleet attacked by German Dive Bombers, those planes having been previously flown from Germany and housed on the Isle of Sicily. The Aircraft Carrier 'Illustrious' and the Heavy Cruiser 'Southampton' were the chief targets. Although damaged by the attack the 'Illustrious' managed to reach port. The 'Southampton' was set on fire and had to be finally abandoned, it was subsequently sunk by our own gunfire.

So much for the first attack by Germany on our fleet in the effort to invade Italy, for we now hear that twelve Dive Bombers were brought down on this attack and a very good effort was also made by the RAF who also attacked the German air base in Sicily and destroyed many more machines.

Monday 20th January

President Roosevelt becomes President of the USA for the third Term of Office.

Wednesday 22nd January - *Fall of Tobruk*

British mechanised unit's, with Australian Infantry close in pursuit enter Tobruk only after thirty hours fighting. The Italian cruiser 'San Georgio' lay disabled in the harbour mouth, having been previously crippled by bombs of the RAF.

Friday 24th January

Heard that the Destroyer 'Hyperion' has been sunk in the Adriatic either by mine or torpedo.

Thursday 30th January - *Fall of Derna*

Friday 31st January

Mr Churchill visited Southampton and Portsmouth.

Friday 7th February

Heard today that Benghazi has fallen to General Wavell's army

Sunday 9th February

Have learnt today that the Western Mediterranean Fleet consisting of the 'Malaya' 'Renown' 'Ark Royal' and 'Sheffield' under the command of Vice Admiral Sir James Somerville have bombarded Genoa causing great havoc. Aircraft from the 'Ark Royal' also bombed some of the main objectives

Monday 10th February

Still getting 'Llandovery' ready for sea, but goodness only knows when we will sail.

Monday 10th March

The last month has been devoted to getting the ship ready and we expect to go in a few days.
Portsmouth and Gosport had their worst raid of the War, a terrible amount of damage was done, apart from the hundreds killed.

Friday 14th March

All is ready and we are off tomorrow morning. We will leave the Quay at 9.00am and proceed to Spithead to await instructions.

Saturday 15th March

We do not sail, ship put back twenty four hours, anything may happen now.

Sunday 16th March

We are not to go to Liverpool, but to stay here another week.

Friday 21st March

Plymouth blitzed.
Sailing day put back another week.

German Battleship 'Gneisenau' reported sunk in Oslo fiord by Coastal Batteries - unconfirmed

Saturday 22nd March

Balance of RAMC staff join us.

Sunday 23rd March

Matron and nurses join us (fourteen in number) all very busy settling down and preparing wards for the patients which we hope will arrive tomorrow.

Monday 24th March - **1st Day Out**

The patients came on board at noon, so we are now ready to leave. We finally leave the berth 101 and move down stream; Off the Isle of Wight we adjust the compass and then drop anchor and await the dawn to move through the Boom to the open sea, may good luck go with us. A very quiet night and no air raid warning.

Tuesday 25th March - **2nd Day Out**

Up anchor at 8.00am and proceed to adjust compasses, anchored again at 10.00am for further instructions. At 6.30pm we get up anchor and make for the Boom, passing through at 7.00pm and then down channel. As a hospital ship we are all lit up, and I should imagine visible for miles. Nobody is saying very much, but no doubt thinking a lot. The weather is particularly bad for this time of year, half a gale blowing, fairly heavy sea, and a large rain. All water tight doors are closed and boats turned out, we are as near as possible ready for an emergency, which we hope will not happen of course!

Wednesday 26th March - **3rd Day Out**

Weather still heavy and still rolling slightly, but really very good weather indeed. It has been too rough for subs to operate and too windy for aircraft, or perhaps that's just wishful thinking, let us hope it may be true. Rain cleared away during the afternoon, the ship is still pitching, but very little really, it seems a lot to the first time trippers!

Thursday 27th March   4th Day Out

Still in very heavy seas, it is pitching a little. Saw a couple of boats this morning away on the horizon, caused a bit of a stir for a moment, but eventually proved to be fishing craft. We had good news this morning, we heard that Keren had fallen, also Harer, and that the Slavs are kicking up and also our Naval forces had engaged the enemy in the battle of the Atlantic. News is scarce these days, but we have to get more details tomorrow.

Friday 28th March   5th Day Out

Sea even worse today; we have stopped pitching and developed a nasty roll. Hopefully one of the dangers has now passed, now that we are out of range of any enemy aircraft. What of the subs? Perhaps next week this time, we may be able to say the same about those. Everyone seems to be settling down apart from a few who are still sea sick.

Saturday 29th March   6th Day Out

Slight improvement all round today and the weather is on the turn. We have at last turned South after making West'ard since Southampton, a distance of about 1,400 miles.

'HMS Warspite' flagship of
Admiral Sir Andrew Cunningham

Sunday 30th March   -   7th Day Out

Heard the good news today that the enemy Navy had a good pasting, with three of their heavy cruisers and two destroyers sunk. No losses to ourselves at the moment; More details tomorrow. The British Battleships in this action were HMS's 'Barham' 'Valiant' and 'Warspite.'

Monday 31st March   -   8th Day Out

Still going along very nicely and things are generally looking quite good. If we can only keep afloat for another week things will be even better and we will more or less be clear of the danger zone.

Tuesday 1st April   -   9th Day Out

Heard today that the Italian fleet outnumbered us by eleven to four but still we went in and beat them up, what a Navy!

Wednesday 2nd April   -   10th Day Out

Very little outside news, things going well on board and I should imagine we are somewhere off the Canary Islands. We may reach Freetown on Sunday if all goes well.

Thursday 3rd April   -   11th Day Out

Heard the bad news today that Benghazi had been recaptured, presumably by German and Italian forces. A great shock to everyone, hope to hear further details later. Personally I expect worse things but one can only hope for the best.

Friday 4th April-12th Day Out

No good news as we had hoped.
Hope to get to Freetown Sunday.

'Warwick Castle'

Saturday 5th April - **13th Day Out**

It's been very warm today, thank goodness we are not too busy. Saw Seagulls this morning, a very good indication of nearing land.

Sunday 6th April - **14th Day Out**

Arrived Freetown.

Paravanes were out this morning, another good sign. At 7.00am a flying boat came out and gave us the once over and then returned to port. We finally sight the harbour entrance at about 10.30am. Passed through the Boom and anchored at about noon. What a collection of ships here, well over fifty, some of the best Merchant Ships. "The Castle Company" is represented by 'Warwick Castle,' 'Stirling Castle,' 'Llangibby Castle,' 'Dromore Castle,' which is a freighter, and us, not a bad gathering! There are many other Merchant Ships of various shapes and sizes. The Navy is also here with two Light Cruisers and the Battleship 'Nelson.' I think the big merchantmen are Southward bound taking troops to the Middle East. Heard today that Germany had declared war on Yugoslavia and had already bombed Belgrade.

Germany and her partner Italy are attacking Greece, and Salonika has already been heavily bombed.

German troops being held in Libya.

British enter Addis Ababa.

Monday 7th April - **15th Day Out**

Terribly hot today, and although we have only been here a few hours we are looking forward to getting away.

Tuesday 8th April - **16th Day Out**

Still very hot, but we hope to get away this evening. We finally get away from our anchorage at 4.30pm, passing through the Boom at 5.15pm. Another convoy has just gone out, this time for home, a total of fifty two ships, so in two days, seventy two ships have left here, not to say anything for the incidentals, not forgetting us!

'Llangibby Castle'

'Dromore Castle'   A. Duncan

Wednesday 9th April   -   **17th Day Out**

Salonika has been occupied by the Germans who, according to the news, entered yesterday. What a terrible thing this German machine.

The fall of Tobruk is only a matter of time.

Although the Yugoslav troops are fighting desperately to maintain their position, the Germans are steadily over running the country.

Our bombers carried out an extensive raid on Kiel, over 30,000 incendiaries and many tons of high explosives were dropped on the big Naval base.

Saw two ships, but they were ours thank goodness!

Thursday 10th April   -   **18th Day Out**

Weather still very hot, but hope to be out of it in a few days.

Heavy raids on England last night. Birmingham and Coventry suffered the most. Germans lost twelve bombers.

Berlin was also attacked last night by our forces, five of our aircraft missing.

In Libya some of our forces have been captured, including three Generals.

Friday 11th April   -   **19th Day Out**

Crossed the Line going South; Still very warm.

Our forces in Greece come in contact with Germans for the first time.

Portsmouth has been blitzed again.

Saturday 12th April   -   **20th Day Out**

Things are going bad for us in Libya, all our chasing of the Italians, all to no avail, apart from prisoners and war material.

The combined forces, German and Italian, moving with ever increasing speed.

Sunday 13th April   -   **21st Day Out**

The combined forces of the enemy have reached the Egyptian frontier, what a nasty set back for us. Still we mustn't despair we must still go on hoping for the best. I wonder what Egypt will do, like the Turks they seemed to be reluctant to do anything.

Greece, together with our Imperial Forces and the RAF are putting up a good show, but I am afraid that the outcome is evacuation.

As I have said for months, in my mind the War will finish in the Middle East.

Monday 14th April   -   **22nd Day Out**

Much cooler today, a little more breeze which is very welcome. I can picture us going through it on the East Coast, that is if we get there in time!

Heavy fighting around Sollum, seventy miles form the Egyptian border.

Our forces in Greece came in contact with Adolf Hitler Division, and gave a good account of themselves; RAF giving every support, I hope the Navy will soon be in the picture also.

Tuesday 15th April   -   **23rd Day Out**

We maybe in Cape Town Saturday.

Weather turned much cooler and we shall change into blues tomorrow. Sea a little choppy, fresh breeze, and we are pitching slightly.

Wednesday 16th April   -   **24th Day Out**

Action in the Mediterranean between our light Naval forces and an Italian convoy, three of their destroyers have been sunk, possibly five. Our losses were 'HMS Mohawk,' and several supply ships were also sunk.

Enemy aircraft blitzed Belfast, their first raid.

Italian resistance in Abyssinia is on the point of giving in.

Thursday 17th April - **25th Day Out**

Heavy fighting in Greece. The fleet bombard enemy transports around Bardia.

Heavy raid on London, the heaviest so far, casualties are believed to be many, and damage considerable.

Friday 18th April - **26th Day Out**

Nearing Cape Town, with luck we ought to be in dock by tomorrow.

Saturday 19th April - **27th Day Out**

Arrived Cape Town

I saw Table Mountain in the distance at 7.30am. Naval trawlers out sweeping the channel, or at least keeping the existing one clear. After picking up the Pilot we go to our anchorage, what a blow, we all took it for granted we would be going alongside. Some of the convoy that left Freetown on the 7th April are here, I presume the others have gone to Durban, to store etc., split things up a bit I suppose. The main escort for the convoy is also here 'HMS Nelson,' but she pulled out this afternoon and headed North.

The 'Capetown Castle' is anchored in the Bay and well down, so I presume she is loaded for home, and will soon be on her way.

London has had it's heaviest raid ever.

Sunday 20th April - **28th Day Out**

Still swinging at anchor and likely to do so for a day or two according to rumour.

The convoy is now leaving the quayside and assembling in the Bay, prior to departure.

This time last year I was on leave from the 'Llanstephan.'

War news not too bad, just about holding our own in Greece, but I fear the ultimate result.

Monday 21st April - **29th Day Out**

Still in the Bay, and hoping to go in.

The 'Windsor Castle' arrived this morning coastwise down, after having been to India with Italian prisoners.

The 'Illustrious' and a County Class cruiser the 'Dorsetshire' also arrived this morning.

Got my cable away at last, hope everything is alright.

Pilot boat came alongside at noon and told us we were going alongside this evening; We were alongside at 5.30pm in the old basin. The 'Carnarvon' is here being patched up after her scrap, just about finished by the look of things.

Tuesday 22nd April - **30th Day Out**

News in Greece not too good, expect to hear the worst at any moment. Possibly leave tomorrow for Durban direct. "Durban Castle" arrived in the Bay outward.

'Capetown Castle' in the Bay homeward. 'Windsor Castle' also came alongside today and the 'Arundel Castle' has arrived in the Bay.

Wednesday 23rd April - **31st Day Out**

Our troops in Greece are still hard pressed, a few days or maybe even hours will decide the issue. Left the quayside at 4.30pm for Durban.

King George of Greece and his government, have been forced to leave for the Island of Crete.

Another raid on Plymouth.

Our Aircraft again attacked Brest, where the two German battle cruisers 'Scharnhorst' and 'Gneisenau' are still lying. This is the ninth raid since the ships have been in dock. Going slowly along the coast, and it is fairly rough with the ship rolling slightly. We will possibly get out to Durban on Sunday.

Thursday 24th April - **32nd Day Out**

German troops advancing South of Lamina within fifty six miles of Athens.

The Admiralty announced tonight that the armed cruiser 'HMS Rasputin' has been torpedoed and subsequently sunk.

Weather a little better today.

'Athlone Castle'

Friday 25th April   -   **33rd Day Out**

German battle cruisers again bombed.
Imperial troops again in Greece.
Weather worse again today.

Saturday 26th April   -   **34th Day Out**

Off East London.
Weather quite good again, and getting a little hot, hope to be at Durban tomorrow.

Sunday 27th April   -   **35th Day Out**

Arrived off the Bluff at 6.00am, awaited Pilot and then entered harbour, tied up at Maydon Wharf just ahead of the 'Athlone Castle.' The other hospital ship the 'Atlantis' is still here and the 'Nelson' is in dry dock having the usual clean up.
Very hot all day, but quite cool during the evening.
Have heard that the Imperial troops are steadily leaving Greece, another country under the German Heel!
German forces have crossed the Egyptian frontier at several points.

Monday 28th April   -   **36th Day Out**

Terribly hot here today, and unfortunately have plenty to do in storing ship.

Tuesday 29th April   -   **37th Day Out**

Still storing ship, but no idea when we will get away.
Things look bad in Greece, have to be getting out of there.
Pompey gets another blitz.

Wednesday 30th April - **38th Day Out**

Mr Churchill declared to the House, that to date 45,000 Imperial troops have been evacuated from Greece but unfortunately some of their heavy gear had to be abandoned.
Still waiting and hoping!
Went to the pictures and saw 'Sailors Three'. - A busman's holiday!!

Thursday 1st May - **39th Day Out**

Finished storing, so for our part the ship can leave, but I have an idea we shall be here for the weekend.
Very hot again today.

Friday 2nd May - **40th Day Out**

Just a game of waiting once more, first one day and then another, but hope to be away by Monday.
Have heard today that we lost two destroyers and two merchantmen in the evacuation of Greece.
Heavy raid on Merseyside last night.
RAF gave Hamburg a good dressing down.
Fighting now taking place in Iraq, but only of a minor character.

Saturday 3rd May - **41st Day Out**

Merseyside raided again last night, but the RAF shot down eleven of them, a jolly good bag. They also shot down five the night before making a total of sixteen in the two nights.

Sunday 4th May - **42nd Day Out**

Mr Bevin, Minister of Labour, is to mobilise the Merchant Navy.
"HMS Nelson" leaves the dry dock. Heard today that the armed liner "Voltaire" has been sunk, through enemy action.

Monday 5th May - **43rd Day Out**

Left Durban for Suez
Hope to leave today for somewhere up North, according to rumour we should leave at noon, but I think it may be later. Very hot again today, it will be nice to get to sea and get a little breeze.
We get away at 5.00pm and with the help of tugs make for the entrance and open sea; I wonder what lies in front of us now, hope for the best, that seems the only thing one can do!

Tuesday 6th May - **44th Day Out**

Well out to sea and steaming due North. At the moment, Aden is to be our first port of call.
Clydeside raided last night. Merseyside was also attacked, for the fifth night in succession, but nine enemy raiders were destroyed.

Wednesday 7th May - **45th Day Out**

Fairly rough today, with plenty of rain. Everything is screwed down and as hot as Old Nick. Passed a freighter, well down, no doubt it is on the way to the War Front.
Lord Moyne stated in the House that our casualties in Greece were at the most 11,500 men of whom a large number were cut off on re-embarking.

Thursday 8th May - **46th Day Out**

Much better today no rain, but a nice breeze.
German planes were destroyed over England during the daylight raids yesterday.
Survivors of the Dutch vessel 'Princess Wilhelmina' which was torpedoed, arrived at Montevideo in a British ship.

Friday 9th May   -   **47th Day Out**

More raids over Britain, thirteen planes shot down during the day and twenty four during the night, and further ten possibly destroyed, jolly good work by the RAF. There was another attack by enemy aircraft in the Humber area.

Saturday 10th May   -   **48th Day Out**

Very hot today, with little breeze, by this time next week we hope to be in Aden.

Sunday 11th May   -   **49th Day Out**

What a day, tons of rain, and everything boxed up enough to kill one, things improved slightly during the evening. A very heavy raid on London, but we gave them a good show with thirty three bombers brought down by the night's highest bag of the war. The RAF raided Hamburg, Bremen, Emden, and Rotterdam. A 7,000 ton Norwegian ship has been captured in the Indian Ocean. After extensive searching by the Netherlands Cruiser 'Leander' and the Australian cruiser 'Canberra' at the same time, a German merchant ship the 'Coburg' 4,500 tons was intercepted and eighteen German officers and fourteen ratings were taken Prisoners of War.

The Royal Navy bombarded Benghazi last Thursday sinking several ships.

The combined aircraft of both Germany and Italy at that moment available, dive bombed our fleet, but nothing happened apart for some of those "Wops" being blown out the skies!

Monday 12th May   -   **50th Day Out**

Still very hot and likely to get worse any moment, hope to arrive on Saturday.

Have just heard that Rudolph Hess one of Hitler's deputies, has been taken prisoner after a flight from Germany to Glasgow. No further details at the moment, if it's true then it is a good sign.

Tuesday 13th May   -   **51st Day Out**

The hottest day so far - .

The landing of Rudolph Hess in Scotland has been confirmed by the Ministry of Defence.

Getting well North, about opposite Mogadishu in what was Italian Somaliland.

Wednesday 14th May   -   **52nd Day Out**

Still going along, and as hot as ever. No doubt the further North we go the hotter it will get. We are now almost opposite Cape Guardajui, about a two day run from Aden.

Thursday 15th May   -   **53rd Day Out**

Passed Cape Guardajui, this morning at 5.30am, and are now steaming almost due West, possibly arrive today. Yesterday was the hottest day ever.

Friday 16th May   -   **54th Day Out**

Arrived Aden

Picked up the land this morning at 10.00am, and a lovely breeze as well thank goodness! We should arrive about noon.

We are now in Aden, this is the second time I have been here; The first time being in January 1919 whilst serving on 'HMS Malaya,' en route to the Federated Malay States, no doubt things have altered some what since then, in more ways than one, but just as hot no doubt!

Arrived in the Bay at 1.00pm, quite a number merchantmen at anchor.

A Dutch boat went out loaded with troops with an Armed Liner as escort. At 3.00pm we get up anchor and proceed inside the Boom, we have to drop anchor and then make fast to a buoy astern.

There is very little activity here at the moment, a few small freighters either loading or discharging, no Naval ships of any description, everything moored North no doubt.

"Whisky" our cat is sent ashore!

Hope to get ashore tomorrow for a couple of hours to get a few whites etc., of which I am sorely in need!

Saturday 17th May   -   **55th Day Out**

Heard we had carried out many raids over Germany, including Berlin. Also that we had bombed the French airfields in Syria which had now been lent to Germany.

We went on shore this morning to buy a few whites etc., left the ship at 9.30am returning at 10.30am.

We get up anchor and cast off from the buoys and finally leave at 12.15pm for Suez where we should arrive on Wednesday with a little luck.

Passed through "Hell's Gates" at about midnight and so on to the Red Sea, to my mind it should be the Red Hot Sea!

Very little news this last two days owing to not being able to use the ships wireless, but hope we are still bombing Germany.

Sunday 18th May   -   **56th Day Out**

In the Red Sea and it is hot, changed my clothes three times today already!

Passed a couple of ships heading South, or, would it be more correct to say they passed us!

Picked up a nice breeze during the night.

Monday 19th May   -   **57th Day Out**

Not quite so hot today, owing to the little extra breeze maybe.

Heard today there has been another raid on the Suez Canal area, hope they don't make it too warm for us!

Tuesday 20th May   -   **58th Day Out**

Passed Deadless Shoal Lighthouse at the entrance to the Gulf of Suez, we are roughly three hundred and fifty miles from Suez it'self, should be there tomorrow at about this time; 11.00am.

Wednesday 21st May   **59th Day Out**

At Suez

Saw Mount Sinai this morning at 6.00am, proceeded up stream and finally arrived at Suez at 12.30pm.

Nearly all the ships which were at Freetown are with us here, that is the convoy with troops, two more hospital ships, two cruisers, and tons of freighters about one hundred ships in all! They had been raided several times here, so tonight we are to observe a strict blackout. Very hot today, a little breeze off the land but that is also hot! Hope to get some letters today.

Had my first letter of the voyage (No.3), I wonder what has happened to the first two? Everything is well thank goodness.

At the moment we are anchored in the Bay, hope to go alongside tomorrow and get away again, too hot for us here in more ways than one! A very quiet evening and night, long may it continue!

Thursday 22nd May   -   **60th Day Out**

Still in the Bay, awaiting instructions I presume. Another hospital ship came in today, quite a gathering, so possibly the War will move South, once they get Crete, Malta, and Cyprus in their hands.

Fierce fighting in Crete, impossible to say what's really happening at the moment . Our Navy made contact with two enemy transports with a Destroyer as escort, and sank all three. Immediately afterwards a convoy of twenty ships were attacked by our Naval forces the result of which is not yet known.

Friday 23rd May   -   **61st Day Out**

Very heavy fighting in Crete, the Navy doing our share as usual. Went on shore yesterday just to have a look at the town. Went from Tewfik to Suez by army lorry returning the same way. Particularly hot on shore with a warm breeze blowing in from the desert.

Had two warnings last night, but nothing else happened.

All the Aussies and extra nursing staff left yesterday, anything may happen to us now, probably finish up around Port Said; Then look out for squalls!

H.M.H.S. 'Llandovery Castle' off suez

Saturday 24th May - **62nd Day Out**

Heard the bad news that 'HMS Hood' has been sunk by gunfire after being in action with the German battleship the 'Bismarck' no details at the moment.
The battle is still on for the occupation of Crete, today should decide one way or the other.

Sunday 25th May - **63rd Day Out**

Still awaiting details of Naval action in which the 'Hood' was lost.
The battle of Crete still continues and at the moment we are holding our own. Have heard that our Naval forces were still in contact with the 'Bismarck' but I am not too hopeful of the outcome.

Monday 26th May - **64th Day Out**

Very little ships news, playing the usual waiting game, maybe here for months. Had a raid alarm last night but so far nothing of importance has come to light.

Tuesday 27th May - **65th Day Out**

Heard the jolly good news that the 'Bismarck' had been sunk. Mr Churchill deals with the Crete question, and I wonder "shall we hold on to it?"

Wednesday 28th May - **66th Day Out**

Still waiting for letters and some news as to our next landfall.
Still very fierce fighting going on in Crete but I wonder "can our men keep the pace?"
Royal Marines have been landed to help stem the line.
Our troops in Libya have been withdrawn from Hellfire Pass and Sollum is now in enemy hands.
President Roosevelt's speech has been acclaimed throughout the United States and the British Empire, my personal

opinion is, that it will only be a matter of a few months before they are in the War, the sooner the better say I!

Quite a number of ships passing through the canal going South, all travelling light. Most of the convoy we saw at Freetown and were here on our arrival have now left, hope we shall be the next one to leave!

Thursday 29th May - 67th Day Out

Very fierce fighting continues in Crete and we have had to give ground. 'HMS York' which is lying in Suda Bay whilst undergoing repairs has been bombed and subsequently sunk.

The Navy has had a trying time these last few days, it's lost a Battle Cruiser, three Cruisers, five Destroyers, and a Submarine which was the 'Usk,' one of the five destroyers was the 'Mashona,' bombed and sunk by enemy planes after helping to finish off the 'Bismarck.'

Friday 30th May - 68th Day Out

Very much the same news, and things are much the same on board as well. We have heard nothing definite as to where we might go, but if things continue as they are, we might take a load of Aussies or New Zealand troops back home, failing that we will go to Durban with our own, or South Africans.

Saturday 31st May - 69th Day Out

Went for a sail today, which made a pleasant change, have an idea we shall be moving soon, possibly through the canal - then what?

Sunday 1st June - 70th Day Out

Things are going very well in Iraq, taking all things into consideration.

The position in Crete is very serious, all though our forces are fighting well, I think the odds are against them, if only we had the aircraft, or even a base near Crete, from which, the few we have can operate.

We have withdrawn our troops from Crete, one more setback, although we did extremely well in some respects, the fact remains we have lost valuable lives, and costly ships. Planes and more planes must be our aim. Armistice has been signed in Iraq, that is one trouble less!

Monday 2nd June - 71st Day Out

Heard to day that the 'Warspite' and 'Barham' had received damage off Crete. The former is by all account lying at Alexandria, in a very bad way, the latter came through the canal this morning and is at anchor just ahead of us. To what extent she is damaged we cannot say, the tugs and cranes are alongside indicating some upheaval. The 'Dido' also arrived this morning.

Went to the pictures this afternoon on board a Blue Funnel ship not a particularly good picture but it passed away a couple of hours.

No news to date as to what we may do, but the scene seems to have shifted to Durban, personally I don't mind which way we go, provided it's not up or down!

Tuesday 3rd June - 72nd Day Out

'HMS Barham' pulled out and went South.

A cruiser of the Neptune class came in from the South and went direct through the canal. I went for a sail today and got horribly sunburnt.

RAF raid Berlin and the Kiel canal.

Wednesday 4th June - 73rd Day Out

It has been very hot again today; I sent a letter by Photo - Airmail, a new idea!

Still no news from home, still no news as to when we may move out, been here exactly a fortnight today.

The German Kaiser died today after being a fugitive since the last War.

Thursday 5th June - 74th Day Out

Heard today that we maybe here another week, we are going to load more wounded or go to either Durban or Australia.

Dogfight off Crete 2nd June 1941

Moses Well near Suez 8th June 1941

Alexandria had it's worse raid of the War, over one hundred and fifty killed and five hundred wounded, the scene of War is gradually coming nearer, I mean travelling East and South. These may be light days for us, but we shall be busy here before this is finished.

Friday 6th June   -   75th Day Out

The hospital ship 'Atlantis' arrives form Durban.

Saturday 7th June   -   76th Day Out

Nothing to report.

Sunday 8th June   -   77th Day Out

Heard we may leave about Friday, and that mails for Egypt posted before the 4th and 9th April had been lost through enemy action, so good bye to one letter!

Two more transports came in today with troops, there is a steady flow of ships in and out, something is going to move soon. Had a day out today and with twenty others had a sail to the Mecca pier and then tramped inland for about two miles to see "Moses Well". It was very interesting, more so if you let your imagination run away with you. The tramp was over sand and by the time I got back I was nearly cooked, in more ways than one, still although very hot and tiring I think we all enjoyed it.

Somewhere in the Sahara !

The Free French Forces backed by Britain, marched into Syria, about time we made a move before the fun begins! Once more the 'Scharnhorst' and 'Gneisenau' are bombed lying in Brest harbour.

Monday 9th June   -   78th Day Out

Our troops still advance into Syria, having met almost no opposition.
Daylight raid over England.

Tuesday 10th June   -   79th Day Out

Heard today that two destroyers the 'Howard' and the 'Imperial' and one Aircraft Carrier the 'Calcutta' were also lost in the battle in Crete. Our losses were about 1,500 men altogether.
Enemy losses about 1,700 and about 400 planes. Royal Marines fought the rear guard action, and most of them were either killed or taken prisoner.

Wednesday 11th June   -   80th Day Out

The Italian hospital ship, that was brought in the other day, has been turned over to the Navy. Upon investigation she was found to be an ordinary merchant ship painted hospital ship colours and trying to escape with several Italian Generals, she is quite safe now.
Plenty of activity through the canal, big preparations going on somewhere, ships come and go every day. Had an air raid warning yesterday, and one has just gone now, things are beginning to warm up, they are just getting the measure of things.
Heard we may go alongside tomorrow and load away for Durban, stopping at Port Sudan and Aden to pick up more details.
I think our chances of getting letters here are now over. Three months yesterday we have been away, and I have had one letter - No. 3.

Thursday 12th June   -   81st Day Out

At last we get up anchor and come alongside, finally tying up at 1.30pm. According to rumour we get the patients

'Through the Porthole' hospital train arrival Port Sudan

on board at 6.00am, and get away as early as possible. It is much warmer alongside, and the flies are a pest. Still no mail!

Friday 13th June - **82nd Day Out**

Left Suez 1st time

We start to take on wounded at 10.00am, amongst them are all the various services, Army, Navy, Air Force and Marines.

Went on shore for a while to the agent and stores etc.

Saw a destroyer come through the canal on tow, having had her stern blown off in the Battle of Crete, the after gun had also been blown over the side. If the Navy had an easy time during the early stages of the War they have certainly made up for it recently. Heard last night that the monitor 'Terror' had been sunk, with another Naval craft 'Ladybird' off the Libyan coast.

We leave the quayside at 4.00pm and proceed to sea. Passed a freighter loaded with War material going into Suez. No mail, so now for Durban to see what await's us.

Saturday 14th June - **83rd Day Out**

Picked up the very hot weather again, roll on Durban lets get in blues for a change!

Sunday 15th June - **84th Day Out**

Possibly arrive at Port Sudan tomorrow.
Even hotter today.

Monday 16th June - **85th Day Out**

Arrived Port Sudan 8.00am and anchored in the Bay. Two freighters already here otherwise things seem very quiet.

After being anchored till noon, we came alongside the Hospital Train bearing the wounded at 6.30pm.
Received my first cable stamped 6th May-Cairo.

Tuesday 17th June - 86th Day Out

This had been the hottest day of the whole voyage.
Very little news from the outside world.

Wednesday 18th June - 87th Day Out

Picked up a little breeze last night, what a day though; Three of our men sick, so that means extra work for all of us, and what with the heat to contend with as well, we are all just on breaking point, still it's got to be done.
Passed the Isle of Pevim last night, so we should be near Aden some when about noon.

Thursday 19th June - 88th Day Out

Arrived Aden

Arrived at Aden, going South (first time) anchored in the Bay at noon, probably go alongside tomorrow to pick up patients, oil and water. There are well over fifty ships here most of them well down with cargo. Two Naval boats are also here, and an eight gun cruiser 'HMS Mauritius' and a destroyer. The heat is almost unbearable, if only it would snow, what a relief that would be! Our rigs this weather are particularly varied;   Gone native almost!
Still without mail.

Friday 20th June - 89th Day Out

Came alongside the oiling berth to oil and also took in water. One or two more patients joined the ship.
No outside news.
The Armed Liner 'Carthage' sailed this morning.

Saturday 21st June - 90th Day Out

Pulled off from Aden going South (first time) at 10.00am, and immediately picked up a little breeze, may it continue to increase as we get out to sea.
The wind did not increase, in fact it fell away, and during the night it was awful.

Chapter Five

Russia Attacked

Sunday 22nd June - **91st Day Out**

Germany attacked Russia at 4.00pm this morning.

Received good news today, RAF shot down twenty eight planes in a sweep over the French coast and the channel. A bit cooler this morning again, quite a nice breeze if it will only last.

Passed the Island of Socotra, East of Cape Guardajui, we are now out of the Gulf of Aden, and in the Indian Ocean steaming almost due East.

The breeze lasted alright, and finally developed into a minor monsoon, all ports had to be closed so we were actually worse off, when not up on deck.

Germany had attacked Russia on a front from the White Sea to the Black Sea.

The usual methods were adopted without even declaring War, German bombers rained down high explosives on the towns, then the armoured divisions got on the move, and then finally the infantry to consolidate the positions, so much for the Mutual Friendship Pact signed so recently by Germany. What will happen remains to be seen, but it is quite obvious that it is a prelude to an attack on these Islands (Great Britain).

Monday 23rd June - **92nd Day Out**

The reported sweep of the RAF over Northern France cost the enemy thirty fighters with a loss to ourselves of two Aircraft, a pilot of one being safe. The Finns are reported to be supporting the Germans in their attack on Russia. In addition to bombs, leaflets were also dropped over a South Coast town attacked by enemy aircraft last Saturday night.

Tuesday 24th June - **93rd Day Out**

Still very hot, and in a heavy sea, having to be battened down makes conditions even worse.

Turkey proclaimed strict neutrality.

The German supply ship captured in the Atlantic, of the 1898 - 1899 class is to be registered for War work next month.

The 4,200 tons Portuguese steamer 'Gander' has been sunk by an unknown submarine.

Wednesday 25th June - **94th Day Out**

The RAF continue to batter Germany at her most vital points. On Monday night, which was the 13th successive raid, industrial targets at Emden, Wilhelmshaven, and Hanover were bombed. Kiel harbour also received attention. German losses this month; one hundred and eighteen planes; Our losses, twenty four fighters and four bombers, five pilots safe.

Thursday 26th June - **95th Day Out**

Crossed the Line last night, going South.

Picked up a beautiful breeze, a real treat after so much hot weather; Hope to be in Durban in about a weeks time. Still waiting to hear that the Russians have bombed Berlin, I very much doubt if they will do great things, time alone will tell. Stalin's boast of clouding the skies with aircraft is yet to come true.

Friday 27th June - **96th Day Out**

At the moment things are not too good on the Russo-German battle front. To my mind the Russians are in a quandary, but very little news is getting through apart from the German version.

Another supply ship of the 'Bismarck' has been sunk by our Naval forces in the Atlantic. This is the eighth supply ship sunk so far.

A Turkish ship has been torpedoed by an unknown submarine, let's see what happens now. The weather is improving, not quite so hot, what a change getting in blues, after being in whites for over two months!

Just heard some Russian news, according to their report they are sticking it out, I only hope that they will put up a good show, and if possible carry the campaign into the winter, this to my mind would be a wonderful asset to the Allied forces, and to Britain in particular. One hundred and forty seven lives were lost when the Turkish liner sank.

Saturday 28th June - **97th Day Out**

Not much news in from the Eastern Front.

Germany seems to be going ahead steadily, let's hope the Russians have something ready for them once they get going!

Still going fairly well in Syria, I suppose Jerry is too busy elsewhere to worry about that yet! He can come down through that way once he gets command of South East Russia.

Passed a ship this morning going North, more stores for the Middle East.

Getting almost cold now, although we are still in shorts, it's really a wonderful change.

Sunday 29th June - **98th Day Out**

Another supply ship of about 3,000 tons has been captured by our fleet in the Atlantic, this is the 9th supply ship disposed of since the sinking of the 'Bismarck.' We lost twelve bombers in our extensive raid over North West Germany.

The Russians are still resisting the bombers on all fronts, but things don't seem too good. The Soviet Airforce has still to come up to expectations.

Weather much cooler with a very high sea running.

Monday 30th June - **99th Day Out**

Doing a steady 12 knots, and I should imagine we are off the Lourenco Marques, should get to Durban Wednesday afternoon, with a little luck.

Quite nice again today, and things are cooling down generally, it's a very welcome change.

One of our patients died today, as a result of War wounds, one more gone, a life wasted to satisfy the madmen of Europe.

Tuesday 1st July - **100th Day Out**

We are in Blues and it's quite nice to be cool for a change.

Things are not working too well in Russia, but we still hope for the best. We are hoping to arrive at Durban Thursday morning, and get some good news by then.

Wednesday 2nd July - **101st Day Out**

Everyone looking forward to Durban, if only to get some letters from home, and to know everything is alright.

Been a really nice day, more or less a calm sea with a little breeze, what a welcome change after weeks of heat. The hospital ship 'Dorsetshire' passed us at 6.00pm going North, after being in Durban a fortnight storing and oiling etc.

Thursday 3rd July - **102nd Day Out**

Arrived Durban from Suez

Arrived off the Bluff early this morning and came alongside to a berth at the Point (our old Mail berth) at about 9.00am. Plenty of ships in the Bay, also in the harbour. It's raining like nothing on earth and it's a real change. It is the first rain we have seen for many weeks.

I am waiting anxiously for my mail, I expect now that we are here, they have sent it North to Suez!

Received one letter - No.1, posted the 30th March that's just over three months, goodness knows where the others have got to.

Italian cruiser 'Gorizia' 10,000 tons sunk by our forces in the Mediterranian

Friday 4th July - 103rd Day Out

Having disembarked all patients we move out in the stream, and proceed to Maydon Wharf to tie up, all berths are filled so we have to tie up alongside the 'City of Canterbury.' The harbour is full of ships of all kinds, another Convoy having come in yesterday. The 'Barham' is here, having a minor refit after her Crete episode, two other Cruisers are also here. The Russia news is not too bright and any day I expect to hear the worst.

Saturday 5th July - 104th Day Out

Getting the ship tidied up and waiting for Mails. Very little local news.

Sunday 6th July - 105th Day Out

Had a very quiet day, just ticking over.
Our Naval forces in the Mediterranean have sunk the 10,000 ton Italian cruiser 'Gorizia', also three other Merchant supply ships.
Russia claims to have beaten back the Nazis at the River Dwina, in White Russia.
Our air blitz continues unabated over many parts of industrial Germany.

Monday 7th July - 106th Day Out

Southampton Blitzed
Things very much the same, still no news as to what we may do, and still no mail.

Tuesday 8th July - 107th Day Out

Heard over the wireless that Southampton had another sharp raid Monday night; Hope that everything is alright but it's almost too much to expect.

Wednesday 9th July - 108th Day Out

Another hospital ship came alongside today, the 'Amra' from Bombay. We hear we are to leave tomorrow for East London, the main reason being, to have our repairs done. At Durban the demand is so great that less essential jobs

'S.S. Mauretania' Cunard White Star Line launched 1938 top speed 25 Knots

are being passed to other ports. The Navy as usual takes first place. There were six ships, all Naval, in port for minor repairs. 'Barham,' 'Hawkins,' 'Cornwall,' and three other Cruisers, also a Free French torpedo boat.

We get the order to store ship in readiness for sailing, and we go all out until 8.00pm, what a game!

Thursday 10th July - 109th Day Out

This morning at 8.00am the Pilot came on board, tugs were alongside, and we are hauled to deep water and make for the Bluff exit. As we proceed, we go past the Union Castle Mail berth, where there are three transports tied up, they are bound for the Middle East with troops. The transports are the new 'Mauretania' 'Ille de France,' and the 'Amsterdam.'

Once past the Bluff we pick up a choppy sea, a reminder of our Mail Ship days!

Hope to make East London by daybreak tomorrow.

The RAF continue to bomb Germany.

Russia seem to be doing a little better.

Friday 11th July - 110th Day Out

Arrived East London

Arrived East London at 8.00am and tied up alongside the old Mail Berth.

Very little activity here, compared to Durban. A lull has developed in the Russo- German War.

British peace terms rejected by the Vichy Government.

The RAF made a heavy raid on Naples Wednesday night.

Saturday 12th July - 111th Day Out

Another quiet day as far as the ship is concerned.

War news a little brighter.

Oxford Street East London
13th July 1941

Native Homestead known as 'Rondavels' visited whilst on a day out courtesy of the Ladies of East London

According to the news, the Vichy has ordered a cease fire, fourteen French War ships go to Alexandria and are interned by the Turks. American troops reported to have landed in Iceland.

Heavy raids by the RAF on enemy bases in France and North West Germany.

Sunday 13th July - 112th Day Out

According to this morning's radio news the Vichy Government signed the British Armistice in relation to Syria.

Had a very pleasant run out today, the ladies of East London put fifty private cars at the ships disposal, and these in numbers of about five to fifteen took us out for the afternoon. Our convoy in cars is five in number, and took the road North to the Transki; The native reserve. Unfortunately never made that far, but having gone over forty miles in that direction we had a good idea of what it would be like. About half way we had to halt for a few minutes and view a few Rondavels, which are native mud huts. We took a few snaps of the native women in the raw almost! We saw very few men folk, these I presume were away in the towns at work. At the end of the second jaunt we pulled up and had tea, each individual car having made this necessary arrangement before hand. This proved very interesting in more ways than one, and after tea we left the scene as individuals. We came back in good style our car being a Ford V8, and at times we were driving at over 70mph!

We were on board by 8.00pm, so ended a very pleasant and interesting day.

Monday 14th July - 113th Day Out

Fairly busy today, what with repairs, stores, etc.

Ship being painted once again and made presentable.

Tuesday 15th July - 114th Day Out

Russians reported to have sunk thirteen Nazi troop ships.

Reported rift between Hitler and Goering.

Allied troops enter Beirut.

Very little ship news, repairs being steadily completed.

Wednesday 16th July - 115th Day Out

Very heavy fighting between Russo - German troops.

Thursday 17th July - 116th Day Out

Things very much the same.

Friday 18th July - 117th Day Out

The Germans claim to have captured Smolensk.

Saturday 19th July - 118th Day Out

Still very heavy fighting on the Eastern Front, and Russians doing better than was first anticipated.

Famous Italian Air Ace killed; Seignor Ferrarin, who was the Schneider trophy winner in 1926.

Sunday 20th July - 119th Day Out

"V Sunday"

Went for another drive, this time to Bonza Bay, and had a nice time, played darts, and after tea went for a row in the river. Came back to town at about 5.00pm, and our hostess took us home for a sundowner and dinner, at about midnight we were brought back to the ship, so ended another pleasant day at East London.

Several Nazi transports sunk by the Russians in the Baltic.

RAF continue to batter at Axis shipping, eight ships to their credit during the weekend.

Monday 21st July - 120th Day Out

A steady day, very little news locally.

Tuesday 22nd July - **121st Day Out**

The Finnish four masted barquentine 'Lawhill' arrives from Perth Australia, after sixty one days out.

A Vichy ship is brought in and anchors in the Bay.

Heard today that Moscow had been bombed for the first time.

Wednesday 23rd July - **122nd Day Out**

Japanese issue an ultimatum to Vichy for the occupation of the whole of Indo-China.

Another raid on Moscow in which one hundred and fifty planes took part.

Ten German ships sunk in the Baltic by Soviet bombers and Naval craft.

Thursday 24th July - **123rd Day Out**

Moscow raided for the third time.

Friday 25th July - **124th Day Out**

Heard today that the RAF had carried out their biggest raid of the War, chiefly over Northern France, and paid particular attention to Brest and La Pallice. The German Battle Cruisers 'Scharnhorst' and 'Gneisenau' had a terrific hammering. This last effort by the RAF should keep them quiet for some time. The whole raid lasted from Wednesday morning until Thursday afternoon. American Flying Fortresses took part, also our new Halifax bombers.

We lost fifteen bombers and seven fighters, whilst Jerry lost thirty four Fighters.

Things seem to be getting worse in Indo-China, anything may happen now.

Another enemy convoy attacked in the Mediterranean, but unfortunately we lost a destroyer through enemy dive bombing; 'HMS Fearless.'

Berlin bombed, no details as yet.

Saturday 26th July - **125th Day Out**

Russians doing very well on all fronts; Huns held up for the time being.

Heard today that Axis Partners had tried to invade Malta, no full details yet.

Sunday 27th July - **126th Day Out**

Several E boats (fast motor boats carrying torpedoes) tried to enter the harbour of Valetta Malta, possibly on Saturday, they were met by fire from coast batteries, and the RAF came in to bomb them, as far as is known twelve boats were sunk. Had a very quiet day and stayed on board, hope to be away next Sunday. Getting a bit tired of East London!

Monday 28th July - **127th Day Out**

The raid on Valetta from the sea cost the enemy seventeen motor boats, in other words the whole fleet had taken part.

Enemy planes over London for the first time since May 10th, no doubt in reply to our bombing in Berlin last Friday.

Tuesday 29th July - **128th Day Out**

Things much the same today, hope to get away during the weekend.

Wednesday 30th July - **129th Day Out**

RAF attack Sicily, without loss to themselves, many planes destroyed.

Things much the same on board, getting repairs done, and painting ship.

Sailing again delayed until after August Monday.

Thursday 31st July - **130th Day Out**

RAF bomb the Finnish Port of Pitsams.

West Street Durban 5th August 1941

Friday 1st August - **131st Day Out**

Russians still fighting back, particularly around Smolensk.
We lose twenty six planes in offensive operations against the enemy.

Saturday 2nd August - **132nd Day Out**

Went to Marina Glen, to the Red Cross fete and what a crowd, back on board at 5.00pm
Berlin bombed.

Sunday 3rd August - **133rd Day Out**

Went for a walk this afternoon for about five miles.
We hear we are leaving at last, probably at daybreak tomorrow, things are moving in that direction anyway.
Russia's still doing very well.
Extra pressure on the Vichy government by Germany, possibly for their fleet etc.

Monday 4th August - **134th Day Out**

Left East London

Pulled out this morning at 7.15am for Durban, nice to be at sea again, wish it was for one month instead of one day!
The weather generally is in our favour, unusual in this quarter.

Tuesday 5th August - **135th Day Out**

Arrived Durban

After a pleasant run we arrive off the Bluff at 8.15 am, unable to find a berth for a while so we anchor until 11.30am then we head for the harbour at noon.

'M.V. Georgic' at Suez after being bombed
She was salvaged and seen here on the way to dry dock

We are going to the oiling wharf on the Bluff side of the bay to connect up ready for oiling first thing in the morning. Had an answer to my cable; All is well.

Wednesday 6th August - **136th Day Out**

We start to store ship, and if possible will get away today. After a very hard day, what with stores etc, we hear the ship will not leave until tomorrow at noon!
Went on shore for the last time for a few weeks.
We hear Suez is coming in for a few raids, and that the White Star Liner 'Georgic' has been hit and burnt out, a total loss more or less, this happened quite a while ago by all accounts

Thursday 7th August - **137th Day Out**

Sailed from Durban for Suez for the second time.
After completing our storing we pull out and make for sea. We are now in for a hot time, and in more ways than one apparently, that is, if Jerry has his way!   Fairly cool at the moment and we are still in Blues.

Friday 8th August - **138th Day Out**

Still nice and cool, but unfortunately we expect a change any moment.
The White Star Line confirm the loss of the 'Georgic' through enemy bombing. The RAF again raided Hamburg and the Essen steelworks. We lost ten fighters and Jerry lost seven. Berlin has been bombed by Russian planes for the first time.

Saturday 9th August - **139th Day Out**

Berlin again bombed by Russian planes, give them plenty I say!
Not much ship board news; I hear our first stop is in Aden.

Sunday 10th August - **140th Day Out**

Still going along and making our usual 13 knots. We should make Aden by this time next week.

Monday 11th August - **141st Day Out**

We go into Whites, and we are now in for a hot time, this being the hottest time of the year in this quarter. Russians still falling back, but I hope they will hang out until the winter. There is the reported lost of another Destroyer.

Tuesday 12th August - **142nd Day Out**

Reported sinking of an 8,000 ton freighter in the Suez Canal by German Aircraft. So we may have to look to our Laurels!
Crossed the Equator going North - second time.

Wednesday 13th August - **143rd Day Out**

Fairly cool at the moment considering the position of ship.
Very heavy fighting on the Russian Front.
In an offensive sweep over France and North Germany the RAF lost twelve bombers and eight fighters.

Thursday 14th August - **144th Day Out**

The RAF lost another thirteen bombers over Germany.
We hear Mr. Churchill has gone to America to consult Roosevelt - probably the Jap question.

Friday 15th August - **145th Day Out**

The RAF send a force of over three hundred bombers to blast Berlin, twelve reported missing, but a very good feat really. Hope Berlin will soon look like London, see what they think about it!
Mr. Churchill back in England after seeing Mr. Roosevelt.

Saturday 16th August - **146th Day Out**

Passed Cape Guardajui early this morning picked up a very strong breeze, possibly a minor monsoon, the breeze is very welcome but it's worse below, having the ports shut.
Hope to arrive at Aden 9.00am Monday.

Sunday 17th August - **147th Day Out**

Inside the Gulf of Aden it is particularly hot, we lost our breeze as soon as we turned West. Not much War news, due to bad reception, but we have heard that the RAF had bombed industrial targets in Germany, sending over a large force to do so, fourteen of our bombers are missing and we accounted for nineteen enemy fighters during the course of the twenty four hour operation.
Mr. Roosevelt back at the White House after a meeting with Mr. Churchill somewhere in the Western Atlantic.

Monday 18th August - **148th Day Out**

Arrived Aden

We've eased down and put out Paravanes in readiness for making port. Came to anchor at about 10.30 am to await instructions. There are over fifty ships here, of all types and nationalities. There appears to be one or two Naval craft in the inner harbour. It's very hot now and of course much worse at anchor. We were hoping to be here for one day, but according to rumour it may be a week. So much for our haste at East London and then Durban!
The Polish Liner 'Polaski' is here loading with troops, whilst writing this she has been pulled out for Suez. 'Arundel Castle' is alongside and oiling, and also has about 1,500 troops for Suez. She pulled out and made Northwards at 6.00pm, 'Monarch of Bermuda' has taken her place at the oiling jetty.

Tuesday 19th August - **149th Day Out**

Still out in the stream and no one seems particularly interested as to our welfare. Nearly killed ourselves in storing ship at Durban to get away, then we get here and nobody wants us!
Very hot during the day, but the early mornings are nice, although I don't see much of that of course.

Inside Aden Harbour Monday 19th August 1941

'Arundel Castle'

Wednesday 20th August - **150th Day Out**

Two more transports came in today, full of troops for the Middle East.   Aden seemed to be their stopping place, until such time they can deal with them at Suez, avoiding the raids no doubt.

Thursday 21st August - **151st Day Out**

I think this is about the hottest day we have had so far, fortunately we do not have much work to do.
Usual War news.

Friday 22nd August - **152nd Day Out**

Very little news, just wasting time.

Saturday 23rd August - **153rd Day Out**

Very little news generally, wasting time and wasting away!

Sunday 24th August - **154th Day Out**

A day of rest in more ways than one, a jolly good War for some of us!
Heard the Russians are still at it, although the War news is scanty these days.

Monday 25th August - **155th Day Out**

A Greek Cruiser arrives.
Heard tonight that the Allied forces had marched into Iran, the Imperial Forces from West and South and the Russians from the North. This has been acclaimed as a good move generally, stalling the Nazis in their drive Eastward.
Still lying in the bay, and likely to remain so for a good while yet. Still without letter, I have just had the two so far, goodness only knows where they have got to.

Tuesday 26th August - **156th Day Out**

'HMS Exeter' comes into port, after having been in a few hours she leaves again.
Airborne troops were used in the march into Iran.   The RAF has raided industrial Germany, and Russia is still hitting back.

Wednesday 27th August - **157th Day Out**

Went ashore to see the town, and buy a few things.
We have heard that a convoy has been attacked in the Atlantic, and we have lost several ships.

Thursday 28th August - **158th Day Out**

We move into the oiling berth for oil and water, we hope to be leaving soon.
No further news.

Friday 29th August - **159th Day Out**

Thank goodness we are to leave on Monday!

Saturday 30th August - **160th Day Out**

The RAF is again busy over Germany.
Slight raid at home.

Sunday 31st August - **161st Day Out**

Left Aden for Suez

Suddenly received orders to standby and make ready for sea. Left the oiling berth for an anchorage in the Bay, we finally leave at about 6.30pm.

Our mail is still coming so now it's Suez or nothing!

Monday 1st September - **162nd Day Out**

Very hot today but fortunately there is a little breeze.

The RAF lost seven bombers over Germany.

Suez and the Canal were raided Monday night, we hope to make Suez by Friday morning.

It's like being home again to be in a raid or two!

Tuesday 2nd September - **163rd Day Out**

This is the hottest day we've had so far, just imagine being in the Red Sea during September!

Slight raid over Germany, lost one bomber.

Romanians are on the outskirts of Odessa.

Russia admit's the fall of Tallim.

Wednesday 3rd September - **164th Day Out**

The Germans are battering at Leningrad.

Berlin was raided last night by the RAF, also Frankfurt, and Mannheim.

The War to date has lasted two years, and I wonder what the next two shall bring!

I hear we are not arriving until Saturday now.

We have ARP drill.........so what!

Thursday 4th September - **165th Day Out**

First day of the third year of the War, may it all be finished by this time next year.

Heavy battle still raging in and around Leningrad and Russian aircraft raid Berlin.

We had a lovely breeze with us, a most unusual thing in this quarter at this time of the year.

Hope to make Suez tomorrow and so get our longed for mail!

Friday 5th September - **166th Day Out**

Passed through the neck into the Suez Canal at about midnight, and we had previously been warned to stand by for enemy air attack. Every precaution has been taken and nothing left to chance. At 12.30am we are all nicely settled down when the air alert alarm is sounded. We take up our various stations and stand by for what is to come, two planes appear but leave us alone, after about forty minutes the "all clear" is sounded, so this is our first minor raid after many months, and it passed off very well!

Six enemy fighters have been shot down over Malta.

Suez area raided during the night, and two people were killed.

Saturday 6th September - **167th Day Out**

Arrived Suez

A 23,000 ton Italian Liner 'Dullio' which was on the Cape run before the War has either been sunk or badly damaged by torpedoes in the Mediterranean.

Picked up the pilot at 4.00pm, and got away again at 4.15pm heading for our anchorage.

Left our anchorage at 6.00pm, and went alongside, ready to take on patients.

At 9.00pm we have a raid warning, but nothing further develops. At last we get our mail, the first for months; All is well.

Sunday 7th September - **168th Day Out**

Left Suez

All the patients came on board first thing and we sailed at 10.00am, that's something like business! Passed the Cunard White Star Liner 'Georgic' on the way out; What a mess, she was bombed a month ago and then caught fire, she is now a hopeless wreck, I very much doubt if anything can be done in the way of salvage.

Steaming well at the moment and hope to be out of the danger area by midnight.
Went to ARP stations.

Monday 8th September   -   169th Day Out

Had another scare this morning at 1.30am. Enemy planes passing over the ship but no bombs were dropped, we were all at our stations in case anything happened, perhaps some of the Jerrys are human after all, but I would rather say they had already dropped their bombs and were on their way home!

Tuesday 9th September   -   170th Day Out

The biggest raid ever by RAF on Berlin, several other towns were also bombed. We lost twenty one planes and I think this is the most we have lost in a single raid, but let us hope that Berlin will soon look like London.
We are now eased down so as to make Port Sudan at daybreak, it is still extremely hot, and I'm getting a bit fed up with it.
Reported landing of an Allied force in Spitzburgen.

Wednesday 10th September   -   171st Day Out

Arrived and left Port Sudan 2nd time.

An American freighter is bombed and sunk in the Red Sea, the 'Steel Seafarer.'
Two Flying Fortresses have been lost whilst on reconnaissance work over Germany, I think this is the first aircraft of this type to be lost.
We meet the Free French Liner 'President Doumier' once again, this time she is taking details to Mogadishu.

Thursday 11th September   -   172nd Day Out

Extremely hot today, and we are all walking around like drowned rats, may pick up a little breeze tomorrow, I hope to goodness we do!
Russians still doing very well and putting up a resistance around Leningrad, if only they can hold out another month or so, then things may be alright.

Friday 12th September   -   173rd Day Out

A little cooler at the moment, but I am still looking for the welcome breeze.
RAF raided several towns in Northern Italy, Turin being the chief target.
Britain had a free night from raids.
Passed through "Hells Gates" this morning at 11.00am should arrive at Aden tomorrow morning at about 9.00am.

Saturday 13th September   -   174th Day Out

Arrived and Left Aden 2nd Time.

Went in alongside this morning to water and oil and take on a few patients.
It really got busy and we were away by 5.00pm; Next stop Durban.
Received letter number twelve written on the 13th June!

Sunday 14th September   -   175th Day Out

Steaming very slowly for reasons best known to others; It's fairly warm and no doubt our speed has something to do with it. Hope to pick up a breeze of sorts sometime tomorrow, once we get around the corner to Guardajui.

Monday 15th September   -   176th Day Out

Passed Cape Guardajui at 10.00am, and picked up a very welcome breeze. Have heard the RAF has gone to Russia, planes and personnel.
Battle for Leningrad still raging.

Tuesday 16th September   -   177th Day Out

What a welcome change, a drop in the temperature of seven degrees, it's really a treat not to be wiping away perspiration. A fairly heavy sea running, but fortunately we are able to keep our ports open.

Wednesday 17th September   -   178th Day Out

Much the same again today, really quite cool considering where we are. Russians still holding around Leningrad, I only hope they manage to keep it, not that it will be much good to anyone!

Thursday 18th September   -   179th Day Out

The RAF carry out many raids over Northern France in occupied territory, over three hundred planes used. German troops said to be massing at Bordeaux, possibly with an eye on French Africa. RAF fighters in action with Russians around Leningrad, against the Luftwaffe.

Friday 19th September   -   180th Day Out

Russians are still holding Leningrad, but by all accounts a terrific battle is raging for mastery. Going along very nicely at the moment and should be in Durban a week today.
Passed the Cruiser 'Hawkins' heading North.

Saturday 20th September   -   181st Day Out

Very little news apart from the Eastern Front, where very fierce fighting continues.

Sunday 21st September   -   182nd Day Out

Heard the news that the Southampton Docks had been attacked, let us hope there were not too many casualties. Almost cold today, but it's a welcome change.

Monday 22nd September   -   183rd Day Out

Things much about the same, the Russians are still doing very well, and let's hope they hold out until the bad weather starts.

Tuesday 23rd September   -   184th Day Out

We are now well South opposite Lourenco Marques the weather has taken a turn for the worse with a heavy sea running and she is just beginning to pitch nicely. What a treat to have it a bit cool, but unfortunately it's a little uncomfortable for the troops and patients, with all the tossing about.   We should be alongside Friday morning, I wonder if there will be any mail?
The Russians seem to be doing very well, I only hope all we hear is somewhere near the truth for the Russians point of view!

Wednesday 24th September   -   185th Day Out

What a night, if it was a change we wanted we certainly got it, the worst so far but it's quite decent again this morning.

Thursday 25th September   -   186th Day Out

Things much about the same, hope to make port tomorrow.

Friday 26th September   -   187th Day Out

Arrived Durban from Aden 2nd Time

Went in alongside at about 8.30am and tied up at the old Mail berth, the hospital train was awaiting with the patients, and had the all clear by noon.
According to the news, Russia is still holding Leningrad and putting up a good show, apparently the Germans have altered their tactics somewhat and are now making a thrust for the Crimea, lets hope this new move will prove as costly as their other efforts!

Russian Battleship 'Marat' was beached at Avtovo to defend Leningrad

Saturday 27th September   -   **188th Day Out**

Left the Mail berth this morning at 7.00am, and proceeded to the Maydon Wharf, finally making fast alongside the hospital ship 'Amra,' altogether there are now four hospital ships in, so if we are to leave in order of arrival I can see us being here for a month or thereabouts.
The Russians are still doing very well, and what a surprise this is, and to the whole world I should imagine!

Sunday 28th September   -   **189th Day Out**

A quiet day really with most of the staff and crew etc., away on shore.
The War news seems a little better.

Monday 29th September   -   **190th Day Out**

Went on shore for a few hours, a welcome change.

Tuesday 30th September   -   **191st Day Out**

The Russians are putting up a fine resistance in defence of Leningrad. The RAF bomb Steltin, which is the German supply base for their troops in Northern Russia.
Soviet Battleships the 'October Revolution' and 'Marat' have been beached near Avtovo, South of Leningrad to help in the defence of the city.

Wednesday 1st October   -   **192nd Day Out**

War and local news much about the same, we have heard today we are here for another week.

Thursday 2nd October   -   **193rd Day Out**

A fairly heavy raid over England after weeks of comparative quietness, I hope it wasn't too bad around Southampton.

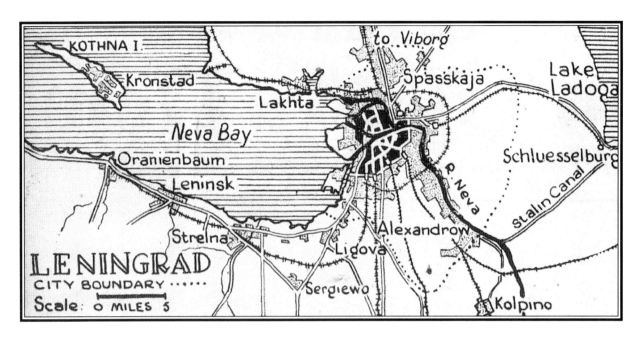

Map of Leningrad and surrounding area

Friday 3rd October - **194th Day Out**

A big convoy arrives presumably for the Middle East with 'HMS Nelson' for escort.
German battleships again visited by the RAF.

Saturday 4th October - **195th Day Out**

Fierce fighting continues around Leningrad. In the Crimea, may Allied resistance arrive in good time. America should declare War on Germany as a tonic for all Russians!

Sunday 5th October - **196th Day Out**

Russians counter attack in the Ukraine, and push the Nazis back a few miles, Germans trying to stem the flow by mass air raids.
RAF bomb invasion ports, Rotterdam, Antwerp, Dunkirk, Brest, Calais, and Boulogne, a good show!

Monday 6th October - **197th Day Out**

Nazis started their big offensive against the Russians, a final throw before the winter sets in, presumably their main objective is Moscow, let's hope history repeats it'self !

Tuesday 7th October - **198th Day Out**

Terrific battle raging along the whole Eastern Front, hope the Russians manage to keep the Nazis out of Moscow, but I very much doubt it.

Wednesday 8th October - **199th Day Out**

Had a fairly heavy day today, storing ship.
Went on shore in the evening, to Mr. Langmead's farewell party, and had quite a nice time.

Thursday 9th October - **200th Day Out**

Battle for Moscow still continues. Air raids on Britain very slight, we seem to have eased off too. Next few days will tell their own story.
According to rumour we shall be leaving here on either Monday or Tuesday.

Friday 10th October - 201st Day Out

Russians still doing fairly well in spite of German advances, anything may happen within the next day or two.

'HMS Colombo' came in yesterday, also the 'Ilex,' a Destroyer damaged from the Crete operations.

Weather fairly cool inspite of being in Whites.

Very busy storing ship, and getting ready generally for sea, several rumours going around as to our final destination, some say home, some say Bombay, we shall see!

Saturday 11th October - 202nd Day Out

Over two hundred planes of the RAF carry out extensive raids over the Rhineland, and invasion ports. Nazis still gaining ground in direction of Moscow.

Had a fairly quiet day, we are now stored up and ready for sea.

Sunday 12th October - 203rd Day Out

Heard this morning that we leave on Tuesday, or at least that they are trying to get us away by then.

Monday 13th October - 204th Day Out

Another big raid by the RAF over Germany, over three hundred planes took part. Russians still retreating and not doing too badly. Heard we may call at Mombassa.

'HMS Nelson'

Tuesday 14th October - 205th Day Out

The big German drive for Moscow continues and they are now within sixty five miles of the city.

Had a very busy day preparing to leave.

Wednesday 15th October - 206th Day Out

Left Durban Northwards 3rd Time

Once again we leave Durban (Northwards) we are proceeding to Mombassa with coloured RAMC and fifty South African Nurses.   We have two sittings, an unheard of thing almost these days!

We pick up fairly heavy weather and some are feeling homesick, at least so they try and make us believe!

Thursday 16th October - 207th Day Out

Germans nearing Moscow, and it seems only a matter of time before it falls, what then I wonder, I doubt very much if they will continue the struggle in any big capacity.

Romanian troops are reported to have entered Odessa.

Things a little better on board today, the sea is down and we shall soon be running into hot weather, a few more restless nights again; and days for that matter.

Friday 17th October - 208th Day Out

Russians still holding out for Moscow, whether it falls or not I think they have done very well.

The American destroyer 'Kearny' has been torpedoed about three hundred and fifty miles off Iceland. What of the "re-action?" (eleven men killed)

Gradually getting warmer, soon be in shirts and shorts again.

Odessa evacuated by the Russians and military forces moved to other sectors.

Saturday 18th October - **209th Day Out**

Battle for Moscow still continues unabated.

Britain was bomb free last night.

Things going fairly well on board but very busy, myself in particular, owing to the fact of having two jobs to do.

Sunday 19th October - **210th Day Out**

Should be a day of rest, but that's alright for a few.

War news much the same.

Monday 20th October - **211th Day Out**

Marshall Voroshilou still holding out for Leningrad. Russians generally are doing equally as well before Moscow, the Russian government has been established at Kujbyshev about five hundred and fifty miles South East of Moscow.

Still fairly cool considering where we are.

Tuesday 21st October - **212th Day Out**

Had a very busy day, what with one thing and another.

The German drive on Moscow possibly easing up.

Wednesday 22nd October - **213th Day Out**

Arrived Mombassa 1st Time Northwards

Prisoners of War from all parts of the Empire in enemy hands, is estimated at about 660,000.

Arrived at Mombassa and went alongside at 2.00pm, roughly thirty officers disembarked, and fifty one nurses and sixteen other ratings joined the ship for Suez. Quite a number of merchantmen here, also the County Class Cruiser 'Fiji.'

Thursday 23rd October - **214th Day Out**

Very busy again, and looking forward to Suez to get rid of some of these people.

Friday 24th October - **215th Day Out**

Enemy planes raided North Wales and Merseyside, three brought down.

Russians still holding out before Moscow.

Saturday 25th October - **216th Day Out**

News generally much the same.

Monday 27th October - **217th Day Out**

Weather still comparatively cool despite our position, we should be somewhere off the Italian Somaliland coast; Or should it be British by now?

Russians still holding out before Moscow but no doubt the Nazis are gathering their forces to make another drive.

Monday 27th October - **218th Day Out**

Picked up an SOS at midnight from the Greek ship 'Anna Marcou' to say she had broken down, and that she was in need of assistance. After steaming seventy miles off our course we found her and proceeded to take her in tow. From 8.00am to late afternoon we were making fast, and finally got under way at about 6.00pm, we are now doing about 10 knots.

Tuesday 28th October - **219th Day Out**

This afternoon the 'Anna Marcou' broke adrift and caused quite a panic for a little while. After hours of patient labour by all sailors, she was eventually made fast again, and once more we proceed on our way, this time at a much reduced speed, hope to goodness she doesn't break away during the night.

Securing a line to the greek ship 'Anna Marcou' after receiving her S.O.S.

Wednesday 29th October   -   220th Day Out

Germans reported to have penetrated into the Crimea.

A new German thrust begins for Moscow.

At the moment we still have the 'Anna Marcou' in tow and doing about 8 knots, if all goes well we should be in Aden tomorrow afternoon, one night there and then I presume we will be away again. Weather conditions very good considering our position, not too hot at the moment.

Thursday 30th October   -   221st Day Out

The old tub is still with us, we shall now lose her tomorrow morning, at which time we hope to be at Aden, normally we should have been there on Wednesday, but salvage operations naturally delayed us.

Much warmer today, but not nearly as bad as the last voyage, but there is the Red Sea to face yet; Hope Jerry is too busy in Russia to send bombers over this time, not a very pleasant feeling to see them over the ship trying to make up their mind whether to drop bombs or not, still, as usual we hope for the best.

Friday 31st October   -   222nd Day Out

Arrived Aden 3rd Time Northwards

Alexandria area raided last night.

Renewed activity all along the Eastern Front.

Arrived at outer anchorage at 10.00am and after disposing of 'Anna' to the safe keeping of a tug, and finally dropped anchor. Moved into the inner harbour at 4.30pm to oil and water. Very few ships here this time, quite a noticeable feature, after having seen so many here on our previous course.

Possibly get away tomorrow direct for Suez. There are a lot of stories going around as to our next destination; Possibly Bombay!

Saturday 1st November - **223rd Day Out**

Left Aden 3rd Time Northwards

Pulled out this morning at 11.00am for Suez.

Had a very busy time last night owing to the ship being open for shore officers.

Sunday 2nd November - **224th Day Out**

Going along nicely again, now that we are rid of 'Anna.' Very warm today, although there is a bit of a breeze.

Heard that an American Destroyer had been torpedoed and sunk off Iceland.

Monday 3rd November - **225th Day Out**

Hottest day so far this voyage, but we live to tell the tale, possibly get to Suez about Wednesday.

Tuesday 4th November - **226th Day Out**

A little cooler today, having picked up a breeze.

Wednesday 5th November - **227th Day Out**

Heard that two more American Destroyers had been torpedoed and sunk off Iceland.

Arriving tomorrow morning, by all accounts staying two days then away again. I wonder if we will go to Bombay direct.

Blackout tonight as we are in the danger area, I wonder what's in store for us,

Bombay or Bombed out!!

The two American Destroyers sunk off Iceland have been named as the 'Rueben James'

and the 'Salinas.'

Thursday 6th November - **228th Day Out**

Arrived Suez 3rd Time

Arrived Suez, and went alongside to discharge cargo that we have brought from Mombassa.

At 4.00am I was awakened by A.A. gun fire; In less than three minutes two bombs were dropped, heavy ones at that, for our special benefit!

I thought it was all up, I heard them screaming down and with seconds to spare, I thought "they must hit the ship!"

Fortunately they both just missed, one on the quayside about twenty feet from the bow and the other a little further along.

The first bomb exploded and sent showers of cement and stones aboard, which fell on our awnings, and several of our men owe their lives to this fact, several were also injured, but none seriously.

The second bomb came almost through the centre of a cargo bed killing two soldiers and badly injuring several others, so once more we live to tell the tale.

Saturday 8th November - **230th Day Out**

Left Suez 3rd Time Southwards

Italian prisoners, wounded and medical come aboard 6.00am, there are about three hundred of them.

Pull out at 9.00am and proceed straight to sea, next stop Bombay.

Sunday 9th November - **231st Day Out**

The RAF raid Berlin, Cologne, Mannheim, and several other German towns, thirty seven of our planes are missing, I should imagine this to be the most we have lost in any single night.

Passed a Trooper going North with a Cruiser as escort.

Monday 10th November - **232nd Day Out**

Very warm again today, I should think we are somewhere off Port Sudan.

Once more the Navy has given "Musso" a nasty smack, this time ten ships of the convoy sunk and two escorting destroyers.

Bomb landed on quayside, a very near miss whilst at Suez

Tuesday 11th November - **233rd Day Out**

Still very warm but hope to run into cooler weather any day now.

Wednesday 12th November - **234th Day Out**

Passed through "Hells Gate" this morning at 7.00am and picked up quite a nice breeze, I hope it will last, by what I can gather we should be in Bombay a week today. I only wish they would turn the old tub Westwards for a change, getting a bit fed up with things now, sun and sweat for months on end without a break, enough to drive one to drink; That's one excuse anyway!

Thursday 13th November - **235th Day Out**

'Ark Royal' Sunk 30 Miles off Gibraltar
A little cooler at the moment and very much appreciated.
Passed Aden last night.

Friday 14th November - **236th Day Out**

A heavy raid on Fayoum, sixty miles from Cairo, sixty four persons killed and ninety five injured.
Russians still holding out in the Moscow and Leningrad sectors, may the weather prove to be an asset to them, and history repeat it'self.
Britain had another quiet night.

Saturday 15th November - **237th Day Out**

The Admiralty announces that the Aircraft Carrier 'Ark Royal' was sunk in the Mediterranean; Casualties are believed to be light. Apparently she was returning to Malta from normal operations and torpedoed by a U-boat. Towing operations proved unsuccessful.

Sunday 16th November - **238th Day Out**

Russians still doing very well at the end of the 22nd week fighting. Very few people realised in, or out of the service for that matter, that they could possibly hold out for so long, it will now possibly turn into trench warfare.

Only one casualty reported in the sinking of the 'Ark Royal.'

Still fairly warm, with a little breeze, by all accounts we should be at Bombay on Wednesday morning.

Monday 17th November - **239th Day Out**

American Navy seized in the South Atlantic the German motorship the 'Odenwald,' she was trying to make Bordeaux with a general cargo of war material, something else for Hitler to shout about!

Britain raid free last night.

Tuesday 18th November - **240th Day Out**

Very little general news, and things on board much the same.

Italians on board have been very good regards behaviour.

Hope to arrive tomorrow sometime, then what?

Sincerely hope there is a chance for transfer as I hear the 'Windsor' is here for repair, and I'm getting a bit fed up, as I said before sun and sweat for months on end.

Wednesday 19th November - **241st Day Out**

Arrived Bombay

Arrived about noon and went in alongside about 3.00pm to disembark Italian prisoners, but we had to keep them on board for one more night.

This is my second visit to Bombay, the first occasion being in 1919 whilst serving on 'HMS Malaya,' then there was very little time to see the place, but I hope to be able to do so properly this time, it looks a very nice place, first impression.

Thursday 20th November - **242nd Day Out**

Heard the good news today that the Imperial Forces had started advancing into Libya again, I hope they will finish off Jerry the same way they finished off the Italians. According to the local paper here, we have already advanced fifty miles. This is not a bad start if we can keep it up, and we should be able to if we have sufficient aircraft. Time alone will tell.

Friday 21st November - **243rd Day Out**

British still giving the Nazis a shake up in Libya, furious fighting continues West of Fort Capuzzo. Nazis reported to have lost one hundred and thirty tanks already.

Saturday 22nd November - **244th Day Out**

Reported capture of Rostov by the Germans. Fierce fighting before Moscow.

There's a fierce tank battle raging in the Tobruk area, I wonder what the outcome of it will be. So far, yesterday was the worst day spent aboard ship, full of workman, and to crown it all there are about one hundred men chipping away at the paintwork, the din was worse than a blitz, and that's going some, thank goodness we move into the stream tomorrow. I have learnt that the 'Windsor' is here for another two months!

Sunday 23rd November - **245th Day Out**

Good news from the Western Desert. New Zealand troops have captured Fort Capuzzo, and British troops have occupied Bardia. The main battle between tanks is still proceeding.

Monday 24th November - **246th Day Out**

Moved out into the stream, possibly finish off repairs and store whilst at anchorage, then sail for Suez, calling at Aden en route.

Still very warm although we are away from the Quay but we have got rid of the dust and some of the flies.

*HMS 'Barham' 35,500 tons, struck by four torpedoes
and sank within four and a half minutes in the Mediteranean*

No decision reached between the rival forces in the tank battle, it still continues unabated, but I think we should come out on top, things seem to point that way.

Moscow at the moment is taking the full force of the new German thrust, and I doubt very much if they can keep them back much longer; Anyway they have done extremely well.

Things on board going with a swing, as far as workman are concerned, but I expect we shall be here another week.

Tuesday 25th November - 247th Day Out

'HMS Barham' Sunk

Two Allied vessels arrive with Italian prisoners, they are safe for a little while. Fierce fighting around Moscow. Tank battle still continues in and around Tobruk.

Wednesday 26th November - 248th Day Out

'HMS Revenge' arrives, presumably for the Far East, she started to store immediately on arrival, so it looks a bit business like. Tension existing at the moment between America and Japan, War between these two nations possible within a week.

British tanks in action in Russia for the first time.

Fierce fighting still going on in the Western Desert, particularly for mastery in tanks.

Thursday 27th November - 249th Day Out

A very busy day getting stores on board and attending to things generally.

War news on all fronts a trifle conflicting, but I think we are on the upgrade.

Friday 28th November - 250th Day Out

Grave Japanese and American tension, it looks as though it's going to be War.

Russians still sticking it out; And our people in the Western Desert doing as well as can be expected, there again I think we shall finally bottle them up, but it may take time.

Saturday 29th November - 251st Day Out

Gondar Fortress, the last Italian strong hold in East Africa capitulates, (Thursday). Over 20,000 men were taken prisoner, so ends Mussolini's East African Empire.

Over forty one vessels sunk in the Mediterranean in the month of November, a particularly good feat on the part of the Navy.

Russians still doing well in the Kalinin area, the Germans are reported to have been pushed back.

The Russians are also doing well in front of Moscow, lets hope they manage to keep Jerry out: Should he eventually take it, it can't possibly be of much use.

Sunday 30th November - 252nd Day Out

Russia is reported to have pushed back Jerry in and around Moscow. Our forces in Libya trying to contact the remnants of the Nazi tank forces; Generally speaking things are going very well.

Report of Naval action in the English channel not confirmed yet.

Monday 1st December - 253rd Day Out

'HMS Devonshire' sinks a raider in the South Atlantic, another one out of the way!

Russia still going well.

Tank battle in Libya still going ahead, but I think it is definitely in our favour.

Japanese-American talks still going on, anything may happen.

HMS 'Revenge'

Bombay Yacht Club
Saturday 29th November 1941

Tuesday 2nd December - 254th Day Out

'HMAS Sydney' has sunk by gunfire a heavily armed raider in the Indian Ocean, the 'Sydney' in turn has been sunk and so far no trace of her has been found, it is believed from many quarters that the 'Sydney' has been engaged by a Pocket Battleship; The hunt is now on.

Germans before Tobruk gained a slight success, according to the Cairo news, this can only be a temporary success!

Things on board much the same, waiting to sail, getting a bit tired of Bombay.

Wednesday 3rd December - 255th Day Out

'HMS Prince of Wales' arrives at Singapore. Nazis recapture Sidi Rezegh.

Italian destroyer 'Alvise da Mosto' sunk in the Mediterranean.

Mr. Churchill announced the call up of all unmarried women between the ages of twenty and thirty for work of National importance.

Thursday 4th December - 256th Day Out

Russians still driving back the Germans in the Rostov (Crimea) area.

Bitter fighting continues on the outskirts of Moscow.

In Libya both forces have seemed to come to a standstill after many days of desperate fighting, possibly gathering strength to renew the struggle at any moment. Things on board about the same, all repairs done, and stores finished; Hope to leave tomorrow at noon.

HMS 'Devonshire'
Built 1929 9,850 tons. Top speed 32 Knots

Charles E Brown

Friday 5th December - 257th Day Out

Left Bombay

Pulled out at noon and made for the open sea; What a treat to be at sea once more, may this be the last time I see Bombay, and that goes for the rest of the crew I think! Fancy being stuck in this hole for just over a fortnight, and not being able to get ashore any evening. Now I suppose it's Aden, with it's usual wait and see methods, what a lovely War for some people! Personally I hope we go back on our usual run, Durban to Suez, but I somehow have an idea we may go through the Canal this time, to pick up our wounded, or even be a base hospital ship near the Tobruk area.

Saturday 6th December - 258th Day Out

Very warm again today, one would imagine that we should be used to this particular weather by now, but personally I don't think I shall ever get used to it; Gumboots or snow shoes for me in future, if this is the Middle East, then here's hoping to go West.

Still no news as to what we may do, not even a mention of Durban, roll on this ruddy War, and let me get out of it; Same old thing day after day sweat, sweat, sweat, with no possible hope of a change!

Sunday 7th December - 259th Day Out

Another raider has been sunk in the South Atlantic by 'HMS Dorsetshire'

Britain free of raids for the 3rd successive night.

Japan attacks the United States 1520 hours E.S.T.

The Japanese have attacked Pearl Harbour in Hawaii, in the second attack, army and navy bases in Manila were hit!

HMS 'Prince of Wales' Battleship 35,000 tons sunk off Malay Peninsula

Monday 8th December - **260th Day Out**

Great Britain declares War with Japan.

USA will probably do so within the next few hours.

The Dutch East Indies also at War with the Allies against the Axis. What a terrible thing War is, almost the whole world involved, I wonder; Will it shorten the war?

I sincerely hope so, instead of us going home, it is possible we shall go to the Far East; Another three years of this......... my God, what I would like to do to Hitler and Co!

Tuesday 9th December - **261st Day Out**

Japan going all out to do as much damage as possible before the Yanks get into their stride.

The heavy raids in Pearl Harbour Hawaii caused untold damage 'The Oklahoma' was set on fire, and many other ships damaged. Heavy casualties are reported.

British gun boat 'Petrel' sunk off Wake Island by the Japs.

The War in Libya seems to be turning in our favour again.

Russians doing well on both fronts.

Things on board much the same, plenty of rumours floating around, but time will tell as to which is correct, one thing is certain we shall not be going home, probably the Far East is now on the cards.

Wednesday 10th December - **262nd Day Out**

Have heard the terrible news that the 'Prince of Wales,' and 'Repulse' have been sunk by Japanese bombers, no actual details yet apart from the fact that the bomb caused internal explosions. It is a setback and no mistake about it, apart from the terrible loss of life, our position is considerably weakened from the Naval point of view in the Far East.

Thursday 11th December - **263rd Day Out**

Arrived Aden 4th Time (from Bombay)

Arrived Aden, and straight to oil and water.

Hoping we would be away immediately after being told we were leaving at 6.00am for Suez. Then we get another order to say; "Go out to anchor, and probably you'll be there for Christmas".

More muddle!

Friday 12th December - **264th Day Out**

Finished oiling and watering and came to anchor at 7.30am, now I presume we swing around the buoy for a couple of weeks, if some of us are not crazy before this is over, then I must be already mad to think it!
One thing in our favour;   It is very cool here at the moment.

Saturday 13th December - **265th Day Out**

War news much the same, with the Yanks getting into position after being caught unawares.
There are now four Hospital Ships with us here including the 'Amra' and 'Atlantis.'
Just heard we may sail today, this time still further North.
Still here, we may go tomorrow.
A big convoy arrives with troops for the Middle East.

Sunday 14th December - **266th Day Out**

Left Aden

Once more we leave Aden, and I sincerely hope for the last time. By all accounts we are going still further North. I understand that Port Said will be our base.
Entered the Red Sea last night, also for the last time I hope! Fairly cool at the moment, I wonder how long it will last. According to local rumour we are calling at Massawa to pick up a complete Hospital Unit (Australian).

Monday 15th December - **267th Day Out**

The cool weather soon left us, today it's as hot as hell again, with a following wind to make things worse.
War news very good generally.

Tuesday 16th December - **268th Day Out**

Arrived off Massawa and anchored. Not very impressive at first sight, several scuttled ships here and there, the original intention being to block, or to try and block the main entrances. Considering the place has been bombed and shelled it doesn't look too bad.
Russians still doing well.
In Libya we appear to be holding our own, but Hong Kong seems to be on the danger list.

Wednesday 17th December - **269th Day Out**

Arrived Massawa

Up anchor at 7.00am and came alongside to find the Hospital Unit awaiting us, no doubt all concerned will be very pleased to get away, even if it does mean the Western Desert or thereabouts. All ratings including twenty nine nurses, twenty officers and two hundred and thirteen lesser ranks who joined at 8.00am.
It's terribly hot here at the moment but I believe it's fairly cool at night. Very little here in the way of entertainment. It rained tonight, only the second time I have seen it in over six months, and as we were led to believe, it was fairly cool!

Thursday 18th December - **270th Day Out**

Pulled away from the Quay at 8.00am, now for Suez I presume. At 8.30am we anchor owing to rain and bad visibility, as we have to pass through mine infested waters, it was finally decided to be too dangerous, so here we are swinging around the buoy, more or less, until tomorrow morning 7.00am; Then Suez.

Friday 19th December - **271st Day Out**

Left Massawa

Up anchor and away at 7.00am. Heavy raid on Brest by the RAF. More success in Libya and on the Eastern Front.
'HMS Dunedin' has been torpedoed and sunk in the Atlantic.
Fairly cool again at the moment if only it will last, things won't be too bad.
Hong Kong in a precarious position.

The Quayside at Massawa

Saturday 20th December - **272nd Day Out**

War news fairly satisfactory apart from the Far East, there I think it's men and lack of materials, still, it will avail them nothing providing we win the War!

Not much local news, probably get to Suez on Monday and then through the Canal; May be!

Sunday 21st December **273rd Day Out**

Derna captured, and the Axis Forces are now being driven to Benghazi, where they may make their final stand. The weather is really quite cool, what a welcome change.

Monday 22nd December - **274th Day Out**

Even cooler today, so much so that some are back in Blues, may it continue.

Hope to arrive at Suez in the morning, with luck, and Luftwaffe willing. Fairly certain we shall go through the Canal, but no doubt we shall know tomorrow.

Tuesday 23rd December - **275th Day Out**

Arrived Suez

Arrived at Suez at 8.00am, and immediately discharged the complete Australian Unit. Took on water and away again.

Into the Canal at 11.30am; Our quickest move since being in commission! I wonder what is in store for us, a few scares if I know anything about it, time alone will tell. Anchored at Ismalia for the night.

Wednesday 24th December - **276th Day Out**

Arrived Port Said 1st Time

Got under way at 6.30am, arriving at Port Said 1.30pm. Tied up at oiling berth and proceeded to oil and water.

United Services Club Ismalia

Arrived at Port Said Christmas Eve

Italian Cruiser 'Sans Georgia'

Devastation at Tobruk

Thursday 25th December - **277th Day Out**

CHRISTMAS DAY; And what a day.

Heard we had taken Benghazi and also that Hong Kong had been lost.

We were to leave today but it has been postponed, no doubt we shall leave tomorrow.

Friday 26th December - **278th Day Out**

Pulled out at 5.00pm and picked up bad weather almost at once, anyway it's a change from the continual heat, the first real change of weather since leaving home.

All blacked up apart from the Convention Lights, also all water tight doors shut down and ports closed as a precaution; A Hospital Ship doesn't mean much to the Axis crowd!

Saturday 27th December - **279th Day Out**

Had a pretty rough night last night, but it was cool, that's the main thing.

No scare so far, but we expect it at any moment. Still, why worry over something that may not happen!

Sunday 28th December - **280th Day Out**

Arrived Tobruk 1st Time

Weather improved today, still nice and cool with a moderate sea running.

Russians still doing well, but things are not too bright in the Far East.

We arrive at Tobruk, or at least off Tobruk and are taken into the harbour inside the Boom, we are now lying almost alongside the Italian Cruiser 'Sans Georgia' which was sunk during our first assault in the early days. Quite a number of other ships, although those that have not actually been sunk or damaged, have been beached.

Several sloops and destroyers are here, but by what I can gather, they actually left harbour at night and came back in the morning, possibly doing a twofold job in getting away from bombs and watching the coast.

At the moment, the Army is in command, all civilians having left months ago. We had a raid free night last night, the first one for quite a while.

The patients are coming on board first thing in the morning.

Monday 29th December - **281st Day Out**

Patients came on board this morning, and what a business having to bring them in our own lifeboats, they were in a terrible condition and filthy dirty. I hear we are taking them to Alexandria. Then possibly go back for more, going a bit further West next time, maybe to Derna.

Got under way at 5.30pm, and should make Alexandria easily by Wednesday morning.

Possibly a fairly heavy raid over England, three enemy planes were brought down.

Tuesday 30th December - **282nd Day Out**

Had a scare during the night, had to stand by for a raid at 1.00am, planes were heard by several people but fortunately nothing happened, luck is still with us, and how we need it.

Wednesday 31st December - **283rd Day Out**

Arrived Alexandria 1st Time

Came into harbour and tied up. Red Cross train awaiting us, all patients are off by 4.30pm. After a little more muddle, we finally pull away from the quayside and tie up to a buoy in the inner harbour.

Chapter Six

1942

HMHS 'Llandovery Castle' at Alexandria

Thursday 1st January 1942 - **284th Day Out**

NEW YEARS DAY.

Friday 2nd January - **285th Day Out**

Still swinging around the buoy, but hope to move out very soon. The weather is particularly cold but I think in keeping with the particular run of things at this time of the year. Have not been ashore so far, but hope to make contact on our next visit. Owing to bad weather the ship slipped, or at least broke away from the buoy and had to be re-moored.

Just heard we may possibly leave tomorrow.

Saturday 3rd January - **286th Day Out**

Left Alex for Tobruk 2nd Time

We pull out at about 4.00pm and I presume for Tobruk. I wonder what is in store for us this time, last time we did not have actual raids and I think we were rather lucky, as raids had been pretty frequent, almost a nightly occurrence until our arrival; The previous Hospital Ship 'HS Somersetshire' had a narrow escape being straddled by a stick of bombs, but no material damage was done.

Sunday 4th January - **287th Day Out**

A day of rest.

Things on board very much the same, perhaps it would be as well if something did happen to cause a slight diversion! Weather quite good in comparison to our last voyage to Tobruk.

Monday 5th January - 288th Day Out

Arrived Tobruk 2nd Time

Arrived this morning at 9.30am, and immediately proceeded to embark the wounded, nearly 600 altogether. Sailed again at 5.30pm for Alex, where we should arrive on Wednesday morning. Had no scares so far but we expect one any moment, I can't see Jerry letting us get away with it every time, without trying to cause us some 'inconvenience'; Time alone will tell!

Tuesday 6th January - 289th Day Out

Had a very quiet night, thank goodness.

Wednesday 7th January - 290th Day Out

Arrived Alexandria 2nd Time from Tobruk

Arrived this morning at about 9.00am, and tied up alongside, usual routine then carried out disembarking patients etc.

Weather particularly good for this time of the year.

Thursday 8th January - 291st Day Out

Under 48 hours notice, but still alongside. Went on shore and had quite a good time.

General War news much about the same.

The Russians are still doing very well.

Enemy casulties being loaded at Tobruk

Stanley Bay Alexandria, reminded me of Bournemouth !

Friday 9th January   -   292nd Day Out

Things very much the same.

Saturday 10th January - 293rd Day Out

Left Alexandria for Port Said

Pulled out at 3.00pm, and finally cleared the Boom by 4.00pm. A fairly heavy sea running and the ship rolling slightly. We should be at Port Said first thing in the morning, but the weather may delay us.

Sunday 11th January   -   294th Day Out

Arrived Port Said from Alexandria 1st Time

In spite of weather etc. we managed to make port and come to rest at the entrance to the canal, we are now anchored with our stern to the shore, and tied there. To go ashore we have to hire a boat so really it is neither one thing nor the other.   Heard that the Japs have made a landing in North Borneo. They seem to be allowed to do as they wish!

Russians still going ahead.

Heavy raid by the RAF over Wilhelmshaven and Kiel.

Leslie Penny ashore for stores Alexandria

Monday 12th January   -   295th Day Out

Things much the same generally; Awaiting orders.

Tuesday 13th January   -   296th Day Out

Still waiting.

Wednesday 14th January   -   297th Day Out

Still waiting.

Thursday 15th January -   298th Day Out

Very little news to hand, just waiting for something to turn up.

War news much the same, with the Russians going ahead and our troops in Malaya going astern, and I thought all the muddle was in the Middle East!

Just heard we may possibly sail on Saturday.

Friday 16th January   -   299th Day Out

RAF raid Hamburg and Emden.

No news from the Far East, Britain raid free again last night.

Saturday 17th January   -   300th Day Out

Still here and likely to remain so for a few days. As much as we would like to get going we are extremely lucky to be here, no raids to worry about, and very little to do and weather above all is particularly cool, a very welcome change from what we have been used to for so many months.

Sunday 18th January -   301st Day Out

Things very much the same.

Tuesday 20th January - **303rd Day Out**

Very little local news, and I think we must be here for the duration.

Russians still doing very well.

Wednesday 21st January - **304th Day Out**

The Yanks seem to be waking up at last, Jap cruisers sunk by U.S. bombers.

RAF again raid Sicily.

Thursday 22nd January - **305th Day Out**

Having a very quiet time still, and the weather ideal.

A reconnaissance plane flew over today and AA Guns went into action, it may be tonight that we have a call, make a change anyway!

Heard we may possibly leave tomorrow.

Friday 23rd January - **306th Day Out**

Left Port Said 2nd Time

We leave at last; Pulled out at 3.30pm, so much for our proposed stay of two days! Possibly it's Tobruk again calling at Alexandria en-route.

Japs making a landing in New Guinea, a jumping off place for Australia.

Russians still chasing the Nazis.

Saturday 24th January - **307th Day Out**

Called at Alexandria en-route

Called at Alexandria this morning having anchored in the outer harbour for several hours, got under way again at about 4.00pm.

With us at the moment are, eight Destroyers, four Cruisers, and a supply ship, four Destroyers either side of us and the four Cruisers astern, we are all wondering what is in the wind, perhaps the 'Iti' navy is out, let's hope so, it will cause some sort of a diversion!

At the moment according to the news a terrific tank battle has begun between our forces and Rommel's, maybe the Navy is going to see what they can do.

Sunday 25th January - **308th Day Out**

Had a stand by this morning for an air-raid, a huge bomber passed over, but nothing worse happened, weather fairly good, sea a bit choppy.

Monday 26th January - **309th Day Out**

Had another alarm this morning at 3.30am, and went to stations, but again nothing happened. Arrived this morning at 8.30am, but the sea was too rough to take on patients. During the morning a sand storm developed and made things even worse, at one time it was so bad you could not see the ships at their moorings. There is sand everywhere even inside the ship and everywhere is covered, food as well. I feel sorry for the poor blighters ashore; Possibly they will stay there all night.

Tuesday 27th January - **310th Day Out**

Left Tobruk for Alexandria 3rd Time

Owing to heavy seas and the sand storm, we were unable to take on patients and remained all night (Monday). Hope to get busy this morning. Things at the moment are not too good this way. I think Rommel has caught us napping. Started to get patients aboard by 10.00am and by 4.00pm all aboard, just over six hundred in total.   Ready to sail at 5.00pm and owing to bad weather and a minor sand storm we were delayed until 9.00pm. Heard that 'HMS Barham' had been lost (officially) she was torpedoed and sunk in November. I think Rommel is doing well at the moment, I only hope we shall be able to check him.

Russians still forging ahead.

Japs still spreading themselves around the Pacific.

Wednesday 28th January   -   **311th Day Out**

Heavy fighting still going on around Benghazi. Very difficult at the moment to say what the result might be.

Japs still pressing towards Singapore.

I wonder "will our reinforcements reach there in time?"

Weather still very cool.

Should arrive Alex tomorrow morning.

Thursday 29th January   -   **312th Day Out**

Arrived Alex from Tobruk 3rd Time

Went alongside at 10.30am, and started to discharge patients, finished by 4.00pm. Heard that Benghazi had fallen to the Axis forces, Tobruk won't be too healthy again now!

Friday 30th January   -   **313th Day Out**

Should have sailed again for Tobruk, but eventually put on twelve hours notice, that may mean several days.

Left the quayside this morning and we are now at the inner harbour moorings.

Saturday 31st January   -   **314th Day Out**

War news very much the same in Libya.

Japs nearing Singapore, they are only sixteen miles away.

Russians still going ahead.

Sunday 1st February   -   **315th Day Out**

Japs in full occupation of Malaya, all troops withdrawn to the Island of Singapore.

Ship news much the same; Waiting to sail.

Monday 2nd February   -   **316th Day Out**

Things much the same.

Tuesday 3rd February   -   **317th Day Out**

Left Alex for Tobruk 4th Time

Pulled out at 2.30pm.

Wednesday 4th February   -   **318th Day Out**

Getting along very nicely, but expect things to happen any moment. Heard that Derna had fallen, that being only seventeen miles from our port of call which is Tobruk, so we maybe in for a warm time. The ship at the moment is pitching rather heavily, but it will help to keep the subs off, if not the aircraft!

Thursday 5th February   -   **319th Day Out**

Arrived Tobruk 4th Time

Arrived at 9.00am and anchored in the usual spot. Got busy immediately, and patients were soon coming aboard. Had a couple of nuisance raids, a few bombs dropped during the last one, but miles away or at least it might have been for all the harm it did to us!

Heard the Jap assault for Singapore has begun. I wonder what the outcome will be, I doubt very much if it's impregnable, as usual I hope for the best.

Friday 6th February   -   **320th Day Out**

Had a real scare today at about 11.00am, a bomber believed to be German dropped a stick of bombs about fifty yards ahead of us. At this particular moment we were doing about 8 to 10 knots, had we being doing our usual speed we should now be in 'Davy Jones Locker' I imagine the pilot took it for granted that a ship of this size must

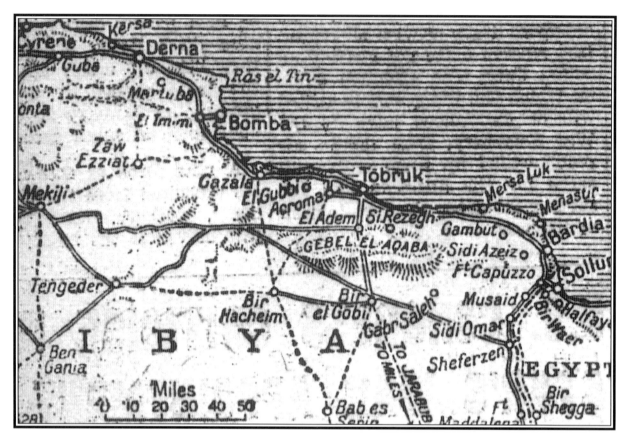

Map of Libya and Egypt

be doing about 15 knots and dropped his bombs accordingly.

At about 2.15pm we had another scare, two planes this time, but fortunately they left us alone, in this I would rather say they had already dropped their bombs. To my mind the only good Germans are dead ones! It is now 10.00pm, and we are going along beautifully, all lights on; I wonder what the morning will bring.

Saturday 7th February - 321st Day Out

Arrived Alex from Tobruk 4th Time

Safe alongside once again. Patients disembark and we are away to the buoys at 4.00pm.

Sunday 8th February - 322nd Day Out

Had a rude awakening this morning at 5.00am. Jerry paid us a visit; Plenty of AA fire for a few minutes but I don't think there were many bombs dropped, if any. Still under six hours notice and still tied up to the buoys. The best day as regards weather for a long time, not that one craves sun after our Red Sea experience!

Monday 9th February - 323rd Day Out

Left Alex for Tobruk 5th Time

Had another scare early this morning, but nothing happened.

War news much the same. Russians advancing with us doing the opposite!

Tuesday 10th February - 324th Day Out

Another raider paid us a visit this morning and dropped a stick of bombs, all misses and no damage, we certainly have a charmed life thank goodness. But it is quite on the cards that we shall get a wallop before this Tobruk stint is finished. The Axis forces are within thirty miles of us, no distance particularly for a plane, still the devil looks after his own

Kittyhawks on a mission over the Western Desert

Wednesday 11th February - **325th Day Out**

Arrived and left Tobruk 5th Time

Arrived 10.00am and left at 5.00pm. A few planes came over whilst loading but nothing exciting happened.
Singapore being attacked to it's fullest extent by Japs, only a matter of days, possibly hours, before it is in enemy hands.

Thursday 12th February - **326th Day Out**

Had a quiet night, although we were expecting otherwise.
Singapore according to the news is making it's last stand, another set back.

Friday 13th February - **327th Day Out**

Arrived Alex from Tobruk 5th Time

Heard the news today that the 'Scharnhorst' and 'Gneisenau' and 'Prinz Eugen' had made good their escape from Brest but were intercepted in the channel heading Northwards. A general battle ensued, the outcome of which is not actually known, to date we lost twenty bombers, sixteen fighters, and sixteen Sherewordfish aircraft whilst Jerry lost eighteen planes, hope to hear more details this evening at 6.00pm.
Singapore still holding out, but the position is still pretty hopeless.
Arrived at 9.00am, and went alongside, discharged patients and went to anchorage at 3.00pm.
Maybe here for a day or two then back to Tobruk or possibly through the canal going South again, the latter I hope will prove to be correct.

Saturday 14th February - **328th Day Out**

Heard we are to remain here four days, for minor repairs etc., and it's quite on the cards that we go back to Tobruk again. I suppose we will continue doing that run until we get a packet, either a bomb or a torpedo.
Singapore still holding out.

'Rowallan Castle' sunk 16th Febuary 1942   *A. Duncan*

Sunday 15th February   -   **329th Day Out**

Mr Churchill has told the world that Singapore has fallen (surrendered). Another military set back, still we must fight on; And win.

Monday 16th February   -   **330th Day Out**

Singapore now occupied by the Japs. Russians still going ahead, about the only bright spot at the moment. Heard that the 'Rowallan Castle' had been sunk whilst in convoy to Malta from Alexandria.

Tuesday 17th February   -   **331st Day Out**

The battle for Burma begins, then India.
Ships news much the same, still doing minor repairs, may possibly sail Thursday.

Wednesday 18th February   -   **332nd Day Out**

News generally much the same.

Thursday 19th February   -   **333rd Day Out**

As for Wednesday.

Friday 20th February   -   **334th Day Out**

Port Darwin bombed by the Japs, the first time the war has struck Australia.

Saturday 21st February   -   **335th Day Out**

Russians still doing very well, and pushing the Nazis back on all fronts.

Japs getting a taste of their own medicine in the bombing of Bali, several cruisers hit and one actually sunk, one hundred and eighty two Jap ships sunk or damaged to date. Fighting in the Philippines still very fierce but the Yanks still seem to be doing very well at the moment.

Sunday 22nd February - 336th Day Out

The sea and air battle of Bali still proceeding, six Jap warships hit possibly one or two sunk. We on the other hand are still waiting for news of sailing, this hanging around ports is enough to drive one mad, nothing to do, day in and day out.

Monday 23rd February - 337th Day Out

Still swinging around the buoy and still waiting.
War news much the same; Heard we may actually go South, I only hope it's true.
We see very little of the War at the moment.

Tuesday 24th February - 338th Day Out

Heard that Bali had been taken by the Japs, and so it goes on.

Wednesday 25th February - 339th Day Out

News much the same.

Thursday 26th February - 340th Day Out

Heard the good news that the Russians have trapped nearly 100,000 Nazis near Leningrad, hope they complete the job in their own way!
RAF raid Kiel and Wilhelmshaven, where the German battle cruisers 'Scharnhorst' and 'Gneisenau' are in dry dock.

Friday 27th February - 341st Day Out

Russians still trying to annihilate the Germans, who they have surrounded near Leningrad.
Naval battle in the Java sea, awaiting outcome.

Saturday 28th February - 342nd Day Out

Lull in the Burma fighting, many Jap planes litter the countryside.
Russian net tightens around Germans, and the Nazis fail to affect relief for the threatened army.
Two planes came over today on reconnaissance, may get a visit tonight. I feel we are in for a good time, sooner or later!
The rumour of our going South seems to be unfounded, possibly going West, in more ways than one!

Sunday 1st March - 343rd Day Out

Japs made landing in Java at three different points. The Naval action has ended and I think a little in our favour.
Reported landing of British paratroops in Northern France. Things comparatively quiet in the Western desert, at the moment anyway. However we expect a flare up at any moment.

Monday 2nd March - 344th Day Out

Have been here now eighteen days, the longest time in port for many a week. We hear we may go tomorrow - Tobruk again! I only hope it's true, one gets so fed up hanging around these places, particularly as we are at anchor in the bay, it wouldn't be quite as bad if we could stay alongside, and walk off and on as we wished.

Tuesday 3rd March - 345th Day Out

Left Alex for Tobruk 6th Time

At last we are going to get underway.
We leave at 5.30pm proceeding Westwards hoping for the best.

Wednesday 4th March - **346th Day Out**

Had another scare this morning at 2.30am. Air raid gong was sounded, but nothing worse than that happened.

Saw two or three floating mines this afternoon, tried to explode the same by rifle fire, but we were unsuccessful.

Thursday 5th March - **347th Day Out**

Arrived Tobruk from Alex 6th Time

Pulled into anchor at 9.00am, very few ships here now, getting a bit too hot no doubt!

The weather on the contrary is quite cold, with plenty of rain reminding of us of an April morning at home.

Friday 6th March - **348th Day Out**

At sea from Tobruk to Alex; A fairly heavy sea running and quite a good few down. Free from bombing raids so far.

Saturday 7th March - **349th Day Out**

Arrived Alex from Tobruk 6th Time

Back in Alex once again; Went alongside at 10.00am, discharged patients and stayed alongside all night.

Sunday 8th March - **350th Day Out**

Left the quay for the buoys, another couple of weeks here I suppose.

Java likely to go any moment, goodness only knows what will happen next.

Monday 9th March - **351st Day Out**

Swinging round the buoy once again.

Java practically finished and Rangoon well on the way.

Tuesday 10th March - **352nd Day Out**

Heard that Rangoon has been evacuated, one more setback. Durban is the next port to get a shake up. Russians still doing well and making a good show.

Wednesday 11th March - **353rd Day Out**

War news much the same, no hopes of our moving yet.

Thursday 12th March- - **354th Day Out**

Same as yesterday.

Friday 13th March - **355th Day Out**

Russians still doing well and the German army is surrounded at Stanaya, Russia is in a bad way.

German battleship 'Gneisenau' bombed and damaged by the Fleet Air Arm, at present in Norwegian port.

Saturday 14th March - **356th Day Out**

RAF resume full scale assault over Germany. Essen was particularly in the limelight. Reported sinking of three German U-boats.

'HS Somersetshire' sailed for Tobruk so we are next on the list, next weekend I hope.

Sunday 15th March - **357th Day Out**

News generally much the same.8

Monday 16th March - **358th Day Out**

Had 48 hours leave, and went to Port Said.

Tuesday 17th March - **359th Day Out**

In Port Said and having quite a nice time, what a welcome change from the boat.

Wednesday 18th March - **360th Day Out**

Back on board again, to the same old dreary round; What a life!

Thursday 19th March - **361st Day Out**

Heard we may sail this weekend.

Friday 20th March - **362nd Day Out**

Things generally much the same, some speculation as to where we may go, possibly Crete.

Saturday 21st March - **363rd Day Out**

Went on shore for a change.
Japanese cruiser bombed and sunk by Flying Fortresses off Java.
Malta had a severe air raid.
Russians still doing well and beating Jerry up!

Tuesday 24th March - **366th Day Out**

Left Southampton a year ago today for the Middle East hope to be able to say left the Middle East for Southampton this time next year!

Wednesday 25th March - **367th Day Out**

Had a sand storm today and naturally it was everywhere, goodness knows what it must be like actually in the desert. Another raid on South Coast towns, we also gave Germany a visit. We are leaving tomorrow.

Thursday 26th March - **368th Day Out**

Left Alex for Tobruk 7th Time

We leave again, having been here for just on three weeks, we shall be back again on Sunday, and for another long stay I suppose.
Weather is quite good, just suitable for an attack, I expect we shall survive; We can only hope so, our luck has held so far.

Friday 27th March - **369th Day Out**

Arrived Tobruk from Alex 7th Time

Arrived at 11.00am, one other ship in the bay but plenty of land activity, possibly our last trip to Tobruk and very few will mind that! Two raids since we were there last time, a second one though only a few minutes duration (actual bombing) was pretty severe, they narrowly missed us several times, one being close enough to make one or two small holes in the ships side. One time the ship seemed to lift and drop again, clocks were shaken off the bulkheads as also were the mirrors. In spite of everything no one was hurt, and we got the patients away. I saw one man being picked up in the water. We were just leaving when the attack started and I think they would have liked to have sunk us and blocked the entrance; Still, we live again to see another day.

Saturday 28th March - **370th Day Out**

Everything very peaceful, and everything ideal, sincerely hope both will last till Alex.

Sunday 29th March - **371st Day Out**

Arrived Alex from Tobruk 7th Time

Safely at Alex once again, went straight alongside to discharge patients. I think we will remain here for a few days.

Damage sustained to Fo'castle during raid on Tobruk 27th March 1942

Monday 30th March - **372nd Day Out**

Heard today that we are going on a different run, probably to Turkey to exchange Prisoners of War.

Tuesday 31st March - **373rd Day Out**

It has been confirmed today that we shall sail for Turkey on Saturday with 900 Prisoners of War, hoping to bring back the same amount of our boys.
Plenty of bustle on the ship, repairs etc., a rather heavy day getting stores in.

Wednesday 1st April - **374th Day Out**

Still busy what with one thing and another. More rafts sent on board today, in case of accidents, I don't like the idea really, I presume we will be allowed to get to our destination with Italian prisoners. What of coming back with ours? Still we shall see.
Weather getting much warmer, wearing whites again.

Thursday 2nd April - **375th Day Out**

Getting ship shape now, in readiness for our new adventure.
Reported massing of armies on the Eastern Front for the big spring battle.

Friday 3rd April - **376th Day Out**

Shifted ship in readiness to embark.

Saturday 4th April - **377th Day Out**

Started to take on over 900 Italian Officers and men - Prisoners of War. By what one can gather we are taking them

Italian Pow's at Alex

to someplace in Turkey in exchange for our men.

Heard the news tonight and 'someplace' is to be Smyrna or Izmir, should arrive there sometime Tuesday.

Easter Sunday 5th April - 378th Day Out

Left Alex for Smyrna 1st Time

Left this morning at 7.00am with our motley crowd for Smyrna. There are about one hundred and fifty actually wounded, the others being equivalent to our RAMC no fighting unit's. We are having at the moment particularly good weather, expect to go into whites at any time. I expect we shall get a few scares of various degrees, we should know more about that this time next week, when we hope to be back at Alex.

Monday 6th April - 379th Day Out

Uneventful so far, passed quite a large island away to starboard possibly Rhodes.

This island proved to be Casa!

Away to port is the island of Crete, we passed it at 9.00am.

Arrived Freetown twelve months ago today.

Passed many islands during the afternoon most of which appeared to be uninhabited.

Tuesday 7th April - 380th Day Out

Arrived Smyrna

Saw the Italian hospital ship at 10.00pm last night, coming up astern, and it passed us during the night. She was well lit up and all ports open, we on the other hand, irrespective of weather had to darken ship, that's all ports closed and unnecessary lights out, just hospital ship lights on only, with Red Crosses illuminated. They of course are sure of not being attacked!

Italian Pow's boarding 'Llandovery Castle' at Alexandria

Instead of getting warmer it is getting much colder, so it's still blues. Ceylon raided for the first time, possibly on Sunday night, fifty seven planes were either damaged or lost, a particularly good first effort. According to the news Madras was also raided.

Got well in amongst the islands at noon and at 1.40pm picked up the pilot. Several came on board as a matter of fact.

Just Heard that 'HS Somersetshire' has been sunk how far true we don't know, no details, she has been our opposite number on the Tobruk run since 1st January this year, if she hasn't gone it's a case of only a matter of time before one or the other of us does go.

Nearing Smyrna and in the main channel, the country from first glimpse appears very fertile, with plenty of trees and shrubs, reminding one of home, maybe wishful thinking though.

'The Somersetshire' has been attacked (official) probably hit by a torpedo, she's down by the bows and they have taken to the boats, so much for being on hospital ships; A safe job, I don't think so!

Arrived at Symrna, and anchored at 4.45pm, quite near the Italian hospital ship 'Gradisca' which had arrived a few hours before, bringing British POW's in exchange for the Italians we brought.

Leave given to RAMC and crew, exchange of POW's to take place first thing in the morning.

Wednesday 8th April   -   381st Day Out

Left Smyrna 1st Time

Started to disembark Italian POW's at about 7.00am. Our first batch came on at 10.15am. Exchange of POW's by noon.

We have on board one hundred and thirty nine of our own POW's in exchange for over nine hundred Italians, seems rather a poor deal to me, should have been the other way round. We leave at 4.00pm after taking on the pilot, whom I presume will see us clear of the channel. I wonder what fate holds for us on our return journey, possibly a different story to tell, we shall see.

Just heard there was a raid on Alex Monday night fifty two killed and eighty injured, another raid last night but only slight damage done, it seems as though things are warming up, as I thought they would.

Thursday 9th April   -   382nd Day Out

Malta had it's biggest raid ever. Heard that resistance in the Philippines had ceased, the Americans being finally overcome.

An Italian cruiser has been sunk in the central Mediterranean, by one of our submarines.

Rommel's forces are on the move, look out Tobruk!

H.S. 'Gradisca' bringing British Pow's for exchange

British Pow's waiting to board HMHS'Llandovery Castle'

Italian Warship severely damaged by our Naval Forces

Italian Warship in the process of being sunk by our Naval Forces

They gave it out over the news that we had been to Smyrna, so that our people know where we are at last, or at least know we are safe for the time being.

Heard that two British cruisers have been sunk in the Indian ocean by Jap aircraft the 'Dorsetshire' and the 'Cornwall.'

Friday 10th April - 383rd Day Out

Malta heavily raided once again.

American troops finally cease to resist the Japs at Bataan.

We had an alert at 10.30am, but the aircraft passed over us without dropping bombs.

Weather getting warmer again, with our usual luck we should be in Alex tomorrow morning.

Saturday 11th April - 384th Day Out

Arrived Alex from Smyrna

Went alongside at 9.45am and just aside of the 'Resource' Naval depot and repair ship. It appears our stay may be short.

Shifted ship at 1.00pm and went to the buoys.

Sunday 12th April - 385th Day Out

Particularly heavy raid over Germany last night.

Tuesday 14th April - 387th Day Out

Doing general repairs and awaiting orders.

Wednesday 15th April - 388th Day Out

Laval reinstated to the Vichy government

Thursday 16th April - 389th Day Out

Heavy raids on Germany and occupied France.

Saturday 18th April - 391st Day Out

Heard the very good news that several towns in Japan have been bombed, Tokyo included.
I wonder how they like it!

Sunday 19th April - 392nd Day Out

Heard that we may sail tomorrow, I wonder!

Monday 20th April - 393rd Day Out

Still here, and likely to remain so.

Wednesday 22nd April - 395th Day Out

Shifted ship this morning to an outer anchorage, no one at the moment seems a bit interested in our welfare. All sorts of rumours are circulating round the ship, some gone as far to say we may go home. Wishful thinking says I!

Thursday 23rd April - 396th Day Out

War news much the same, Japs still gaining a little headway in Burma.

Russian and German troops getting ready for the spring offensive.

Friday 24th April - 397th Day Out

Thirty three thousand tons of French shipping seized by Japan and Indo China. Another very heavy raid on Malta,

The Captain has got married

Germans lost twenty three bombers, and eleven fighters since Sunday.

Can Malta continue to take these heavy raids and hold out? It is almost certain death or sinking, for a ship to approach her coastline.

RAF carry out another heavy raid on Rhineland.

Saturday 25th April - 398th Day Out

RAF continue to batter German industrial towns.

Rostock and Lubick on the Baltic coast are coming in for a particularly good hammering. I wonder how they like it. It's about time they had a taste of their own medicine!

Sunday 26th April - 399th Day Out

Still waiting, but hear we may sail Tuesday for Tobruk.

A big convoy came in today.

Had a raid alarm last night, but nothing happened.

Monday 27th April - 400th Day Out

Very heavy raids on Bath as a reprisal for our bombing on Lubick and Rostock. Captain married to Sister Llewellan.

Tuesday 28th April - 401st Day Out

Heavy raid on Alex, over one hundred people killed, no damage to any ship, which was rather remarkable considering that the harbour was full of them.

At last we are (I really believe) going to sail.

Wednesday 29th April - **402nd Day Out**

Left Alex for Tobruk 8th Time

Left at 7.00pm, three raiders were shot down during Tuesday's raid over Alex. English Q.A.'s join the ship.

Thursday 30th April - **403rd Day Out**

At sea and everything well so far.

Friday 1st May - **404th Day Out**

Arrived Tobruk from Alex 8th Time

Arrived at 8.00am and walking cases were coming on board within ten minutes, it looks as if we are to get away early thus avoiding air raids.

Got away at 2.00pm, the earliest ever; Just behind us came a merchantman escorted by two destroyers, and a squadron of our fighters. Had an alarm at 4.00pm but the two planes proved to be ours, thank goodness!

Saturday 2nd May - **405th Day Out**

Arrived Alex from Tobruk 8th Time

Had another scare this morning at 3.15am, but our luck still held. Picked up the merchantman this morning with her two escorts just outside Alex, so she's safe once again, she proved to be the 'Empire Patrol' an ex Italian vessel. Went on deck this afternoon and sat in the sun, got quite sunburnt.

We did the run from Tobruk in twenty seven hours, we usually take thirty eight hours, extra night in port. Now what of the raids thought?

Sunday 3rd May - **406th Day Out**

Went out to anchorage for another week or two I suppose.

Wednesday 6th May - **409th Day Out**

Occupation of Madagascar by United Nations.
Stirling bombers raid Skoda works.

Thursday 7th May - **410th Day Out**

Official announcement of Corrigidor having fallen.

Sunday 10th May - **413th Day Out**

Hospital Ship 'Ramb 4th' bombed and set on fire fifty miles outside Alex, whilst on her way with the wounded, over one hundred and fifty casualties, subsequently sunk by torpedoes from one of our naval vessels.

Monday 11th May - **414th Day Out**

Japs get a setback through Naval action in the Coral sea.

Tuesday 12th May - **415th Day Out**

In the battle for Malta, ninety three Axis planes were destroyed or damaged within forty eight hours.

Wednesday 13th May - **416th Day Out**

Russians still fighting back.
Three British destroyers lost in the Mediterranean they are the 'Lively' 'Jackal' and 'Kipling.'

Thursday 14th May - **417th Day Out**

German aircraft accounted for the destroyers lost yesterday, the attack lasted for over four hours and three ships were lost out of four.

Friday 15th May - **418th Day Out**

Fifteen enemy planes shot down by our fighters in a sweep over the Mediterranean; A little of our own back!

Sunday 17th March - **420th Day Out**

Russians still going ahead.

Monday 18th May - **421st Day Out**

RAF raid Boulogne

Tuesday 19th May - **422nd Day Out**

At last we prepare to sail, all is ready by 4.00pm; At 4.30pm, the order is cancelled for reasons best known to powers that be, maybe several days now.
Thought we were in for another blitz, but the planes didn't get this far thank God.

Wednesday 20th May - **423rd Day Out**

Battle for Kharkov continues with unabated fury. Italians plan to occupy Corsica.
Heavy raid on Mannheim by the RAF.

Thursday 21st May - **424th Day Out**

RAF make a big raid on Mannheim, dropping over 40,000 incendiaries, I wonder how they like it.
Tank battle developing on Kharkov front.

Friday 22nd May - **425th Day Out**

Sailing again delayed, what a game!
The ex French ship the 'Ille-de-Strasbourg,' has been taken over by Union Castle. It has just arrived in Alex.
Jap cruiser of the 'Kako' class sunk by torpedoes.

Sunday 24th May - **427th Day Out**

(Empire Day) Left Alex for Tobruk 9th Time
Sailed at 7.00pm, and all on our own as usual, although there were several rumours re-escorts etc.
I wonder; Will our luck hold?

Monday 25th May - **428th Day Out**

Had our usual scare, and flares were dropped each side of us, thought our turn had come, but they were apparently trying to find out if we had any kind of escort, the planes were quite low and could have easily bagged us had they wished, but somehow we appear to get away with it every time, at night they certainly can't take us for anything other than what we are, still why worry!

Tuesday 26th May - **429th Day Out**

Arrived and Left Tobruk for the 9th Time
Arrived at 7.00am, and left at 1.00pm had an alert with a little gunfire.
Had a pleasant night, no raids or alarms, we certainly are lucky. Weather has been beautiful, not too hot with a little breeze.

Wednesday 27th May - **430th Day Out**

Arrived Alex from Tobruk 9th Time
All is well again today, no sign of any aircraft whatsoever. Picked up the pilot at 5.00pm, came alongside at 6.00pm, and discharged patients. Went to the buoys at 9.00pm. Heard that Axis had started an offensive in the Western Desert, forty six miles from Tobruk. I wonder what shall happen now and how many more trips we shall make.

Particularly heavy fighting around Kharkov.

Thursday 28th May - 431st Day Out

Fierce tank battle raging in the Western Desert in and around Bir Hachim, the news is very confusing at the moment. The offensive has resumed against Kharkov where a terrific battle raging.

Friday 29th May - 432nd Day Out

Fierce tank battle raging twenty five miles from Tobruk, I wonder what will happen next, personally I think he will give Tobruk a miss, concentrating all forces for his Eastern drive at Egypt and the Suez Canal. I can see us getting a move soon, Port Said or Haifa.

Saturday 30th May - 433rd Day Out

The RAF carried out the heaviest raid of the War over Germany, using over a 1,000 bombers, the main target being Cologne. This will give them something to think about. Fierce fighting still going on in the Libyan desert, Tobruk may be cut off again.

Sunday 31st May - 434th Day Out

Mexico declares War on the Axis.
Position in Libya not favourable.

Monday 1st June - 435th Day Out

Heard that Canterbury had been raided as reprisal for the raiding of Cologne.
Cologne still burning after 48 hours.
Still on top in Libya, Axis unable to get at Tobruk.

Tuesday 2nd June - 436th Day Out

Hospital Ship 'Aba' arrives from Tobruk with wounded from the desert campaign. I hear we sail today, may we be so fortunate.

Wednesday 3rd June - 437th Day Out

Left Alex for Tobruk 10th Time
Still here, but I think we shall be away this afternoon
.Left 6.45pm.

Thursday 4th June - 438th Day Out

Tank battle still raging twenty miles South of Tobruk anything may happen, but at the moment we are doing very well, one more day should see which way things are going.

Friday 5th June - 439th Day Out

Arrived Tobruk from Alex 10th Time
Arrived at 7.30am, and anchored in the usual spot, fairly quiet, but in the distance there is the continual rumble of gun fire so the battle must still be raging. Planes flew around us last night at several different times, may have been our own, in any case we kept jogging along, the only thing we could do, and all is well so far. Heard that a convoy is expected to arrive today, let's hope we get away before the fun starts, as it surely will as soon as Jerry gets to know they are here, had some of that mixture before, and it doesn't taste too good! All patients aboard and away by 12.30pm. We should with luck be able to discharge the same tomorrow night. Very quiet and peaceful at the moment.

Saturday 6th June - 440th Day Out

Very peaceful night, and things generally going very smoothly, hope to make port at 6.00pm.
Arrived at 6.30pm, and anchored in the bay, it being too late to start unloading.

Sunday 7th June - **441st Day Out**

Arrived Alex from Tobruk 10th Time

Went alongside at 9.00am, discharged patients, and they were all away by noon. 'Aba' still here but leaving this evening at 7.00pm.

Things eased up a little on the Russian Front.

RAF continue to batter Germany.

Our troops in Libya still doing well.

Monday 8th June - **442nd Day Out**

Another quiet night, but fairly on the warm side, let's hope it doesn't get too much so!

US Navy in action with Jap forces off Midway Island. Two aircraft carriers sunk, one damaged, other heavy ships damaged also.

Tuesday 9th June - **443rd Day Out**

Battle for Sebastopol gaining in strength, both sides massing for a general onslaught.

Libyan battle still raging, both sides strained to the upmost. French people warned to leave coastal areas in view of present heavy raids by the RAF, and possible landing forces.

Another quiet night here, probably a little too busy in the desert. Jap navy breaks off the engagement.

Wednesday 10th June - **444th Day Out**

Much the same more news from Libya and the Eastern Front. RAF continue to raid the Ruhr. Submarine 'Turbulent' well known to us here in Alex is reported to have sunk an Italian destroyer and three merchant ships in a patrol off the Mediterranean.

Thursday 11th June - **445th Day Out**

Heard today that Bir Hacheim had been evacuated by the Free French after sixteen days battle.

Sailing postponed until tomorrow.

Friday 12th June - **446th Day Out**

Left Alex for Tobruk 11th Time

Left at 7.00pm, and with our usual luck should be in Tobruk Sunday morning.

Japs trying to make a landing on the Aleutian Islands.

In the Coral Sea battle, the Japs lost fifteen Warships, the Americans lost the aircraft carrier 'Lexington' the destroyer 'Sims' the tanker 'Nosheo.' Four Jap aircraft sunk in the Midway battle.

Saturday 13th June - **447th Day Out**

Everything at the moment is going according to plan, no interference from any source so far.

Derby run today, managed to secure 3rd prize!

Sunday 14th June - **448th Day Out**

Arrived and left Tobruk 11th Time

Arrived at Tobruk at 7.00am, and left at 1.00pm, saw a British merchantman bombed and set on fire a few miles out, and a destroyer is standing by, but it's a hopeless proposition I think.

Monday 15th June - **449th Day Out**

Arrived Alex from Tobruk 11th Time

Still on top doing nicely so far.

Went alongside at 9.00pm, and unloading tomorrow.

Tuesday 16th June - **450th Day Out**

Left Alex for Tobruk 12th Time

After unloading we are away again to Tobruk. Finally left at 6.00pm.

At the moment the Navy is coming back to port having been out looking for Musso's fleet.

Had a bit of a scare at 9.30pm, a few bombs dropped, but all missed thank goodness!

Wednesday 17th June - **451st Day Out**

It is now just beginning to get hot in this part of the globe.

War news generally much the same, but I think Tobruk is on the danger list, one more place we shall have to give up, at least I think so.

Thursday 18th June - **452nd Day Out**

Arrived Tobruk 12th Time

Arrived and dropped anchor about 8.00am, I have an idea this will be the last time we shall see Tobruk, and in which case we shall eventually go South.

Stayed at anchor all night.

Friday 19th June - **453rd Day Out**

Left Tobruk for Alex 12th Time (possibly the last)

Remained here longer than usual to pick up extra wounded if possible, have had a quiet time considering what is going on, which is far different from what we expected.

As much as I hate to say it, Tobruk is on the danger list and as far as I can see, people here, servicemen that is, generally are not interested one way or the other. Middle East muddle, my God how true, our lads in the desert fighting for their very existence and in Cairo they have ceremonial parades for the King's birthday!

Saturday 20th June - **454th Day Out**

Left Tobruk last night at 6.30pm, I doubt very much whether we shall see that place again, in which case we shall lay up somewhere, possibly at Haifa or Port Said, or we may go to Suez to dry dock, or maybe even take a load of patients to Durban and go in dock there.

Sunday 21st June - **455th Day Out**

Arrived Alex from Tobruk 12th Time

Heard the news that Tobruk was no more, as far as we were concerned. After all the many lives lost, Merchant ships as well as Naval we are compelled to give way. We left there Saturday and maybe it was just as well, what luck we do get. I suppose we are here now for an indefinite period. We are likely to be bombed at any moment, and can not possibly serve any useful purpose here now. Why don't they move the ship at once to a much safer place? No, they will wait until we are blitzed or the harbour entrance is temporarily blocked then they will think about it; Too late was ever thus!

Monday 22nd June - **456th Day Out**

Tobruk has gone. One more bitter pill for us to swallow. Egypt, I suppose, is next on the list to have to stand up to Hitler and his hordes. I expect we shall be blitzed here at any moment, but things seem to be going on just the same, the harbour is absolutely full of ships, why the hell they don't move some of them is beyond me.

Tuesday 23rd June - **457th Day Out**

Russia still resisting the force of Sebastopol, but the position is rather desperate, just a matter of time before it falls. Still they made a stand that's more than I can say for our forces at Tobruk.

At the moment we are at the buoys, and I should say until next Tuesday, when we shall be ready for sea and possibly Port Said to go South or maybe Durban.

Wednesday 24th June - **458th Day Out**

Particularly warm today, I wonder if we shall see the summer through in this sphere, I very much doubt it. Desert news not too good, and we seem to realise the serious position in which the Suez Canal and Egypt are now placed. My words of a year ago are now coming true, the War in the East is only just beginning. Once we leave here (Alex) we shall not see it again this side of the War, of that I feel certain. Russia is still holding out in spite of severe German attacks but Sebastopol is likely to go any day.

Thursday 25th June - **459th Day Out**

Heard today that we are leaving this area next week, and are going through the Canal to Suez, then either Bombay or Durban. I would think the latter is probably correct.
Germans crossed into Egypt once again.

Friday 26th June - **460th Day Out**

Things much the same, and we now await orders. I think we shall make Port Said in the very near future, or possibly Durban.

Chapter Seven

Going South Again

Saturday 27th June - 461st Day Out

Heard we are sailing tomorrow and possibly to go through the Canal.

Sunday 28th June - 462nd Day Out

Left Alex for Port Said

Left Alex for Port Said at 6.30pm, probably this is the last we shall see of Alex and in many ways I am sorry, about the only thing in our favour is getting away from the flies and heat.

At the moment doing a fairly good speed and should arrive at Port Said about midday possibly stay there the night.

Monday 29th June - 463rd Day Out

Arrived Port Said from Alex going South

Arrived Port Said at noon and went straight through and down to the bitter lakes, where we anchored for the night. Plenty of activity along the Canal, Army on the move, plenty in the Canal, Naval ships going South to a safe anchorage, still retreating. Isn't it all very depressing? Not a bright spot anywhere at the moment.

Negotiating for stores in Port Said

Tuesday 30th June - 464th Day Out

Arrived Suez from Port Said.

Axis forces now only ninety miles from Alex.

Got under way this morning and proceeded to Port Tewfik, went straight alongside ready to embark patients on Thursday.

Wednesday 1st July - 465th Day Out

Storing and making ready generally.

Axis forces now seventy five miles from Alex.

Thursday 2nd July - 466th Day Out

Left Suez for Durban

All bustle this morning, and started to embark at 5.00am. We pulled out for 2.00pm, and made for down channel. Passed the 'Princess Kathleen' with the Q.A's and hospital staff evacuated from Cyprus, they may possibly come South if only to the Sudan.

At the moment we have two destroyers with us, can't quite see the idea yet.

Friday 3rd July - 467th Day Out

Things on board fairly quiet, and settling down for our run South. Battle for the Suez Canal continues and the

Princess Kathleen at Suez

Germans are steadily driving South and East, their intention being to bypass Alex and Port Said and try to reach Suez it'self, when the Nile valley would automatically fall into their hands. I wonder where it will all end, and when!

RAF make another heavy attack on Bremen losing thirteen bombers.

It's terribly hot today, roll on next week when we shall begin to run into cooler weather.

Saturday 4th July   -   **468th Day Out**

Very little local news, but terribly hot again today.
We hope to pick up a little breeze tomorrow.

Sunday 5th July   -   **469th Day Out**

Still terribly hot, and no breeze.
Heard the Axis forces in the desert were being held for the time being, I only hope our forces can hold them for good. We will arrive at Aden on Wednesday morning, and should leave again the same day, ought to be in Durban about the 22nd or even before. Won't it be wonderful to feel cool again, unfortunately we have to come this way a few more times.

Monday 6th July   -   **470th Day Out**

Still very hot, about the worst ever.
War news much about the same, Axis forces at a standstill at the moment.

Tuesday 7th July   -   **471st Day Out**

Passed "Hells Gate" this morning at 10.30am, so we are now in the Gulf of Aden, and picked up a little breeze, I hope it will get cooler as we go along and in a week's time I hope we are in blues, had enough hot weather to last me a lifetime!

Wednesday 8th July   -   **472nd Day Out**

Arrived and left Aden from Suez 1st Time in 1942

After cruising around all night we make harbour at 8.00am, and proceed to oil and water. Quite a number of small merchantmen here. Navy is represented with their usual sweepers, drifters etc. and the cruiser 'Enterprise' is here on station.

Barrage Balloons are now in use here, an addition since we were here last in December 1941. We all hope to be saying goodbye to Aden for the last time, how far this proves to be correct remains to be seen. Passed the Hospital Ship 'Tiarea' at 7.00am on the way up to Suez.

Hope to get away at 5.00pm and should run in to cooler weather immediately.

Pulled out at 6.00pm and should be Durban direct now, but we may have to stop for water. Getting a little breeze now also.

Thursday 9th July - 473rd Day Out

Heard the Germans had forced "The Don" but the Russians are putting up a stiff resistance.
General conditions in Libya very much the same.

Friday 10th July - 474th Day Out

Still waiting for the breeze and cooler weather.
Passed Cape Guardajui and so out into the Indian Ocean.
Breeze getting steadily stronger and sea gradually rougher, we have had to start to batten down and close weather side ports, almost as bad as in the actual hot weather.

Saturday 11th July - 475th Day Out

Heavy sea running, and we are doing about 7 knots, it will take us another fortnight to get to Durban at this rate!
No major operations have taken place in the desert, slight activity in the El Alamein.
Our Airforce still very busy in the forward areas.
Germans have advanced some ninety miles in the Voronezh sector. Chinese still resisting the Japs on all fronts even pushing them back is some places.
Arrived in East London twelve months ago today.

Sunday 12th July - 476th Day Out

Still a fairly rough sea, and we are doing about 6 knots. Very little chance of us getting to Durban!
Russians giving ground but resisting stubbornly.
Allied Forces make a small Western advance in the desert, and capture some prisoners.

Monday 13th July - 477th Day Out

Very much cooler today and life again seems very much worthwhile. We were to be at Durban on the 23rd, but owing to engine trouble, it will be any day after 25th .
War news much the same, Russians steadily giving ground, whilst things in the desert seem almost at a standstill.
Lull before another storm I suppose; Let's see what happens this time.

Tuesday 14th July - 478th Day Out

Still ambling along, goodness only knows when we shall get to Durban, if we ever get there!
War news much the same.
Getting cooler gradually.

Wednesday 15th July - 479th Day Out

Russians still fighting a rear guard action, and giving ground.
Fighting in the desert almost at a standstill. Both sides gathering strength as a prelude to an attack. RAF fairly active.
Big scale raid on the 'Ruhr' we lost five machines.

Thursday 16th July - 480th Day Out

In Egypt another attack was made on our forces in the El Alamein area, at the moment the situation is well in hand; We hope!
A little cooler again today.

Hilindi Road Mombassa

Friday 17th July - **481st Day Out**

Rommel launches his second counter attack (Wednesday).
Allied armies holding out. Airforce very active.
Heard we may reach Mombassa tomorrow.
Another raid by the RAF on German Baltic ports.

Saturday 18th July - **482nd Day Out**

Arrived Mombassa from Aden

Arrived off Mombassa and picked up the pilot, went in at noon, and tied up alongside a Clan Boat. Had a pleasant surprise as the 'Warwick Castle' was in, having brought troops out from home and now loading general cargo, with a few ratings for Cape Town.
A cruiser of the 'Southampton' class is here with two destroyers, and several merchantmen.
Weather fairly cool, but still in shirts and shorts.

Sunday 19th July - **483rd Day Out**

Left Mombassa for Durban at 3.00pm

Busy getting in stores oil and water. Got away at 3.00pm. 'HMS Resolution' and a Dutch Cruiser came in to anchor.
At the moment we are steaming South at about 8 knots, fairly calm sea and a light breeze and so to Durban.

Monday 20th July - **484th Day Out**

Hope to be in Durban a week today.
War news is much the same.

Tuesday 21st July - **485th Day Out**

RAF busy over Northern France.

Fierce fighting in Russia (Donetz).

Holding our own in the desert at the moment.

Wednesday 22nd July - **486th Day Out**

Running into fairly cool weather and unfortunately into a rough sea, it will possibly put us back a day or so.

Desert news fairly satisfactory.

At the moment we are off Madagascar and doing a steady 8 knots.

Royal Navy bombed Mersa Matruh for the third time in four days.

Thursday 23rd July - **487th Day Out**

Sea still fairly rough with a cool breeze blowing. Still in our tropical clothes.

We may possibly arrive Monday with a little luck

War news much the same.

Friday 24th July - **488th Day Out**

We are moving South still, that's about as much as one can say. Weather getting steadily cooler.

Japs made a fresh landing on New Guinea and increased their threat to Port Moresby.

Allied Forces and the Axis Forces still engaged in heavy fighting in the El Alamein sector.

Saturday 25th July - **489th Day Out**

Heavy fighting still going on in the desert.

Russians still fighting back.

We are now into cooler weather, what a treat after many months of sun and sand!

Sunday 26th July - **490th Day Out**

Heard we get to Durban tomorrow ...... thank God!

Monday 27th July - **491st Day Out**

Arrived Durban from Mombassa

Arrived off the Bluff at 10.30am, the pilot came on board and we went alongside. Patients were disembarked to a hospital train at the quayside.

Things appear very much the same here, the only addition being as far as one can see, that there is a total blackout.

Plenty of Merchant ships here, over twenty anchored at the sea anchorage, and as many inside the harbour.

Several Naval ships are here including two battleships.

Hospital Ship 'Atlantis' is here tied up at the Maydon Wharf.

Heavy raid on Hamburg by the RAF and twenty nine of our bombers were lost.

Rostov taken by the Axis forces.

Tuesday 28th July - **492nd Day Out**

Left the disembarkation quay at 6.30am, and went with the assistance of tugs to the Maydon Wharf to tie up, possibly to lie up.

'Atlantis' pulled out this morning on her way North.

According to the news there were widespread raids over Britain, Birmingham being the chief centre of attraction.

Heard we are to go to Port Elizabeth.

Wednesday 29th July   -   **493rd Day Out**

Left Durban for Port Elizabeth
After getting in a few stores etc., we leave Maydon Wharf and so to Port Elizabeth (at 6.00pm).
Another big raid on Hamburg, we lost forty two bombers.

Thursday 30th July   -   **494th Day Out**

Ambling along at our usual speed, about 6 knots, we ran into some heavy weather, so it's quite possible we are not doing that now.
General War news much the same.

Friday 31st July   -   **495th Day Out**

Arrived Port Elizabeth from Durban
Came to anchor at 2.30pm to await further orders, we may go alongside later in the day.
Desert fighting eased considerably.
Russians still hard pressed.
RAF raid Saarbruken, nine bombers missing.

Saturday 1st August   -   **496th Day Out**

Came in alongside at 8.00pm, tying up at our old berth. Very little shipping here, a few freighters and the 'Mauretania.'

Sunday 2nd August   -   **497th Day Out**

Things very quiet on board, and the War seems very far away these days. Blackout came into force.
Russians still retreating in several sectors but still fighting back.
RAF busy over Northern France and Western Germany.

Monday 3rd August   -   **498th Day Out**

War news much the same. Russians sticking it out.
Fairly quiet in the desert, although the R.A.F are rather busy.

Tuesday 4th August   -   **499th Day Out**

Started ships repairs, and we hear that we maybe here a month or five weeks - Ye Gods!
War news much the same.

Wednesday 5th August   -   **500th Day Out**

Russians still retreating, but in some places they have fought back and regained ground.
Situation serious in the Southern area.
Fairly quiet in the desert, both sides playing for more time and presumably more stores.
Still waiting for mail, having had the last in Alex on 1st July.
Minor raids over Britain in various areas.

Thursday 6th August   -   **501st Day Out**

News much the same, things much the same on board too. Repairs going ahead, and many of the staff on leave.
Possibly get a day myself later on. Weather very cool, what a wonderful change from the Middle East!

Friday 7th August   -   **502nd Day Out**

Russians still being pushed back, and Germans still going forward.
RAF raid Ruhr for the third night in succession.
Still fairly quiet in the desert, apart from the air War. Tobruk again bombed.

Saturday 8th August - **503rd Day Out**

General news, ship's and otherwise much the same.
Russians getting into desperate position.
Desert news very scarce.

Sunday 9th August - **504th Day Out**

Serious development in India relating to Ghandi and his followers for a free India. Ghandi arrested with many of his people. Minor riots in Bombay and Allahabad. Several people killed and many more injured.
United Nations attack Solomon Islands.

Monday 10th August - **505th Day Out**

Soviet armies in the Ruban area are being forced still further back by a string of forces of German tanks.
American forces including marines land on the Solomon Islands.
Situation grows worse in Bombay. Police and troops fire on mobs in the city.
University students causing most of the trouble.

Tuesday 11th August - **506th Day Out**

Germans still making steady progress against the Russians on almost all sectors.
Battle for Stalingrad in progress.
United Nations meeting with strong resistance from Jap forces in the Solomon Island battle. Anyone may claim victory at the moment, losses heavy on both sides, naval and otherwise.

Wednesday 12th August - **507th Day Out**

Heard that 'HMS Eagle' the Aircraft Carrier had been sunk in the Mediterranean possibly whilst in a convoy to Malta. War news much the same.

Thursday 13th August - **508th Day Out**

Situation much quieter in India.

Friday 14th August - **509th Day Out**

Heard of the loss of 'HMS Manchester' in the same convoy as 'Eagle.'
Some of the ships got through to Malta apparently.

Saturday 15th August - **510th Day Out**

Fierce battle raging in the Caucasian mountains.
Nazi tanks get a minor setback.
Fighting in the Solomon Islands, at the moment fairly satisfactory.

Sunday 16th August - **511th Day Out**

British warships of the Mediterranean fleet shell the island of Rhodes.
American marines go ahead in the Solomons.

Tuesday 18th August - **513th Day Out**

Heard that I was to proceed to Durban, prior to joining the 'Llandaff Castle' at Mombassa. Left Port Elizabeth by the 8.40pm train.

Friday 21st August - **516th Day Out**

After having spent two days on the train journey, I arrive at Durban at 6.15am, but owing to some mistake I find I have to return to the 'Llandovery Castle,' so I decided to stay here for the weekend.

West Street Durban

South Beach Durban

Saturday 22nd August - **517th Day Out**

Going places!

Sunday 23rd August - **518th Day Out**

At "Beach Hotel".

Monday 24th August - **519th Day Out**

Left Durban by the 8.05pm train to rejoin 'Llandovery Castle.'

Tuesday 25th August - **520th Day Out**

Making Port Elizabeth
We have heard that the Duke of Kent has been killed in an air crash.

Wednesday 26th August - **521st Day Out**

Arrived Port Elizabeth at 5.00pm and rejoined ship.

Thursday 27th August - **522nd Day Out**

Great battle raging for Stalingrad, Germans thirty miles from the city.
Russians counter attacking, but Axis forces coming steadily on.
Japs attack the Yanks in the Solomons hoping to push them out again.
Great air battle going on; Japs suffer losses in men and lose five ships, including a destroyer.

Friday 28th August - **523rd Day Out**

Terrific battle raging around Stalingrad.
Russians advancing in Ryhev sector.
Solomon islands battle still going on, nothing decisive yet.
Very little activity in the Western Desert, apart from air patrols.

Saturday 29th August - **524th Day Out**

Position around Stalingrad slightly better, the Russians at the moments seem slightly to be holding their positions and in some places moving forward.
Things going fairly well in the Solomons.

Sunday 30th August - **525th Day Out**

RAF busy over Germany.
War news generally much the same.

Monday 31st August - **526th Day Out**

Smashing counter attacks by Russians before Stalingrad; Position improving.
Berlin bombed by Soviet planes, also Konigsberg.
Japs lose one hundred and four planes and eighteen ships in the Solomons battle.
Reported Allied landing near Crete.
Brighton and Swindon reported as being bombed by the Nazis.

Tuesday 1st September - **527th Day Out**

United Nations doing very well in Milne, New Guinea.
Germans still trying to batter their way into Stalingrad.
Chinese troops doing fairly well at the moment.
Rommel starts his new offensive for the battle of Egypt.
Malta had twenty four hours without a raid for the first time since January.

Wednesday 2nd September - **528th Day Out**

Fighting now goes on in the Western Desert, and Rommel's forces attack South of El Alamein.
Russians still fighting hard on all fronts, the RAF raided Saarbrucken and lost three machines.
Heard we may possibly leave here next Tuesday.

Thursday 3rd September - **529th Day Out**

Situation in the desert eased slightly.
Heavy fighting going on for Stalingrad.
RAF raid on Karlsruhe but eight planes are missing.

Friday 4th September - **530th Day Out**

Terrific fighting still going on around Stalingrad.
Temporary lull in the desert, although aircraft of the Allied Nations have been very active.
The 'Largs Bay' arrives loading fruit and then home.
Heard we are here until 16th now.
Things in New Guinea at the moment going in the favour of the Allies.

Saturday 5th September - **531st Day Out**

Germans checked at Stalingrad but they continue to throw in men and material in the hope of breaking through.Germans making some progress in the Caucasus.
Things going fairly well in the desert.
Good news from the Solomons.

Sunday 6th September - **532nd Day Out**

Axis forces being pushed back Westward in the renewed desert battle.
RAF raid Bremen dropping over a 1,000 bombs, we lose eleven planes.
Soviet troops doing well before Stalingrad.
Budapest raided by Soviet planes for the 1st time.

Tuesday 8th September - **534th Day Out**

Situation in Egypt satisfactory.
Axis powers being gradually pushed back.
Soviet army checks the drive on Stalingrad. Germans loose 3,000 men.
'Arundel Castle' arrives.

Wednesday 9th September - **535th Day Out**

Position in Egypt and Russia very much the same.
Heavy raid on Frankfurt by the RAF.

Friday 11th September - **537th Day Out**

Operations commence in Madagascar. General attacks made on three ports.
Critical position at Stalingrad.

Saturday 12th September - **538th Day Out**

Heavy RAF raid on Dussledorf, with thirty one bombers missing.
In the fighting around the Solomons, the U.S. bring down ninety six Jap planes in one day!
British landings in Madagascar.

Sunday 13th September - **539th Day Out**

Russians fighting desperately before Stalingrad.

Advance continues in Madagascar, slight opposition from the French forces.

Monday 14th September - **540th Day Out**

The 'Arundel Castle' leaves for home via Cape Town.

Germans doing all possible to get Stalingrad, with over a million men employed, but the Russians are still hitting back, and at the moment holding them in check.

British troops making good progress in Madagascar.

Bremen heavily pounded by the RAF.

Very little ground activity in the desert.

Tuesday 15th September - **541st Day Out**

Position around Stalingrad growing serious, the enemy steadily moving forward.

Allied landing in Tobruk, on 13th and 14th September, we lose two destroyers on withdrawing, the 'Sikh' and 'Zulu.'

The French in Madagascar are offering very little resistance.

Wednesday 16th September - **542nd Day Out**

Enemy in Madagascar ask for Armistice.

Germans still throw in more troops in hope of getting Stalingrad.

Things are getting now to completion on board and we hear we may sail on Tuesday for Durban, we've been here now for seven weeks.

Thursday 17th September - **543rd Day Out**

Critical moment for Stalingrad, Germans throwing in masses of aircraft to blast their way through. Allied Armistice Terms have been rejected by the Vichy Government. With reference to Madagascar, the fight is to go on.

Heard we sail for Durban next week possibly Thursday, first it's one day, then the next!

Friday 18th September - **544th Day Out**

Street fighting in Stalingrad.

Other War news much the same.

Saturday 19th September - **545th Day Out**

Things generally much the same.

Sunday 20th September - **546th Day Out**

Ship under fumigation and all hands are accommodated in the 'Ile - de - France.'

Went to the Marine Hotel to stay.

Monday 21st September - **547th Day Out**

From the hotel we went into town, combining business with pleasure. Stopped and had lunch and came aboard ship; Back to the hotel by 6.00pm.

Went to the pictures in the evening but home by 11.00pm. One day less!

Tuesday 22nd September - **548th Day Out**

Joined ship at 7.30am, and commenced storing, had a fairly busy day.

Stalingrad fights on.

British now thirty seven miles from the capital of Madagascar.

Wednesday 23rd September - **549th Day Out**

Left Port Elizabeth for Durban

Stalingrad still fights on and even making a little progress in some places.

The 'Windsor' came into port, down from Durban and homeward via the Cape.

We shift ship at 9.00am, and go alongside the 'Empire Night' finally pulling out at 5.00pm.

Thank goodness we left Port Elizabeth, never to return I hope.

At the moment we are well out to sea and it's nice to feel the motion once again.

All blacked out and water tight doors closed.

We should get to Durban on Saturday morning and get to dry dock.

Thursday 24th September - **550th Day Out**

At sea.

British Forces enter the capital of Madagascar.

Friday 25th September - **551st Day Out**

Arrived Durban from Port Elizabeth

After a fairly good trip we arrive off the Bluff at noon, no connection with the shore so we go to anchor and will possibly stay all night, going in tomorrow morning.

Fairly heavy swell running, and we are rolling slightly.

War news much the same, Stalingrad still in the balance.

Saturday 26th September - **552nd Day Out**

Still in the Bay and I presume waiting orders.

In the big convoy to Russia several Merchant ships were lost, of the escorting vessels one destroyer and one patrol boat was sunk.

Stalingrad still doing very well.

Sunday 27th September - **553rd Day Out**

And still at anchor in the Bay and what a farce!

They hurry us away from Port Elizabeth as if the War depended on it and when we get here we just hang around.

Quite a number of ships come and go, but we remain stationery; More or less.

War news much the same.

Monday 28th September - **554th Day Out**

At the moment still at anchor, possibly going later

Later

Still of no interest to anyone!

Germans gradually getting into the outskirts of Stalingrad.

Still fairly quiet in the desert.

Tuesday 29th September - **555th Day Out**

Heard we may go into port today but only at the most for forty eight hours. We were to dry dock but the dock apparently is not available, so we go to the wall.

A convoy arrived this morning, nine big ships, escorted by a County Class Cruiser; Our chances of going in now are even more remote, most, if not all the berths are taken....... what a life!

Tobruk raided by the RAF, once again, this is ninety five raids in one hundred days, there wasn't much whilst we were there, goodness only know what it looks like now.

Wednesday 30th September - **556th Day Out**

Came in alongside Maydon Wharf, supposed to be here for two days, but I gather it may be two weeks before we are away!
War news much the same.

Thursday 1st October - **557th Day Out**

We are lying alongside the 'Empire Trooper.'
Very busy storing in readiness for leaving.

Friday 2nd October - **558th Day Out**

Situation getting gradually worse in Stalingrad, but the Red Army still fights on.
US bombers attack Northern France.
Slight land activity in the Western Desert.

Saturday 3rd October - **559th Day Out**

War news much the same. Battle for Stalingrad still continues, and a great tank battle is in progress North of the city.
Japanese Naval Force attacked in the Solomons.
Three light cruisers and two Merchantmen hit

Sunday 4th October - **560th Day Out**

Things generally much the same.

Monday 5th October - **561st Day Out**

Battle for Stalingrad continues.
Allies advancing in New Guinea.
'Llandaff Castle' arrives from Madagascar.

Tuesday 6th October - **562nd Day Out**

Heard the news today that we are to go into dry dock, that means another three weeks here; One day we shall sail.
The battle for Stalingrad still continues, Axis using 1,000 planes to force the issue, but the Red Army still hold out.
RAF raid Osnabruck.
War activity in Egypt.
Minor raid on Sark in the channel islands.
Allied forces in Madagascar meeting with a little more opposition.
United States Battleship has been torpedoed and sunk off Cape Verde (possibly the 'Idaho.')

Wednesday 7th October - **563rd Day Out**

War and general news much the same.

Thursday 8th October - **564th Day Out**

Position in New Guinea becoming more favourable to the Allies. The whole of Stanley area has now been cleared of Japs.
Russians doing very well in the Eastern Front particularly in the Southern sector.
Deportation of the Channel Islanders to Germany.
British prisoners taken at Dieppe have been put in chains.

Friday 9th October - **565th Day Out**

United Nations retaliate and place in chains an equal amount of Germans.
Both sides whether right or wrong, are to my mind playing a dangerous game, the ultimate result - Murder.

Saturday 10th October - **566th Day Out**

Stalingrad still subjected to terrific bombing and a daily occurrence of a 1,000 planes; The Russians still fight back. Good news from New Guinea Australians going forward.

The Yanks are doing very well in the Solomons.

Flying Fortresses do a good job of work over German occupied France. Apart from bombing Lille, and industrial targets, they shoot down forty six planes, and possibly destroy over eighty, a very creditable performance, two of our bombers were lost though.

Sunday 11th October - **567th Day Out**

Stalingrad's fate still undecided, tension eased somewhat, and no major attack by the Axis in the last twenty four hours.

U - Boats now operating outside Cape Town, twelve ships have been sunk according to the Berlin Radio, one ship being the 'Andalusia Star.'

Russians defeat the Axis forces on the Don.

Monday 12th October - **568th Day Out**

Russian news still much the same.

Air blitz on Malta started again, and fifteen Axis planes destroyed.

Three USA cruisers are reported sunk off the Solomons on 8th and 9th of August, they are the 'Quiney,' 'Vicennes,' and the 'Astoria.'

Tuesday 13th October - **569th Day Out**

War news much the same.

Wednesday 14th October - **570th Day Out**

Russia still doing well in and around Stalingrad, advanced slightly in some sectors. The Japanese lose five warships in the Solomons battle.

Strong raid by British bombers on Kiel, but nine are missing.

General Smuts reported as being in London.

Thursday 15th October - **571st Day Out**

Went into dry dock this morning, at long last! Now I presume once out of here we are ready for anything.

'HMS Revenge' also in dock with us.

Big land, sea and air battle commenced in the Solomons.

Continued air raids on Malta.

Stalingrad assaults continue.

Friday 16th October - **572nd Day Out**

Battle in the Solomons still continues.

One hundred and six German planes have been shot down over Malta in six days.

Eastern Front War news much the same.

Saturday 17th October - **573rd Day Out**

War news still much the same.

Fairly quiet in the Western Desert apart from air activity

Sunday 18th October - **574th Day Out**

Stalingrad facing greatest crisis of all.

A ferry boat has been torpedoed off Newfoundland by a U-boat, one hundred and thirty seven lives have been lost.

Lull in the Western Desert continues.

United States troops land in West Africa, as an important strategic move to encounter U-boats.

Monday 19th October   -   575th Day Out

Germans still trying to force the issue before Stalingrad, 50,000 Germans killed in five days.
Malta attacked by ninety planes.
Fighting still very fierce in the Solomons.

Tuesday 20th October   -   576th Day Out

General Smuts has a busy day with War Ministers etc.
According to Mr. Alexander, First Lord of the Admiralty, five hundred and thirty Axis U-boats have either been damaged or sunk.
US heavy bombers busy over Tobruk.

Wednesday 21st October   -   577th Day Out

General Smuts addresses British Houses of Parliament.
Heavy rains hold up Nazi's advance.
Japs forced to retire in the Stanley area.
Malta has withstood 1,660 raids.

Thursday 22nd October   -   578th Day Out

Allied forces mass North of Lake Chad.
Other War news much the same.

Friday 23rd October   -   579th Day Out

Germans eased up before Stalingrad and forced to regroup again before the next attack.
Dakar in the news again, possibly an attack in the future.
Left dry dock for the Bluff to oil at 1.00pm.

Saturday 24th October   -   580th Day Out

Should have left at 6.00am this morning for Suez, calling at Aden en route. Owing to a minor defect we will pull away from the quay at the oil site and then anchor mid stream to have the same repaired. We may not even get away today.
Three ships came in this morning loaded with troops.
The Hospital Ship 'Veta' came in this morning, last saw her at Mombassa in July on the way South.
We may sail tomorrow at daybreak.

Sunday 25th October   -   581st Day Out

Left Durban for Suez 4th Time (1st Time this Year)

After lying at anchor for twenty four hours we make ready to leave.
Got up anchor and away by 6.45am. We have been South, at least in coast ports for three months, thank goodness we are away at last, where to I wonder, or where to from Suez?
At the moment the sea is a bit choppy, quite a nasty day altogether really, apart from our getting away!
Two years ago today I was on the 'Roxburgh Castle' nearing the Cape.
Last year this time we were on our way to Aden, opposite Italian Somaliland. Today we are going North again.
Heard last night that an offensive by the Axis forces had commenced, Navy also shell the enemy rear positions.

Monday 26th October   -   582nd Day Out

Weather conditions a little better today, and a slight breeze with a moderate sea.
Steaming very well, most unusual!
At the moment the War news from the Western Desert is quite satisfactory.

Tuesday 27th October   -   **583rd Day Out**

Getting a little warmer again today, otherwise things are much the same.

The battle in Libya (Egypt really) is gradually gaining force, I wonder what will happen this time, we made the attack, can we keep it up?

Wednesday 28th October   -   **584th Day Out**

Actually in the warm weather, sea fairly smooth and little breeze.

Steaming very well indeed; 13 Knots.

Thursday 29th October   -   **585th Day Out**

Everything going smoothly should make Aden a week tomorrow.

Friday 30th October   -   **586th Day Out**

Desert War going fairly well; Solomons not too good though.

Heavy attacks to the North of Stalingrad.

In the daylight raid on Milan, the second city of Italy, over 80 Lancasters took part.

Saturday 31st October   -   **587th Day Out**

Tank battle in the desert anticipated in the last few days, so far nothing has developed.

Solomon battle in it's critical stages as far as the United Nations are concerned.

At the moment the Yanks are still holding out, a day or so should decide the outcome.

Sunday 1st November   -   **588th Day Out**

In Egypt our infantry have increased their hold and more prisoners have been taken.

The destroyer 'Veteran' has been reported sunk.

Reported daylight raid over South East England, fifty German bombers took part.

Stalingrad holds out.   For three months the Germans have been attacking Stalingrad with a continuous stream of reinforcements coming in, over one hundred divisions are taking part.

Monday 2nd November   -   **589th Day Out**

War news generally much the same, Russia, Solomons, Egypt, and New Guinea.

Tuesday 3rd November   -   **590th Day Out**

Passed Cape Guardajui at 4.00am, should be at Aden tomorrow.

So far the trip has been quite good and not too hot, a breeze moderate or otherwise is with us all the time.

Wednesday 4th November   -   **591st Day Out**

Arrived Aden from Durban 4th Time (1st Time this year)

Picked up the pilot at 8.00am, and proceeded to inner anchorage straight away, short stay possibly. We did the trip from Durban to Aden in ten days - record time!

We were just calling for orders and water, now oil is added to the list, we will possibly stay the night but what for, goodness only knows.

Now I have just heard we may leave at noon, wish they would make up their minds.

Very few ships here, not even half a dozen. Far different from a year ago when it was the usual thing to see fifty or more.

Still fairly cool considering the position, must be the cool season.

'HS Atlantis' left here five days ago for Durban. 'Llandaff Castle' left yesterday for Suez.

Got away at 1.00pm, our shortest stay ever!

Plenty of rumours going around as to what we may or may not do, possibly through the canal or to Bombay or Durban, even home. Perhaps someone is going to be right!

Thursday 5th November - **592nd Day Out**

We are now in the Red Sea having passed through "Hells Gate" at 4.00am, should make Suez by Sunday, all going well.

Heard the extremely good news of our 8th Army in the desert; If only half is true it will not be too bad.

Italians ask for an Armistice to bury their dead, don't worry about the dead, bury the live ones I say!

Friday 6th November - **593rd Day Out**

Vichy French in Madagascar asked for Armistice; Request has been granted by the United Nations, this means all ports in the island will now become available for ships Naval as well as Merchant, thus ensuring a safer passage for ships taking men and material to the Middle and Far East, a significant fact too for South Africa generally, Durban being our principal port at the moment.

War news from the desert very encouraging after so many setbacks in this theatre of war. We are at long last able to take the offensive. General Montgomery Commander-in-Chief Middle East and 8th Army, calls on all troops to keep up their pressure, not to relax, and victory will be ours!

Amongst the Axis prisoners, that currently number 13,000, are some well known Axis generals, the most notable being German General Von Thoma who at one time was in sole command of the Axis forces during the absence of Rommel in Germany.

Tobruk again raided by German medium bombers. German attack on Stalingrad easing somewhat.

A minor German raid took place on an English South Coast town, slight damage done and a few casualties.

Fighting has begun East of the American positions on Guadalcanal Island after additional enemy landings, United States Naval Forces came to the rescue.

Russians are holding firmly in the central Caucasus, and are regaining ground near the Black Sea coast.

Saturday 7th November - **594th Day Out**

United Nations forces (i.e. 8th Army) doing extremely well in the present Desert fighting. Rommel's Afrika Korps are steadily but surely being pushed back, at the same time being blitzed by day and by night. Aircraft of all types and from all nations playing an extremely important part in the present operations. The latest figures of Prisoners captured are well over 13,000 and continue to rise.

Over 300 tanks have either been captured or put out of action.

At the moment things are going well on board and the ship is making good progress.

Sunday 8th November - **595th Day Out**

Arrived Suez from Aden 4th Time

Heard the good news that American troops have landed in Morocco, no details yet.

Italy again raided by the RAF from home, results awaited.

The battle in Egypt going very well indeed, if all we hear is correct the end is in sight.

The enemy has now been driven out of Egypt and our forces are past Mersa Matruh and well on the way to Sidi Barrani.

According to the latest news some resistance has been put up in opposition to United Forces landing in North Africa, but no details to any great extent.

Arrived at the entrance to the Gulf of Suez at 1.00am, to put our Paravanes out, proceeded up stream in the company of other vessels, taking in Paravanes at noon. Examination boat came along side at 2.30pm - all clear given - got underway again and came to anchor in outer harbour. Quite a number of Merchant Navy vessels here and all nations represented, very few Naval craft though, hope they are busy doing their stuff in the Mediterranean!

Weather generally really quite good and fairly cool. From the War point of view, things have been very quiet here of late, not even an air raid for the last two months!

According to the latest rumour before arrival, we were to go straight through the canal, now I believe we are doing a trip down the Red Sea to Port Sudan with patients and then back here again.

I wonder where we shall go next.

Monday 9th November - **596th Day Out**

Got up anchor at 9.00am, and came alongside at 9.30am, tying up at our usual berth. Heard we are to load patients at daybreak; Four hundred and Fifty officers and men to take to Port Sudan.

The War at the moment seems to have taken on a different aspect.

Powerful United States Army, Navy and Airforce supported by unit's of the Royal Navy and the Royal Airforce made large scale landings at numerous points in the French North African and Atlantic coast in the early hours of last Saturday morning, stretching from Southern Morocco to Tunisia.

The idea is to forestall the Axis powers from taking over this area and menacing our trade route South - the direct threat to South America - and above all to assist in defeating Rommel's forces, now being pushed back by the 8th Army.

Vichy French forces have resisted in several places, but an Armistice has already been signed in Algiers.

A sea battle has taken place between United Nations Fleet and the Vichy navy, losses on both sides particularly the French.

The 8th Army still advancing and all Axis forces are now out of Egypt.

Australians doing well in New Guinea.

Americans also doing well in Guadalcanal Island.

Tuesday 10th November - 597th Day Out

Left Suez for Port Sudan

Everyone up and doing this morning, patients ready to come aboard at 5.30am, starting at 6.00am we finish off at 9.00am, having taken on board twenty four officers and three hundred and forty one other ranks. We are bound for Port Sudan where they will disembark. Then I think we shall be returning to Suez.

Finally pull out at 9.30am, and make for down stream; All very peaceful at the moment.

Air raid alarm last night, but no raid. American forces gradually overcoming the resistance of the Vichy French in North Africa, and are reported to have landed within one hundred miles of the Tunisian border.

The sea battle raging yesterday by the Vichy French so far unconfirmed by the United Nations.

British troops reported to have landed on North African coast; RAF in particular.

This morning we heard that the Navy had taken Tobruk, or at least the Royal Marines have, so far this is also an unconfirmed report, but of course as things are going now it's only a question of time.

Wednesday 11th November - 598th Day Out

Still making good headway (13 knots) and should be at our destination tomorrow late afternoon. Out of the danger area by 6.00pm last night; i.e.; Gulf of Suez and into the Red Sea. Weather definitely in our favour at the moment; Comparatively cool light wind and a following sea what more can a sailor ask?

Axis forces still retreating before our 8th Army, rear guard action being fought in and around Sollum and Sidi Barrani.

In the West, the United Nations are steadily overcoming the French Resistance; Tangiers is in our hands and Casablanca surrounded.

In the Naval engagement off Casablanca, the Vichy battleship 'Jean Bart' was set on fire and is still burning.

Permission has been granted to the American forces by the Chief of Tunisia to pass through his territory en route to Libya.

Thursday 12th November - 599th Day Out

Arrived Port Sudan from Suez

On the order of Hitler, German troops have marched into unoccupied France, their objective being to take over the French Mediterranean coast.

All is now quiet in North Africa, the Vichy French have been given the order 'Cease Fire'.

An unconfirmed report says airborne troops from the Axis forces have made landings in Tunisia.

The 8th Army still advancing into Libya. General Alexander, Commanding Officer of the 8th Army has estimated that 59,000 German and Italians have been killed or wounded, and of these, 34,000 were Germans and 25,000 were Italians.

The enemy lost about 500 tanks and over 1,000 guns, British losses were 13,000 officers and men.

Arrived off the port at 12.45pm, the pilot came aboard and we went in alongside, tied up by 1.30pm, disembarked half the patients and the remainder will be leaving tomorrow.

Particularly hot this afternoon but fortunately quite a nice breeze blowing.

Two or three Merchant Navy ships here otherwise things very quiet.

'Queen Elizabeth' Cunard White Star Liner entering her home Port of Southampton
after having been reported as sunk !

Friday 13th November - **600th Day Out**

Left Port Sudan for Suez

Disembarkation completed this morning by noon.

Owing to our being required in Suez by the earliest possible moment, tugs were standing by during the latter part of the disembarking. On completion of the same we were towed to mid stream, and immediately got under way passing through the outer boom defence at about 1.00pm. Once clear of the breakers a noticeable feature at the port, we turn Northwards and to Suez. We hope for enlightening news from all battle fronts today, stretching from Murmansk in the Arctic Sea to the Solomons in the South Pacific.

Tobruk the scene of so much bitter fighting and remembered by the Navy and the Merchant Marine alike in their endeavours to keep open the trade route and supply lines to our desert army, has once again fallen into our hands. Bardia has also been occupied. Our advance columns are now moving West and South West of Tobruk into Eastern Cyrenaica.

According to the Italian radio, an Italian sub has sunk the 'Queen Elizabeth,' Cunard White Star Liner. So far unconfirmed by United Nations.

United States Forces reported to be within the fifty miles of the Tunisian-Libyan border and still moving Eastwards.

Saturday 14th November - **601st Day Out**

Things on board going to plan, and in all haste for Suez, to what fate I wonder, possibly Port Said, Durban or even Bombay. Allied reinforcements arriving in Tunisia.

Admiral Darlan late C.N.C French Navy has joined the Allied cause in North Africa.

The 8th Army still going Westwards.

Sunday 15th November - **602nd Day Out**

Arrived Suez from Port Sudan

Our 8th Army has now passed Gazala, fifty miles to the West of Tobruk. Our 1st Army gradually consolidating positions and moving steadily Eastwards.

As to what may happen to the French fleet is still in the balance, at the moment they are still anchored at Toulon.

Reported Axis movements reaching Tunisia by air and sea, possibly the greatest resistance will be met with here.

Canal entrance at Port Tewfik

Axis subs active in the Mediterranean, particularly towards our convoys in that theatre of War.

Church bells were rung today over the whole of Great Britain in honour of the victories in North Africa.

Entered the Gulf of Suez this morning at 3.00am.

A very strong headwind blowing at the moment, most welcome after yesterday's hot session.

Arrived at the examination area at 3.00pm, pilot came on board, and away to our anchorage. On the way we passed a Greek battleship and the White Star Liner the 'Mauretania,' the latter being on Prisoner of War duty.

On anchoring we immediately began to take on board water and the usual native boat was hoisted on board in readiness for the Canal, to tie up if necessary thus allowing another ship to pass. Total blackout observed.

Monday 16th November - 603rd Day Out

Arrived Port Said from Suez

Pilot came on board at 3.00am, and after various preparations all is set for the journey through the canal. At daybreak (roughly 5.30am) we up anchor and are away, we make for the clear channel and enter the canal at Port Tewfik about a mile inside the canal. We can see Suez away on our Port beam. At 8.00am we pass one of the many Italian Prisoner of War camps situated along the canal banks.

Entered the Bitter Lakes at 9.30am, and in the distance saw Gebel Genefa, here being the number nineteen British General Hospital, Prisoner of War camp, RAF station, and general store depots.

Once through the Bitter Lake we enter the canal proper again and so into Lake Timsah leaving Ismalia well away to Port.

Passed number one General Hospital at Kantara at 1.30pm.

Arrived Port Said, and to outer anchorage at 6.00pm.

Good news from all War fronts, 8th Army still moving Westwards , our 1st Army getting ready to move East.

Yanks give a good account of themselves in the Solomons Naval Battle, eleven Jap warships and six transports sunk, with several more damaged, the situation is now well in hand.

Tuesday 17th November - **604th Day Out**

Our desperate hurry Northwards seems to be of little avail as we are now at anchor and by all accounts likely to remain so for several days. Quite a good deal of shipping here including some of our acquaintances of Alex days, Hospital Ship 'Maine', depot ship 'Woolwich' and decoy ship 'Centurion,' these were despatched here last June when Rommel was threatening the Alex area.

We go into blues, a sure sign of cooler weather.

Sea, land and air battles taking place off the coast of Tunisia, with the United Nations forces preparing to take the initiative.

Wednesday 18th November - **605th Day Out**

News this morning of our paratroops having been dropped well inside the Tunisia border, the attack has begun. Rommel reported to be there to take charge of operations.

Hitler getting the wind up and sending all available troops to Southern Europe particularly Greece, and possibly reinforcing Crete.

Derna has fallen to the 8th Army, and advanced forces are within striking distance of Benghazi.

Today the ship was put to twenty four hours notice, a sure sign we are here for a day or two. Having a general clean up after our long stay South.

Thursday 19th November - **606th Day Out**

Desert War news much the same, the 8th Army still advancing. From the West comes news of the final clash with Axis forces inside the Tunisian border. Air battles pretty frequent, both sides in desperate hurry to gain control of the various airfields and the mastery of the air, thus ensuring the control of the Mediterranean.

Australians doing very well in New Guinea, the Yanks doing equally well in the Solomons.

On the Eastern Front the Russians are even advancing in some sectors in spite of continued German pressure.

We are on six hours notice, leave any day now.

Friday 20th November - **607th Day Out**

Still playing the waiting game but should get under way this weekend sometime. Various rumours as to what we may do, probably finish up on the old run. War news much the same in all theatres.

RAF raid Turin, a strong force having left Britain for this special task, no planes lost in this attack.

Had two alerts here last night, but nothing happened.

Just heard we may sail today possibly this evening.

Saturday 21st November - **608th Day Out**

Left Port Said for Tobruk

Had quite a nasty sand storm here yesterday, which may account to some extent our still being here, but if rumour is to be believed, we shall most likely sail this afternoon. Things this end of the Mediterranean are beginning to take shape once again.

Hospital and depot ships are returning to Alex to take up their normal stations. The Hospital Ship 'Maine' left this morning for Alex, and other ships are to leave in the very near future.

We get under way at about 4.00pm, pass through the boom defence and so out to sea. Boat stations and general emergencies at 4.45pm.

Orders passed to close all watertight doors and ports, usual precaution. We are bound for Tobruk and should arrive daybreak Monday morning, if nothing unforeseen happens! At the moment we are doing a steady 12 knots, we have a steady breeze with a moderate sea. Come what may, panic bag is ready!

Sunday 22nd November - **609th Day Out**

Benghazi had been reoccupied by the British 8th Army.

The British 1st Army is closing in on Tunisia.

Home based night bombers have made the biggest raid of the war on Italy, with Turin as the target again, three planes are missing.

Russians are still doing very well on all fronts.

General Hertzog has died in South Africa.

England has been free of raids for the past fortnight.

At the moment all is quiet on the 'home front' I should image we are somewhere off Alex and making good progress, a moderate sea still running and the weather still generally quite good. So far we have neither seen a plane or a ship, a vast difference in the days before Rommel's advance to Egypt. The main activity has of course shifted Westward leaving us a clear field; We hope!

Our main worry is still with us, of course, that being the mines, I wonder; Will good luck still favour us or history repeat it'self? Time alone will tell.

Monday 23rd November - 610th Day Out

Arrived Tobruk from Port Said 13th Time (and left again)

Sighted the coast at 11.00am turned due South and made for our anchorage. To ensure our safe passage through the boom defence, or what's left of it, a Naval boat came out to meet us, and instructed us to follow in her wake, we eventually arrived safely at our anchorage at 8.20am. Mostly Naval men here at the moment, and busy getting things straight again.

We were here five months ago, and one can see a vast difference, particularly in the way of destruction, what buildings were left standing have had a good blitz, and there are five additional wrecks, also two three masted schooners and an Italian sub.

We see a few planes from time to time (our own) possibly on patrol. The Navy here consists of a few patrol boats, invasion barges, and anti sub chasers. One Merchant ship is here discharging stores.

Last night we heard the good news from the Stalingrad Front. The Russians have not only stopped the German advance, but have actually punched them back to an extent of over forty miles, at first this seemed to me to be incredible, but the news of this morning confirmed the report of last night.

News from the Solomons and New Guinea still favourable.

British 8th Army still advancing in spite of very bad weather conditions.

The 1st Army operating from the West has had a brush with the Axis in Tunisia, the result of which ended in our favour. RAF very active bombing Tunisian airfields at present used by the Axis forces.

Our first batch of wounded arrived alongside at 10.30am. Invasion barges being used for this purpose.

Finished loading at 4.00pm, and got underway, passed through the boom, (unaided this time) so to sea and Alex.

At 9.00pm a beautiful clear night, slight breeze but a smooth sea, everything going according to plan.

Tuesday 24th November - 611th Day Out

Arrived Alex from Tobruk 13th Time

Have just heard the good news that Dakar has come under control of Admiral Darlan, this means all French North and West Africa is now inside of the United Nations.

Russians doing extremely well in and around Stalingrad.

Favourable news from New Guinea.

Arrived off Alex at 2.00pm, pilot came aboard, we then proceeded to the inner harbour. Taken in tow by a tug and eventually tied up at the hospital quay. Hospital train waiting for us and by 5.00pm all patients had been disembarked.

Things are much the same here, and still fairly quiet and no air raid for over two months, may it continue!

The French War ships are still here and the British Eastern Med. fleet returned here three days ago.

The 'HS Maine' which left Port Said the same day as us arrived Sunday and has taken up her usual billet.

Wednesday 25th November - 612th Day Out

Particularly good news from Russia, offensive in full swing and according to latest reports the Russian Army around Stalingrad has advanced over fifty miles in some sectors.

The 8th Army is still advancing.

Remained alongside the quay last night, a sure sign we shall not be here long.

Possibly sail tomorrow.

Thursday 26th November - 613th Day Out

Owing to the renewed efforts of the Russians, Stalingrad has been relieved after three months of siege.

The Russians continue to make progress and apart from many thousands of Germans killed, they have taken over 30,000 Prisoners.

French West Indies fleet joined Allies.

No news as what we may do. At the moment we are still alongside and undergoing minor repairs, possibly get away on Saturday.

Friday 27th November - 614th Day Out

Position of United Nations in Tunisia very satisfactory; Air and land battles are now raging.

Russians still forging ahead in the Stalingrad area.

British 8th Army advancing on El - Agheila.

Heard that the Axis forces had marched on Toulon, the last Vichy French territory. Part of the French fleet that was in Toulon harbour has been scuttled to save capture by Axis.

Deck department busy getting aboard stores for Tobruk, mostly hospital equipment. Due to leave at daybreak tomorrow.

Saturday 28th November - 615th Day Out

Left Alex for Tobruk 14th Time

Pulled out this morning at 7.00am passing through the booms at 7.45am, Tobruk our destination.

Heard today that the South Africans occupy the Island of Union, an Island in the Indian Ocean 380 miles from Madagascar.

Sunday 29th November - 616th Day Out

Arrived Tobruk from Alex 14th Time

After an uneventful trip we once again make Tobruk, being off the entrance to the harbour at 8.00am, took the usual channel and came safely to anchor at 8.30am. Proceeded to off load the hospital equipment, and to make ready to receive patients, in view of the fact we were to get away before sunset, ships boats, and personnel were put to good account.

War news much the same. With the Russians still forging ahead, and both British Armies in North Africa making steady progress.

After a busy day, for most people anyway, we get up anchor passing the booms at 5.15pm, and so to Alex.

Monday 30th November - 617th Day Out

Arrived Alex from Tobruk 14th Time

At the moment we are making good progress in the direction of Alex. Things are still very quiet as far as hostile activity towards us is concerned, quite a notable feature to what we have been accustomed to particularly in the early days of our going to Tobruk.

I heard Mr. Churchill's speech last night, but it was poor reception, the speech followed much the same vein, and as usual promised us nothing. War news good on all fronts.

British 1st Army are closing in on Tunisia, and we are now only ten to fifteen miles away from the actual time. A big scale operation likely to start any moment with Tunisia as the chief objective.

Arrived Alex, and alongside at 4.00pm all patients clear by 6.00pm, and we go on six hours notice.

Tuesday 1st December - 618th Day Out

We are still alongside with the possibility of our leaving any day, workmen are carrying out a few minor repairs.

I went on shore for a few hours combining business with pleasure.

Soviet Army is still advancing.

Allied forces in North Africa have been reinforced, and are closing in on Tunisia and Bizerta.

Three French subs have managed to get away from Toulon, one arrived in a Spanish port and has been taken over, crew have been interned and the other two subs arrived in Algiers to join the Allied cause.

Wednesday 2nd December - 619th Day Out

Ships news much the same, nothing doing as regards sailing yet.

Still good news from Russia.
Tunis and Bizerta, get a round the clock blitz.
Aussies doing well in New Guinea.

Thursday 3rd December   -   620th Day Out

War news good on all fronts.
In connection with the North African landing, the Navy lost eleven small ships.
Mediterranean Naval forces attack Axis convoy on the way to Tunisia, four merchant ships sunk and two destroyers also, we lost one destroyer 'HMS Quentin.'
Still no news as to when we may sail, possibly here for the weekend.
Colonel Heiron left the ship, also the matron, Miss McWilliam.

Friday 4th December   -   621st Day Out

News generally much the same.
Minor tank battle in Tunisia, Axis gained a little ground when coming into contact with our advanced unit's.
Heard we may sail tomorrow at daybreak. Twenty three Sisters, QA's, and eight MO's joined the ship for passage to Tobruk.

Saturday 5th December   -   622nd Day Out

Left Alex for Tobruk 15th Time

We are away once again. Pulled out from the quay at 7.30am, through the boom by 8.00am, and to sea. I wonder what is in store for us this time, had two quiet trips so far.
War news much the same.

Sunday 6th December   -   623rd Day Out

Arrived Tobruk from Alex 15th Time

Arrived this morning at 8.00am, and proceeded to inner anchorage started to load patients at 9.00am, so we should be away fairly early if all goes well.
Hard fighting going on around Tunisia with the enemy striking hard with tanks and dive bombers at our advanced unit's.
Russians still advancing and have crossed the Don in several places.
American Liberators have bombed Naples.
Finished loading patients at 5.00pm, having taken on over 700, the most ever!
Got away at 5.15pm through the booms and out to sea.

Monday 7th December   -   624th Day Out

Arrived Alex from Tobruk 15th Time

Arrived at 5.00pm, and proceeded to off load, finished by 8.00pm, quite a good effort considering the number of patients.
American bombers attacked Lille.
British bombers raid Eindheven in Holland, over one hundred taking part, the biggest daylight offensive during the War. Twelve machines lost.
Russians still gaining ground around Stalingrad.

Tuesday 8th December   -   625th Day Out

Still alongside with no news of sailing yet.
Very busy today getting in stores etc.
Big tank battle raging in Tunisia, with both air forces very active.
Dakar becomes available to the Allies.
We have heard the 'Llandaff Castle' has been sunk.

'Llandaff Castle'

Wednesday 9th December - **626th Day Out**

Damage to French warships at Toulon were; Fifty sunk or damaged, with fifteen remaining afloat.
War news much the same.
On shore for a few hours.
RAF from home bases have raided Turin.

Thursday 10th December - **627th Day Out**

Australians doing very well in New Guinea, the Gona having been occupied.
Turin was again attacked on Wednesday night by a strong force of heavy bombers, smoke from the previous night's raid still hung over the city.
Things very quiet on board, no news as to when we might sail, possibly a weekend job again.
Desert news very much the same, both sides on the alert, probing each others defences.

Friday 11th December - **628th Day Out**

A year ago today we arrived at Aden from Bombay we heard the news that we were going through the Canal and being based at Alex, one rumour that has proved true!
I wonder what this next year has in store for us possibly the end of the War and home.
Today is my Birthday.

Saturday 12th December - **629th Day Out**

Turin and Naples again bombed.
Axis tanks in clash with Allies in Tunisia.
Renewed air activity over the whole Western battle area.
Russians still pushing ahead in spite of all Axis can do.

Kittybomber taking off in the desert for another attack on El Agheila

Still good news for New Guinea. Japs in a rather hopeless plight.

Heard that the 'Atlantis' had been sunk - unconfirmed.

Sunday 13th December   -   630th Day Out

Left Alex for Tobruk 16th Time

From a German source comes the news that the British 8th Army are on the move again.

Away at 7.45am and for Tobruk; I think.

On the way out we passed a convoy making it's way to Alex (five Merchant ships with Naval escort) - more nails for Rommel's coffin!

Monday 14th December   -   631st Day Out

Arrived Tobruk from Alex 17th Time (and left again)

Strong force of British bombers attack Rouen having a covering force of 300 fighters. We lost four fighters and two bombers, Axis losses twenty fighters. Just heard the good news that the 8th Army has continued it's advance and has taken El Agheila and are now continuing South to Tripoli.

Arrived at 8.30am, started loading at 9.00am, and should be away quite early as I hear that in future we are only to carry 450 at a time, last voyage we took 750!

The Admiralty has announced that one armed Merchant cruiser, one tanker, and two supply vessels have been sunk.

Losses inflicted by subs only, since the opening of the North African offensive are, one cruiser sunk or hit, one destroyer sunk, one probably sunk, one damaged and three hit, four tankers sunk, nine supply ships sunk, one probably sunk and five damaged, four merchantmen were hit while carrying troops or supplies to Tunisia.

Good news from Russia and the Solomons.

Destroyer 'HMS Penynan' has been lost.

Left Tobruk at 3.30pm having taken on board 450 patients, if rumour is to be believed this is our last trip to Tobruk for a while. Benghazi is to be our next port of call.

Tuesday 15th December - **632nd Day Out**

Arrived Alex from Tobruk 16th Time

The 8th Army is on the move again, and Rommel with his Afrika Korps are being driven still further Westward. RAF keeping up a non stop attack on his fleeing troops.

Enemy planes raid a North Eastern town, bombs were dropped causing damage and casualties.

Came alongside at 3.30pm all patients away at 5.00pm.

Wednesday 16th December - **633rd Day Out**

Should have been away today, for some unknown reason we remain alongside, possibly away tomorrow.

Axis forces still retreating and being relentlessly bombed by the United Nations Air forces.

Allies occupy Buna, the last Japanese stronghold on the Eastern Coast of New Guinea.

Naples again raided.

Germans on the Eastern Front making desperate efforts to stem the Russian advance.

Thursday 17th December - **634th Day Out**

Left Alex for Benghazi 1st Time

Pulled out at 11.30am, and through the booms at noon, bound for Benghazi, I wonder what awaits us? Good news from all fronts.

Friday 18th December - **635th Day Out**

At the moment we are off Tobruk 9.00am, and are proceeding according to plan, a much worn phrase! We are due, I say due at Benghazi tomorrow morning at 10.00am. Apparently Jerry pays a visit to this port every morning at daybreak, yesterday morning one of our ships was sunk, the 'Moller', well known to us on the Tobruk run. She was with us in Tobruk last April when we were singled out and bombed. We both got away with it then, now she has gone, so we carry the torch, for how long, well, time alone will tell!

All precautions have been taken as regards the safety of the vessel. We the crew, are on top line too, now he can do his worst, I only wish that we were armed.

Troops of the 8th Army have cut the retreating German army forces in half, about sixty miles west of El Agheila. The Axis are suffering heavy casualties, being strafed by the Airforce and gunned by the ground forces.

So far we are going along nicely and no interference.

Saturday 19th December - **636th Day Out**

Arrived Benghazi 1st Time

After an uneventful trip we arrive off Benghazi at 11.15am. Pilot came on board and we eventually drop anchor near the outer breakwater, or what's left of it! The town it'self as far as one can see from the ship, seems in fairly good state, but the harbour has come in for a good pounding, many ships litter the place, reminding one of Tobruk. Quite a good deal of shipping is here, a convoy having arrived as recently as this morning, this convoy we saw this morning at 6.00am heading in this direction. The Navy here is as yet not represented to any great extent, apart from sweepers and invasion barges, the usual motor boats are here, keeping up communications between ship and shore.

Started loading about noon taking on one hundred and seventeen patients including thirty officers.

Got away at 5.00pm putting on all speed to get away before the usual 8.00pm raid starts.

When we were about thirty miles away at 8.15pm, we heard the raiders coming in possibly from Crete. The Benghazi defences put up a wonderful barrage, which could be seen quite plainly from the ship and lasted about half an hour.

All quiet during the night as far as we were concerned, eased down at midnight, as we are not required at Tobruk until Monday morning.

Sunday 20th December - **637th Day Out**

Russians, according to this morning news, have made an advance of thirty miles in the last forty days, capturing tons of guns, stores, etc. Our submarines are very active in the Mediterranean, sinking on average one Axis supply ship a day, apart from damaging very many more.

The 8th Army is now one hundred and twenty miles west of El Agheila, and still advancing.

'Rochester Castle'   B.& A. Feilden

Monday 21st December   -   638th Day Out

Arrived Tobruk from Benghazi

Picked up the land again this morning at 6.00am, and proceeded to harbour entrance, passing on the way, two Merchantmen outward bound for Tobruk and escorted by two destroyers.

Took up our usual station and once inside the harbour, started to take on patients. Six Merchantmen are here off loading, this is the most I have seen here at any one time. A good sign, and sure proof, that the Eastern Med. is practically clear of the enemy.

War news from all fronts much the same.

The 8th Army is now three hundred and fifty miles from Tripoli - one hundred and fifty miles west of El Agheila.

Got away at 12.30pm after taking on over one hundred patients, and completing our complement.

Tuesday 22nd December   -   639th Day Out

Arrived Alex from Benghazi via Tobruk

Rommel's army reported to be in the vicinity of Misurata.

RAF bombed docks at Duisburg, twelve bombers lost.

Russians still advancing.

Came alongside at noon, all patients discharged by 5.00pm.

Saw the 'Rochester Castle,' one of the few ships that got through to Malta in the July convoy, although torpedoed she managed to make port.

I hear we may be here for Christmas.

Wednesday 23rd December   -   640th Day Out

Munich bombed by the RAF.

Rommel still moving West, with no sign of fighting. Air activity on large scale over the Tunis front.

Fighter Bombers getting ready for take off in Tripolitania

Thursday 24th December - **641st Day Out**

Russian army sweeps into Ukraine, Germans give ground along the whole front.
Another large convoy through to Malta.
Admiral Darlan shot dead in Algiers (no details).

British Army vehicle entering Nufilia en route to Sirte

Friday 25th December - Christmas Day - **642nd Day Out**

Reported landing of American troops in Dakar.
Russian forces advanced over seventy five miles in a week.
The 8th Army march into Sirte.

Saturday 26th December - **643rd Day Out**

Yesterday the assassin of Admiral Darlan was condemned to death by court Martial and shot. General Giraud succeeds the Admiral as Governor of North Africa.
Nazis still retreating on the Russian Front.
Japs still being pushed back in the Papua area of New Guinea.
After being alongside since Tuesday we pull to our usual billet, and tie up, here for another couple of days I should imagine.
'Dorsetshire', our opposite number now, has arrived and is on her first trip.

Sunday 27th December - **644th Day Out**

Local news much the same, and on board things are very quiet.
Russians smashing everything before them, and doing very well on all fronts.
The 8th Army now over forty miles West of Sirte.
Germans admit that on the Russian front, they have withdrawn to new positions
(the first time ever)!
General Giraud is now the Supreme Commander of French North Africa.

Monday 28th December - **645th Day Out**

War news from all fronts much the same.
Still at the buoys in the Bay and with no news of sailing yet.

Tuesday 29th December - **646th Day Out**

Russians now eighty miles from Rostov.
Our subs operating in the Med., are still making heavy toll of enemy supply ships, two more were sunk yesterday.
French Somaliland, the last of the Vichy French territory, has joined the Allies.
Very little land fighting in Tunisia but plenty of air activity.
Allied Forces contact the Japs in their drive through Burma
Jap cruiser sunk off Rabaul.

Wednesday 30th December - **647th Day Out.**

Russian advance in Rostov continues and they are within sixty miles of the city.
Bombers based on Malta batter enemy bases in Tunisia.
Seven hundred and fifty Merchant ships built in the U.S. in 1942.
Sir Neville Henderson, British Ambassador in Berlin at the outbreak of War, died today.
British 8th Army still moving Westward, now well to the West of Sirte.

Thursday 31st December - **648th Day Out**

News generally much the same, from all War fronts.
More US troops land at Dakar.

Chapter Eight

The Tide is Turning

One of the first pictures of the Navy's new Seafire aircraft leaving an aircraft carrier

Friday 1st January   1943   -   **649th Day Out**

Good news from Stalingrad - German bombers for this city have been completely liquidated.
In total 95,000 Germans have been killed, and 72,000 captured.

Saturday 2nd January   -   **650th Day Out**

Russians still going ahead.
Weather eases the situation in Tunisia.

Sunday 3rd January   -   **651st Day Out**

The Velikie-Luki has been taken by the Russians, and furious fighting continues.

Monday 4th January   -   **652nd Day Out**

Russians now seventy miles from the Latvian border, and retake Mozduk in the Southern sector.
The 8th Army advance has been held up by extremely bad weather.
We are still in the Bay and at anchor with no sign of moving yet.
The weather very unsettled at the moment.

Tuesday 5th January   -   653rd Day Out

News very much the same from all fronts, with a little more activity in Tunisia.

British heavy bombers carry out heavy raid on the Ruhr.

Still waiting for news to move off, we have now been in port a fortnight.

If rumour is to be believed, we may be going in a different direction soon, anything to get away and to get a change!

Wednesday 6th January - 654th Day Out

Things generally much the same as yesterday.

Thursday 7th January   -   655th Day Out

Russians still advancing, and are now seventy miles east of Rostov.

Free French Forces advancing from the Chad area and have captured an Axis post near Aramed. In Tunisia Axis retake the hill West of Mateur.

The 8th Army are steadily moving forward.

A British convoy to Russia gets through without loss, thanks to the Navy.

Russians make steady progress

Friday 8th January   -   656th Day Out

Good news from New Guinea, Jap resistance almost at an end.

Four Russian armies advance on Rostov.

Fairly quiet in the Western Desert, bad weather slowing down operations on both sides.

Saturday 9th January   -   657th Day Out

Soviet armies now only 60 miles from Rostov.

News generally much the same.

Quiet on the home front.

Sunday 10th January   -   658th Day Out

Allies win air battle in Pacific, eighty five Jap planes shot down.

Russians still going forward.

We are I believe here for quite a while possibly another three weeks!

Hospital Ship 'Maine' sailing for Benghazi first, then the 'Dorsetshire,' and then us.

So it means another three weeks here anyway.   Am I fed up or what?

Another big convoy arrives in Britain from Canada, and a few losses sustained, but two U-boats were sunk. In the convoy to Russia last week, one destroyer was lost but all Merchant ships reached their destination safely.

Monday 11th January   -   659th Day Out

Good news still coming in from Russia.

The 8th Army fairly quiet, air activity increasing.

No news on the home front.

Tuesday 12th January   -   660th Day Out

Things generally much the same.

Wednesday 13th January - **661st Day Out**

Continued raids by the RAF over Germany the seventh one in ten days over Ruhr.

Flying Fortresses bag thirty four Axis planes in one raid, twenty destroyed on the ground and fourteen in combat on the way home, no Flying Fortresses were lost.

Thursday 14th January - **662nd Day Out**

Good news from all fronts.

Friday 15th January - **663rd Day Out**

RAF again over Germany, this is the seventh raid in ten nights. Mr Churchill's promise to Hitler is coming true!

Saturday 16th January - **664th Day Out**

Have been in port now for over three weeks, the longest ever whilst in commission.

Heard we may sail early next week possibly on Tuesday. Heard that the 'Aba' had been either mined or torpedoed, but so far unconfirmed.

Sunday 17th January - **665th Day Out**

Yesterday Iraq declared War on the Axis powers.

Allies doing well in Papua, and also on Guadalcanal.

A Soviet ultimatum has been sent to the Germans in Stalingrad, but was rejected, fighting has been resumed and the encircled Germans are nearing the end.

Berlin bombed by the RAF - unconfirmed - but we hope it's true.

The above has now been confirmed this morning.

Monday 18th January - **666th Day Out**

Russians still forging ahead.

British 8th Army resumed offensive, advancing forty miles in twenty four hours. The offensive began at sunrise on Friday. Berlin again bombed by the RAF but with the loss of twenty two planes.

German planes over London, the first raid for nearly a year, ten planes shot down.

Tuesday 19th January - **667th Day Out**

Good War news from all theatres of war, particularly in Russia and Tripolitania.

More Axis supply ships sunk in the Med.7

Wednesday 20th January - **668th Day Out**

British 8th Army now pass Misurata.

Japs suffer more blows in the Pacific.

Thursday 21st January - **669th Day Out**

London had a daylight raid, the first big raid since the Battle of Britain. Thirteen German planes were shot down.

Light Naval forces in the Med. sink thirteen Axis ships in three days.

Hospital Ship 'Maine' arrives from Benghazi with wounded; We are the next away I presume, as we have been here now over a month.

Possibly go alongside tomorrow to load hospital stores for Benghazi. What of Tripoli, our next port of call? At least we hope so, in more ways than one!

Friday 22nd January - **670th Day Out**

Good news from all fronts, particularly in and around Tripolitania.

Saturday 23rd January - **671st Day Out**

Tripoli, the last of the Mussolini empire, fell to the 8th Army this morning. So ends his dream of colonial domination.

Russia still doing remarkably well.

Heard that we sail for Benghazi tomorrow, and eighteen officers and nine sisters joined the ship this afternoon to take passage to that port.

Sunday 24th January - **672nd Day Out**

Left Alex for Benghazi 2nd Time

Once more we are away after a period of over a month in port. Left our anchorage at 7.30am, and through the boom by 8.00am. At the moment everything is quiet, with the ship very steady doing about 12 knots. Benghazi is our destination, and with luck we should be there on Tuesday morning.

Monday 25th January - **673rd Day Out**

British 8th Army are still advancing and are now well beyond Tripoli.

Good news from Russia, advancing on all fronts.

We are still making good progress and arrive tomorrow morning, all has been quiet so far.

Tuesday 26th January - **674th Day Out**

Arrived Benghazi from Alex 2nd Time

Arrived at about 8.30am, and anchored near the harbour entrance, much the same position as last time. The harbour is quite full of Merchant ships having brought men and supplies. A balloon barrage is now up and the place generally seems to be taken over completely.

Started to load at 9.30am, and should be away fairly early. About 400 officers and men embarking.

Whilst loading, the red flag was hoisted on shore, denoting enemy aircraft in the offing, nothing came of this however, thank goodness!

Wednesday 27th January - **675th Day Out**

Heard this morning that Mr Churchill and Roosevelt had met in Casablanca, and the Allied Chiefs of Staff have reviewed the War situation and decided what steps to take in North Africa and elsewhere. The main idea was to form a plan of operations, thus scattering the German forces and easing the situation on the Russian front. Rommel's forces are now in Tunisia with the 8th Army hard on their heels. Heard that the 8th Army were actually over the Tunisian border heading North West but so far this is unconfirmed.

At the moment we are on the way to Benghazi from Alex. We are now opposite Tobruk, a fairly heavy sea running, with a following wind, ship is rolling slightly, pleasant feeling after so long in port, I had almost forgotten what it was like!

Thursday 28th January - **676th Day Out**

Arrived Alex from Benghazi 2nd Time

American bombers for the first time were in Germany proper, with a concentrated attack on Wilhelmshaven - three bombers lost.

RAF go to Denmark and bomb the engineering works of Copenhagen. Three more Axis ships sunk in the Med., two more torpedoed and possibly sunk also. Came in alongside at noon and discharged the patients, we will possibly stay alongside for a day or two.

Friday 29th January - **677th Day Out**

Good news from all the War Fronts.

The 8th Army less than forty miles from Tunisia.

Saturday 30th January - **678th Day Out**

Russians still advancing on all fronts.

Allied planes attack Sfax, the biggest daylight raid so far.

Berlin bombed for the first time in daylight and by the RAF Mosquito bombers, the fastest in the world, so much for Goering's boast. "That no bombs would fall on Germany, much less Berlin".

Later

Berlin bombed twice today!

Sunday 31st January   -   679th Day Out

Heard over the radio today that the German forces in Stalingrad have surrendered, another Nazi boast bubble punctured!

Their forces in the Caucasus area are now cut off and will possibly meet the same fate as those in Stalingrad.

RAF raid Hamburg, dropping some 8,000lb bombs. US subs active in the Pacific, several more Jap ships sunk.

Sicily again bombed by Malta based aircraft.

Monday 1st February   -   680th Day Out

Lonara, the last of the small ports dotted along the Tripolitanian coast has fallen to the 8th Army.

Russians closing in on Krasnodar. Hitler is now confronted with an even greater disaster than Stalingrad. Mr Churchill has paid a surprise visit to President Inonu of Turkey, and is now in Cairo.

Allies capture town in Tunisia, the Nazis make some progress in another sector, having used some of their most modern tanks, fifty two tonners.

The Guv'nor on walkabout in Tripoli

Tuesday 2nd February   -   681st Day Out

Three Russian armies now converge on Rostov.

Heard that the British mine layer 'Welshman' has been torpedoed off Tobruk - later confirmed.

Mr Churchill called at Cyprus on the way back from Turkey to Cairo.

Wednesday 3rd February   -   682nd Day Out

Russian big guns now shelling Rostov and German forces now numbering some 2,000 men are being cut off in the South of Caucasus.

Sea and air battle raging in the Pacific off the Solomons between USA and Jap forces. Over one hundred two ton bombs were dropped in Cologne last night by the RAF.

Thursday 4th February   -   683rd Day Out

RAF again over Germany, Hamburg bombed.

Germany goes into mourning over Stalingrad.

Not too much activity at the moment over Tunisia, both preparing for a major battle.

Friday 5th February   -   684th Day Out

Russians still advancing on all fronts, doing particularly well in the Caucasus and gradually boxing the Axis forces in.

Russian troops reported to have landed to the rear of the Germans, thus cutting off their only line of retreat.

RAF raid Italy and Germany, also Northern France, a real clash in Tunisia expected shortly.

Mr Churchill visit's Tripoli and congratulates the 8th Army.

Hospital Ship 'Somersetshire' goes into floating dock; She was torpedoed last April.

*After a long and dusty trek, the 8th Army turned out spick and span and put on a parade
to honour the Prime Minister, Mr Winston Churchill during his visit to Tripoli*

Saturday 6th January - **685th Day Out**

Heard gun fire this morning, presumably a Jerry plane was overhead having a look around. This usually is a prelude to a raid but nothing happened.
Russians still going ahead on all fronts.

Sunday 7th February - **686th Day Out**

Mr. Churchill arrives back in London this morning after visiting Cairo and the 8th Army in Tripoli.
Good news from all War Fronts.
Great battle for Rostov in progress, with the Russians steadily gaining ground.

Monday 8th February - **687th Day Out**

Battles now raging in the streets of Rostov. Kursk has fallen to the Russians.
The 8th Army still advancing and have occupied Pisida Lorient on the French Atlantic coast, the German sub base is to be evacuated possibly owing to the RAF raids.

Tuesday 9th February - **688th Day Out**

Russians recapture Kursk.
Other War news much the same.

Wednesday 10th February - **689th Day Out**

Japs evacuate the Island of Guadalcanal in the Solomons, ousted by the USA.
All Axis forces driven out of Tripolitania, ousted by the 8th Army.

Thursday 11th February - **690th Day Out**

Lull in the Tunisian fighting bad weather holding up operations.
Count Guandi, one time Italian Minister to Great Britain, may succeed Mussolini in the near future.
More Allied troops land in North Africa.
The Germans under heavy shelling and bombing, they have already begun evacuation of Kursk.

Friday 12th February - **691st Day Out**

War news much the same.

Saturday 13th February - **692nd Day Out**

The 8th Army and Afrika Korps lining up for major clash.
Russians on the point of taking Rostov, and Nazis fire the city as Russians close in.
Japs retreating with losses in New Guinea.
Minor raids on South East and West Coast towns, becoming a daily occurrence.
Another big convoy arrives in a North Russian port with vital War supplies.
Shifted ship to new anchorage.

Sunday 14th February - **693rd Day Out**

Russian troops capture Rostov and still continue to advance.
Over 1,000 tons of bombs dropped by our heavy bombers on the U-boat base at Lorient.

Monday 15th February - **694th Day Out**

American troops in Tunisia forced back by Axis Panzer division, they have now counter attacked, the outcome of which is waited.
Naples and Palermo again bombed.

Tuesday 16th February - **695th Day Out**

The French battleship 'Richelieu' and the Cruiser 'Montcalm' arrived at New York from Dakar to join the United Nations.
Heard today that we sail tomorrow.
In the afternoon a complete hospital unit, the 48th General, joined the ship consisting of twenty five officers, thirty eight sisters and one hundred and forty seven other ranks.
All equipment got aboard during the early evening.
Today lots of delayed mail arrived, I was very fortunate receiving thirty six altogether, on and off it took the balance of the day and well into the night to read them all.

Wednesday 17th February - **696th Day Out**

After completion of storing etc, tugs came alongside and we pull out at noon through the boom and well out to sea by 1.00pm, presumably for Tripoli, time will tell. A convoy for some North African ports went out this morning at 10.00am, so if they remain in the offing, we may in due course get a visitor, we have been extremely lucky so far, may it continue!

Thursday 18th February - **697th Day Out**

Still doing very well and keeping on top, with luck and continued good weather we should arrive at Tripoli Saturday afternoon.
Off Tobruk at noon.
Rome radio stated tonight that casualties in the RAF raid on Milan on Sunday night were 86 killed and 482 injured.

Friday 19th February - **698th Day Out**

Germans gain some success against the US forces in Tunisia. Later we had heard the Yanks had been forced out of their positions and retreated to a line fifty miles to the West.

Ships litter the Harbour entrance in Tripoli

The 8th Army still advancing and nearing the Mareth Line.

On the home front all is quiet and we are proceeding according to plan, hope to be able to say the same in two days time.

So far have seen nothing of the convoy (twenty ships) that left Alex just before us.

Saturday 20th February   -   699th Day Out

Arrived Tripoli from Alex 1st Time

Continued good news from the Eastern Front.

British 8th Army still moving Northwards and towards the Mareth Line, where the first battle for Tunisia will presumably be fought.

US forces towards the West and on the Tunisian border have formed a new line, after being pushed back for many miles. Three airfields were lost in this retirement, apart from casualties and material losses.

Wilhelmshaven bombed by the RAF Ventura bombers on Friday night, four machines lost.

German U boat sunk by our light Naval Forces in the North Sea. 'Gareth' and 'Montrose' destroyers were involved in the action.

At 7.00am this morning paravanes were put out, a clear indication that we are nearing the danger area and in the Gulf of Sirte, well on the way to Tripoli.

This is the third time we have blazed the trail, first to Tobruk then to Benghazi and now to Tripoli, third time lucky; I wonder?

The 8th Army now over sixty miles into Tunisia.

On getting near to the coast we ran into fog and had to ease down, we actually stopped at times.

Finally at about 11.30am, a motor launch came out and we then proceeded to follow it in. It came to the harbour entrance at about 2.00pm, and found just sufficient room to get through, two ships having been sunk across the entrance almost blocking it, once through we dropped anchor and proceeded to off load. Patients came alongside almost immediately and we started to embark.

The harbour has been terribly knocked about, particularly the breakwaters. Quite a number of big ships lie in various parts of the harbour, some burnt out and beached, others sunk at their moorings. An Italian Hospital Ship 'Arno' has also been partially sunk.

Plenty of activity here, several Merchantmen off loading, all with War material.

The Navy and Army are busy straightening up the quayside, a difficult task I should imagine.

At 6.00pm we pull out and are on the way to sea again, this owing to the nightly visit's of Jerry. We shall cruise around all night with our lights on (safety measure) and return in the morning to complete off loading, then away for good. On other occasions such as this we have remained in port with our lights out, but presumably it is too risky here.

Sunday 21st February   -   700th Day Out

As planned we cruised around all night, very quiet at sea, we rolled slightly. Tripoli in fact had a raid in the night.

Picked up our guide at 8.30am, and followed her in, arriving at about 11.30am. Just started to off load again when we were ordered out, as a convoy had arrived from Alex and wanted the anchorage space. We anchored outside the breakwater, completed our job and then away again. The convoy mentioned, consisted of six Merchant ships guided by as many Naval craft i.e. two destroyers and four escort vessels.

Russians advancing towards Taganrog.

British 8th Army advancing towards the Mareth Line, and have captured Medenin.

Monday 22nd February   -   701st Day Out

After being confined to his room for several days with a slight chill Mr. Churchill is now reported to be well again.

Mr. Gandhi is in a desperate position due to his continual fasting.

The 8th Army still advancing, the Yanks have met with another set back, British 1st Army are rushing assistance to that area.

Naples again bombed by the Yankee Liberators.

Wilhelmshaven again bombed by the RAF.

Tuesday 23rd February - **702nd Day Out**

Bad weather has slowed down the operations in central Tunisia, other War news much the same.

Two United States cargo ships have been sunk in the North Atlantic, with heavy loss of life, over six hundred lost in the first ship, and two hundred and fifty dead or missing in the second vessel.

Last night the RAF dropped over one hundred 4000lb bombs on the big port and U-boat base of Bremen without loss to ourselves.

Wednesday 24th February - **703rd Day Out**

Russians still going ahead.

Germans halted in central Tunisia.

Heard over the news that Tripoli was bombed on Sunday, the day the convoy arrived, and fortunately the day we left.

According to Stalin about nine million men have been either killed or wounded in the Eastern Front. (Axis Forces)

Thursday 25th February - **704th Day Out**

News from Tunisia that an Axis Panzer unit has been heavily defeated outside Thala.

Churchill tanks in action for the first time.

Russians still forging ahead and have retaken two more important towns.

A 12,000ton tanker has been sunk in the Mediterranean by our torpedo bombers, it was estimated to be carrying three million gallons of petrol.

Home front news; We are still battling along and should make Alex tomorrow, this voyage back has taken us two days longer than the outward passage, owing to a minor breakdown in the engine room.

Mr. Churchill reported well again.

Axis forces are in retreat through the Kasserine pass, and being bombed en route by all available aircraft including Flying Fortresses. Several hundred Iti's have been taken prisoner and many more surrounded.

Gandhi's condition serious.

Friday 26th February - **705th Day Out**

Arrived Alex from Tripoli 1st Time

Arrived off the breakwater at 7.30am, and picked up pilot, came in alongside at 8.00am, and all passengers discharged by 11.00am.

Axis forces in full retreat at Kasserine.

Pulled away from the quay at 3.00pm, and went to the buoys.

Saturday 27th February - **706th Day Out**

Continued blitz on Germany and occupied France by the United Nations Airforce.

Rommel's forces still fleeing before the Allied Forces who are advancing on Kasserine. (later reported to be in Allied hands)

Germans break the lull in the North and break the 1st Army's positions, counter attack launched by the 1st Army and heavy fighting reported.

In the South the 8th Army are pushing still further Northwards and towards the Mareth Line.

Heard today that the 'Princess Kathleen,' and old friend of ours of long standing, has been torpedoed and sunk on the way back from Tripoli.

Sunday 28th February - **707th Day Out**

Axis attack in North Tunisia, repulsed by the Allied Forces.

Air blitz still continues on U-boat bases.

Great battles raging in Southern Russia.

Monday 1st March - **708th Day Out**

Today the 'Princess Kathleen' has been reported safe and making port.

War news much the same.

Tuesday 2nd March   -   709th Day Out

Berlin blasted by four-ton bombs, it was the heaviest attack ever made (Monday night). "Go to it" says I. This was the 58th raid.

Russians attack on new front.

'HMS Sussex' sank German tanker five hundred miles off Cape Finisterre, whilst attempting to run the Allied blockade.

Allies advance in Tunis.

Wednesday 3rd March   -   710th Day Out

Russian troops recapture Rhzev.

Italian army leaving Russia, probably with view to the Allied invasion of their own country.

Gandhi ends twenty one day fast.

Allied planes have dealt a shattering blow to the Jap convoy steaming from New Britain to New Guinea.

Thursday 4th March   -   711th Day Out

Wonderful news from the South Pacific.

Russians losing ground in the South but making good progress in the North.

The 8th Army gaining in the South and losing in the North. So for the time being the many battles swing to and fro.

New Britain to New Guinea

British Naval Losses to date

5 Capital Ships - 7 Aircraft Carriers - 25 Cruisers - 14 Armed Merchant Cruisers
94 Destroyers - 14 Corvettes - 44 Submarines.

Friday 5th March   -   712th Day Out

A Jap convoy of twenty two ships, have now all been sunk.

Total number of planes destroyed during the whole action one hundred and nine.

Heavy fighting in North Tunisia.

Saturday 6th March   -   713th Day Out

Good news from all fronts; US shell the Solomons.

Russians take key town on the way to Smolensk.

American troops capture Pichon.

RAF raid Essen.

The 8th Army still advancing.

Sunday 7th March   -   714th Day Out

Heard today that we may sail Tuesday for Tripoli.

Rommel's forces attack the 8th Army near the Mareth line and get a severe setback.

Russians still forging ahead.

Nazis admit great damage to Berlin, and according to the radio, four hundred and eighty six were killed and three hundred and seventy seven injured.

Essen gets it's greatest raid ever.

Two hundred and fifty five Jap ships have been sunk in ten months.

Monday 8th March - **715th Day Out**

Still think we may sail tomorrow.

Medical officers join, and all baggage including hospital equipment is being slung aboard, so the outlook of getting away seems more hopeful.

Continued blitz on Germany and Northern France.

Tuesday 9th March - **716th Day Out**

Left Alex for Tripoli 2nd Time

Underway once again, pulled out at 9.30am, through the Boom and out to sea.

Reports from Vichy, state that in Berlin a week after the extensive raids by the RAF, fires are still smouldering.

In a raid on Rennes and Rouen, Flying Fortresses and Liberators, screened by Spitfires, shot down twenty five German aircraft. Four fighters and two bombers of ours were lost.

Rommel in his latest attack against the 8th Army lost forty five tanks, finally falling back to his original position.

Wednesday 10th March - **717th Day Out**

Russians still advancing in the North and Central sectors, but held for the time being in the South

Big raid on Nuremberg, Germans admit extensive damage.

The 8th Army is still pushing Rommel back, seventeen Axis aircraft shot down near Sicily without loss to the RAF and Flying Fortresses.

Bombs were dropped on the South coast of England today.

Home Front; At the moment all is well, Tripoli is our next stop we hope.

Three Hospital Ships at sea today. With us are the 'Dorsetshire' and 'Maine.'

Thursday 11th March - **718th Day Out**

Bad weather has restricted operations in North Tunisia.

Over 500 tons of bombs were dropped on Munich last night.

Russian news much the same.

Passed the 'Dorsetshire' this morning at 2.00am, from Tripoli bound for Alex .

Fairly heavy sea running, ship rolling slightly.

Friday 12th March - **719th Day Out**

Arrived Tripoli from Alex 2nd Time

Signed on two years ago today.

Picked up the land about 7.00am, and made for the Channel, off the harbour entrance at 10.00am, anchored and waited for Pilot. Went into inner anchorage at 10.30am, and started to load patients at once. All is quiet at the moment from an enemy point of view at least, several Merchantmen here off loading and our old friend the 'Princess Kathleen.'

The weather is ideal, plenty of sun but not at all hot.

Got away at 4.00pm, having taken on board four hundred and fifteen patients (other ranks) and seventeen officers. In the raid on England this morning the Nazis lost nine planes, five over the Thames area, and four over Northern England.

War news much the same.

Saturday 13th March - **720th Day Out**

War news much the same.

Sunday 14th March - **721st Day Out**

Have just heard that we arrive at Alex Tuesday morning.

An RAF reconnaissance this afternoon found fires still burning at Krupps works at Essen.

Raid over North East England.

Fairly quiet in Tunisia at the moment.

Germans have succeeded in their efforts at Kharkov, latest reports say they have entered the town which is in a precarious position.

Mr Eden is in USA .

Another Jap convoy being attacked in the South Pacific by Allied bombers.

Marshall Petain reported to be gravely ill.

If rumours are to be believed Hitler is also on the wane!

Monday 15th March - 722nd Day Out

Late last night the rumour aboard was that we were doing another trip to Turkey for a Prisoner of War exchange.

Germans report to the effect that Kharkov has fallen.

American planes bombed Naples last night. Rome radio said today that six hundred and fifty two people were killed in the recent Allied raid on Caglaine in Sardinia.

The 8th Army is getting into position for the final thrust on Rommel's defences.

Heard today that the Hospital Ship (Italian) now partially submerged in Tripoli harbour is none other than 'Arno' reported sunk off Tobruk last summer by Allied dive bombers.

Passed the 'Dorsetshire' last night at 8.30pm on her way to Tripoli.

Tuesday 16th March - 723rd Day Out

Arrived Alex from Tripoli 2nd Time

Saw the 'Malimes' this morning in tow making for Alex, last saw her in Port Said stern down, caused by a near miss.

Picked up the Pilot at 7.30am, and made for harbour.

Came alongside at 9.00am, and started to discharge the patients.

Confirmed today that Russian troops have evacuated Kharkov, but are doing well on all other fronts.

The rumour of Monday has no foundation apparently.

Wednesday 17th March - 724th Day Out

Today we are in Tripoli and all hands are busy loading hospital equipment.

Sixty six sisters and nine officers (medical) join the ship.

War news much the same.

Thursday 18th March - 725th Day Out

Left Alex for Tripoli 3rd Time

Pulled out at 9.00am, through the Boom and so to sea.

Russians halting German drive beyond Kharkov, and continue their drive towards Smolensk.

French patriots defy the Axis in the frontier state of Savoy.

According to the German news agency the 8th Army launched an attack on the Mareth Line.

Friday 19th March - 726th Day Out

Fierce fighting raging in the Donetz Basin, Russians having to give ground.

Fairly quiet in Tunisia, heavy rains holding up operations.

Unconfirmed reports say the 'Arundel Castle' has been sunk.

Saturday 20th March - 727th Day Out

War news very much the same. Weather pretty bad at the moment with a heavy sea running and the ship at times rolling heavily.

Should make a landing tomorrow morning.

Four German planes brought down over Tripoli.

Sunday 21st March - 728th Day Out

Arrived Tripoli from Alex 3rd Time

Sighted land at daybreak this morning and made for the Channel. Off the harbour at 10.00am, and went to our usual anchorage but had to move to dodge an aerial torpedo that had come to the surface, left over from Jerry's raid on Friday night. Within the two air raids in the harbour last week, we shot down nine bombers, but they got three ships, one of them being the 'Ocean Voyager' full of Ammo; Ship had a direct hit on the bridge, which killed seven men and four hours later it blew up. The ship was still burning this morning. Quite a number of ships here off loading. We started to off load the hospital unit at 1.30pm, and by 3.00pm we were off again, having taken on board 450 patients.

Very heavy fighting in Southern Russia, but in the Northern area the Russians are steadily making their way towards Molensk.

The Yanks backed by a British armoured division are pushing steadily on towards the coast in central Tunisia, whilst in the North and South things are fairly quiet.

The three ships sunk were 'Ocean Voyager,' a Greek Freighter and one of our Destroyers.

Monday 22nd March - 729th Day Out

Mr. Churchill spoke last night, and dealt with mostly the Post War conditions, reconstruction etc. He also informed the world that the 8th Army in Tunisia was on the move again.

The American armoured unit in Tunisia has made more progress toward Maknassy.

An Italian Pilot has bombed German and Italian prisoners on board the British repatriation ship 'Talmer' whilst the ship was half way between Port Said and Messina, the plane sent down Siso bombs, fortunately the ship was not hit.

Tuesday 23rd March - 730th Day Out

Arrived Benghazi from Tripoli 1st Time with Patients

Arrived at 7.30am, anchored outside the breakwater and proceeded to off load immediately.

A fairly heavy ground swell at the moment which may possibly hold us up somewhat. In spite of this we hope to be away by noon and so back to Tripoli where we are very much needed.

Left Benghazi for Tripoli 1st Time

American Flying Fortresses and Liberators attacked Wilhelmshaven in daylight yesterday.

News much the same from the Russian Front.

Wednesday 24th March - 731st Day Out

The 8th Army attacked Mareth Line last Saturday night and the latest news is that our forces penetrated to the depth of one mile, and fierce fighting is still going on.

Some of our forces made a flanking movement and are now behind Rommel's forces. On the Mareth Line the position so far seems satisfactory,. Russians still holding the Germans on the Eastern Front, despite all they can do.

Three hundred of our heavy bombers raid St Nazaire, one is missing.

This evening at 8.00pm we heard the news that the Axis forces in the Mareth Line had countered attacked and regained most of the bridgehead which the 8th Army had driven into their defences, latest news is that very fierce fighting is raging on this front.

Thursday 25th March - 732nd Day Out

Arrived Tripoli from Benghazi 1st Time

No detailed news today so far, only that fierce fighting still continues.

It is reported that the British armoured column has got right round the Mareth position and is fighting more than twenty miles West of Gabes.

The British 1st Army have recaptured Helfa station about two miles West of Djebel Abiod.

Picked up the Pilot at 9.00pm, through the Boom, and to our usual anchorage.

Started to load at 10.00am and took on four hundred and twenty five ratings and thirty two officers, getting away at 1.00pm.

Friday 26th March - **733rd Day Out**

Yesterdays fighting for the Mareth Line took the form of heavy artillery duels between the 8th Army and the enemy.
In central Tunisia the Americans have had some local successes.
Other War news much the same.
USA building five ships a day.
According to Algiers radio, British infantry in the latest attacks, have restored some positions in the Mareth Line.

Saturday 27th March - **734th Day Out**

The 8th Army is still developing it's defences. Results achieved continue to be satisfactory.
Allied bombers keeping up a non stop attack for all the battle area.
Russians still going steadily ahead in the Northern sector, whilst holding their own in the South.
Allied bombers last night raid Ruhr, which is Germany's industrial centre.
Malta based aircraft have carried the War to Rome, shooting up trains and rolling stock.
Home Front; much the same doing a steady 13 knots and should be in Alex about 1.00pm tomorrow.

Sunday 28th March - **735th Day Out**

Arrived Alex from Tripoli 3rd Time

Arrived off the entrance at noon, took on the pilot and proceeded through the Boom to our usual anchorage, as usual the train was waiting for us.
During our absence another Hospital Ship has arrived, the 'Talamba', a converted BI boat, that makes five boats in all engaged on this particular run 'Llandovery Castle,' 'Somersetshire,' 'Dorsetshire,' 'Maine' and 'Talamba' possibly one of them will get a move to a different sphere of War.
Berlin bombed again last night, no details yet.
Unit's of the 8th Army have reached Maknassy and are working in co-operation with the US forces.
Finished off loading at 5.00pm, away to the buoys until tomorrow.

Monday 29th March - **736th Day Out**

Very good news from Tunisia. The 8th Army and USA are all advancing.
The 8th Army takes El-Hamma.
US forces take Fondouk.
Fighting French have occupied the Delta heights.
Hurricanes shoot down ten Japs without loss to themselves.

Tuesday 30th March - **737th Day Out**

Heard the extremely good news that Rommel is on the run again.
Another Hospital Ship joins today which brings the total to six now, possibly something is in the wind.
Axis-held positions in the Mareth Line have been evacuated, and the 8th Army has advanced into and now beyond Gabes.
Berlin got another wallop last night from the RAF, we lost twenty one bombers; The Ruhr was also raided again and twelve bombers are missing from this raid.
Enemy aircraft over a few places along the South West coast.

Wednesday 31st March - **738th Day Out**

Still good news from Tunisia, Russians doing quite well too.

Thursday 1st April - **739th Day Out**

The Navy shells Rommel's columns as they retreat Northwards from Gabes.
British Naval forces land at Sfax (not confirmed).
Six more Axis ships sunk in the Med. and four damaged by our subs.
Russians still holding all attacks on the Donetz.
Home Front; No news of sailing yet, but possibly by the weekend.

Friday 2nd April - **740th Day Out**

A hundred Flying Fortresses visit Sardinia and it gets the biggest blitz ever.

The 8th Army are still going ahead.   American forces pushing Eastwards and trying to link up.

Saturday 3rd April - **741st Day Out**

War news much the same.

Sunday 4th April - **742nd Day Out**

British 8th Army regrouping for new offensive and our advance unit's are in contact with Rommel's rear guard.

US War planes bomb Jap naval squadron sinking two cruisers and one large destroyer, also damaged were several other ships whilst trying to get away.

May possibly get away tomorrow bound for Tripoli.

After a week of sunshine we get our usual heavy weather, very dull and fairly cold. All letters written and got away by parcel.

At 4.00pm, two Naval tugs came alongside and took us from our anchorage to the hospital quay, where we embarked more officers and nurses from the desert hospital, taking them to a forward area. Alongside all night and went to the pictures to see "A man about Town.", quite good and very funny in places.   Came out at midnight and walked back arriving on board at 12.45am, not too bright at the moment, personal reflection!

Monday 5th April - **743rd Day Out**

Left Alex for Tripoli 4th Time

Pulled out about 9.30am, once through the Boom ran into fairly rough weather, and quite a few of the new arrivals were under the weather before long.

Still good news in Tunisia in the Northern and Southern sectors, but in the South the two forces are getting ready for the next move.

RAF raid Krupps works at Essen with a strong force of heavy bombers.

Allied bombers attack a Jap convoy and sink several ships.

Tuesday 6th April - **744th Day Out**

Weather eased a little today and ship quite steady. One hundred Flying Fortresses make a heavy raid on Naples.

The 8th Army launched their attack this morning, the first objective was taken and further operations are proceeding according to plan.

Forty eight Axis planes destroyed for the loss of twelve of ours.

War news good generally from other fronts.

Wednesday 7th April - **745th Day Out**

News generally much the same, the 8th Army have attacked, and are moving forward.

Thursday 8th April - **746th Day Out**

Arrived Tripoli from Alex 4th Time and left again

After a rather rough passage at times we arrive at noon, a few hours later than usual. Work proceeded naturally and we were through the entrance again by 5.00pm, having taken on board four hundred patients including sixty Germans and thirty seven Iti's.

Quite a good number of Merchantmen here off loading, they come and go in spite of all Jerry can do.

Good news today, the 1st Army is on the move.

Friday 9th April - **747th Day Out**

Picked up bad weather again this morning and with a following sea, we are rolling very heavily.

On the home front things are very quiet.

Wounded coming alongside

Saturday 10th April - **748th Day Out**

British 8th Army entered Sfax this morning at 8.15am.

Things a little better today not quite as rough and much warmer.

Good news from all the War Fronts.

A German plane flew around us this morning and we were called to stations, no bombs were dropped, probably for one or two reasons, either they had already been dropped on or near some other target, or that we were recognised for what we are.

We were to arrive on Monday but owing to our having made good progress I hear we arrive tomorrow afternoon I wonder what await's us - reliefs I wonder?

Sunday 11th April - **749th Day Out**

Arrived Alex from Tripoli 4th Time

Came alongside at 5.00pm, and proceeded to off load, finishing by 9.00pm.

Heard some more good news from Tunisia, Axis forces fleeing Northwards with the 8th Army hot on their tail. The latter being forty five miles from Sousse whilst the former are ten miles beyond.

Yesterday the Allied Airforces shot down fifty Axis planes with a loss of three to themselves.

Home front much the same, here in Alex the weather is none too good, quite cold and a strong wind blowing.

Hospital Ship 'Maine' pulled out for Tripoli.

Monday 12th April - **750th Day Out**

Very busy today, getting on very fast with a view to our short notice to sail, possibly Wednesday.

Being as we remained alongside all night decided to go on shore, went to the Royal and saw "The Two Faced Women".

War news good from all fronts.

In the South West Pacific thirty seven Jap planes were shot down in a forty minute battle.

Tuesday 13th April - **751st Day Out**

Had another busy day today what with stores embarking etc.

At 3.00pm another complete hospital unit joined us in transit to Tripoli. About eighty officers and sisters and three hundred other ranks (New Zealand Unit)

News still good from all War Fronts particularly in Tunisia, the 8th Army now twenty five miles North of Sousse.

Wednesday 14th April **752nd Day Out**

Left Alex for Tripoli 5th Time

Pulled out at 9.00am, through the Boom and to sea. Weather much better today, and we are at the moment going along nicely, with luck we should be at Tripoli Saturday morning.

War news much the same.

Thursday 15th April - **753rd Day Out**

According to latest report 175,000 Axis troops are trapped in Northern Tunisia.

General news much the same.

Home based bombers carry out a heavy raid on Stuttgart, we lost twenty three aircraft.

Friday 16th April - **754th Day Out**

Admiral Cunningham declared today that the Naval and Airforces were ready to deal with the situation if Axis troops evacuate North Africa.

Sank two Axis destroyers off Sicily yesterday.

Saturday 17th April - **755th Day Out**

Arrived Tripoli from Alex 5th Time

After the usual routine we finally came to rest at 9.30am. The various barges came out with the wounded and on one of them came a brass band comprising of New Zealanders to welcome their countrymen. Whilst the first batch were being off loaded the bands gave a rendering of martial music including some of the most appropriate airs, needless to say the audience was large, and the music appreciated. Loading continued and we were away once again by 3.00pm, having taken on board four hundred and fifty patients.

Plenty of stores are being off loaded here, from ships of the Allied Nations, British, American, French, Greek, Norwegian and Dutch.

Heard that the RAF had carried out a big raid on Germany (Mannheim) and on the Skoda factory in Czechoslovakia, in both raids we lost fifty five bombers.

Sunday 18th April - **756th Day Out**

War news much the same today, aircraft busy on all fronts.

Things on board much the same, weather ideal and the ship making good progress.

Monday 19th April - **757th Day Out**

British subs in the Mediterranean have, in the past month, sunk twenty one Axis ships.

News from Tunisia much the same, both sides making ready for what will probably be the greatest battle of the whole African campaign.

Heard this afternoon that off the Tunisian coast in one fight alone, the Allied Airforce shot down seventy four Axis planes, this levels things up a bit for the loss of our fifty five over Germany last week. Today we lost seven planes.

Tuesday 20th April - **758th Day Out**

Arrived Alex from Tripoli 5th Time

Usual routine and we were alongside by 2.00pm, all patients off by 5.30pm. I hear we are to make ready and be away again by Friday.

Spitfires and Warhawks chase the Luftwaffe from the skies over Tunisia.

The 8th Army is standing by.

Barges ferrying out the wounded at Tripoli

Italy's Naval base of St. Spezia comes in for another hammering.

Mussolini has a headache - I wonder why?

Wednesday 21st April - 759th Day Out

The 8th Army in their latest drive against Rommel have pushed ahead three miles and have captured the village of Enfidaville. The most difficult battle of the whole African campaign is now in progress.

RAF keeping up their bombing raids on Germany.

Heard that the submarine 'Thunderbolt' ex 'Thetis' is overdue and considered lost.

Thursday 22nd April - 760th Day Out

The 8th Army and the Axis forces still at grips and a few miles north of Enfidaville but the former are going steadily forward.

The 1st Army too is also striking hard at the Axis in and around Medjez-el-bab, yesterday they destroyed twenty five of their tanks during an enemy counter attack.

Went ashore for a change to ship's routine, and whilst there saw the film "Desert Victory" quite good from a filming point of view but terrible in many other aspects.

Received quite a good mail, six letters and three aerographs.

Good Friday 23rd April - 761st Day Out

Left Alex for Tripoli 6th Time

Very good news today from Tunisia, for in spite of all the enemy can do, both armies are advancing.

An entire force of twenty German transport planes were wiped out in ten minutes over the Gulf of Tunis yesterday by our fighters. South Africans were in the thick of the flight flying Kittyhawks and Spitfires.

Ten Axis fighters were also destroyed, but we lost four.

The transports were of the latest German type, six engined with a speed 160mph and can carry ten tons of material or one hundred and forty fully equipped soldiers, four more were shot down over Sicily. A total of thirty four for the day's bag - good work.

Saturday 24th April — 762nd Day Out

Still good news coming from Tunisia, Axis forces being steadily rolled back.

Ten more supply ships have been sunk by the RN in the Med.

It has just been learnt that some of the US airmen who bombed Tokyo last year and were captured by the Japs were afterwards murdered, we take no reprisals by United Nations, but America in particular has promised round the clock bombing of Japan. On the home front we are steaming along merrily and should be in Tripoli tomorrow.

Easter Sunday 25th April — 763rd Day Out

At the moment (8.50am) we are off, but quite near the coast, two hundred miles North of Benghazi. Weather is all one could wish for, and the sea flat calm. If it wasn't for the few Khaki clad figures strolling the decks, War would almost seem forgotten. It hardly seems possible that a few hundred miles away, men are fighting for their very existence.

Still very good news from Tunisia, going steadily forward on all fronts.

The American Aircraft Carrier 'Ranger' reported sunk in the North Atlantic (special from German radio).

Monday 26th April — 764th Day Out

Arrive Tripoli from Alex 6th Time

Arrived off the entrance at 9.00am, and awaited the Pilot, in the meantime a convoy came out, consisting of twelve ships with a destroyer escort bound for Alex. Inside the harbour were several more Merchantmen off loading and one US ship getting out tanks.

Had a very pleasant surprise at 11.00am, I'm being told I can go ashore for one hour. I went and returned in the ship's launch. Once ashore I tried to see as much as possible, really there is very little to see but it was exciting nevertheless not knowing what we might come across. A very few shops that are open sell curios and most of these are of the Egyptian type and probably from Alex or Cairo. Nearly all the other shops are closed for the simple reason there is nothing to sell. People of sorts are gradually drifting into the town possibly from the surrounding countryside, to which they fled during German occupation. The place is extremely busy, but only from a military point of view, occasionally a cart is to be seen and also a number of bicycles.

As in most of the ports, it is the harbour and quays that have been bombed, in the towns there are two or more houses down in every street.

Started loading at 10.00am, taking on our usual number of four hundred and fifty patients, finished and away by 4.00pm.

Saw the Hospital Ship 'Dorsetshire' in the distance, Alex bound from Sfax.

Tuesday 27th April — 765th Day Out

Ran into fog this morning and had to ease down. Later the fog lifted and we steamed merrily on.

US Aircraft Carrier has been reported sunk by torpedo from German U-boat. This remains unconfirmed by US Naval authorities, no carrier was operating in this theatre of war.

Still going steadily ahead in Tunisia, the powers that be report, that inside three weeks the campaign will have ended.

Wednesday 28th April — 766th Day Out

News much the same on all fronts.

Thursday 29th April — 767th Day Out

Arrived Alex from Tripoli 6th Time

According to the news on Algiers radio, the Allied Forces are closing in on Tunisia, the fall of which is imminent. Our forces are now only twelve miles from Bizerta, and twenty one miles from Tunis.

Several places in Italy again bombed by our aircraft. On entering Tripoli we pass a convoy of ships coming out. Today as we were approaching Alex we passed another convoy on our way up (Merchant ships) both these are clear indications that the Merchant Navy is delivering the goods, and we have the Med situation well in hand.

Came in through the Boom at 3.00pm, and had to wait a while as the 'Dorsetshire' was still alongside, discharging patients brought down from Sfax.

'Dorsetshire' finally came to anchorage at 4.30pm, and we were alongside by 5.30pm.

Started off loading and finished by 9.30pm. At last we get the new crew list, and as for me personally it's not quite what I expected, I am to remain on the ship in the same position, when it was clearly defined if I was to remain I should be promoted, but this has not come about.

According to rumour, reliefs should arrive next week.

Friday 30th April   -   **768th Day Out**

Heard today that the 'Windsor' has been lost.

News much the same from all battle fronts.

Liberators attack Messina.

Heavy raid by RAF on Wilhelmshaven and thirty one bombers are missing.

Saturday 1st May   -   **769th Day Out**

Heard we are to do one more voyage before the change over.   A sailing most likely on Tuesday.

Allied Forces in Tunisia pushing steadily ahead, and are now attacking 2nd line of Axis defences.

After meeting with such disastrous results in using transport planes for stores and troops to North Africa, the Axis have reverted to the usual method of ships, strung over a wide area and with fighter cover, possibly one or two get through but the majority are either damaged or lost.

RAF carry out a concentrated raid on Essen, to date this is the most bombed city in the world, - so much for Goering's boast!

Sunday 2nd May   -   **770th Day Out**

Von Arnim issues "no retreat" order.

To date 10,000 bombs have been dropped on Essen.

Rommel reported to be in Rome.

'HMS Resource' the depot ship here in Alex has, after a lapse of nearly a year, returned.

On Rommel nearing Alex in his last year's drive, this ship was sent to Port Said as a safety measure.

General Giraud has predicted that Tunisia will be freed this month and the War will be over next year.

Monday 3rd May   -   **771st Day Out**

Still good news on the main War Fronts, particularly from Tunisia.

Storing ship and making ready generally.

Tuesday 4th May   -   **772nd Day Out**

American troops capture Mateur, and have taken many prisoners.

Other War news much the same.

Wednesday 5th May   -   **773rd Day Out**

Leave Alex for Tripoli 7th Time

Allied Forces are advancing on all Tunisian battle fronts and some elements are reported to be within ten miles of Bizerta.

Heavy raid on Dortmund.

Thursday 6th May   -   **774th Day Out**

British and American forces in Tunisia launched an offensive at dawn today and are making excellent progress.

From the 11th November to the 2nd May, North West African Air Forces have destroyed 1,655 Axis aircraft in the air with the loss of 631 Allied machines, they have also sunk 62 enemy ships by air attack.

Friday 7th May   -   **775th Day Out**

Heard the good news from Tunisia, that Bizerta and Tunis have fallen to the Allies.

Saturday 8th May   -   **776th Day Out**

Arrived Tripoli from Alex 7th Time

Arrived off the entrance at 10.00am, and dropped anchor to allow a convoy of sixteen ships to clear the port, these are making for Alex, presumably this is the same convoy as we saw a few days ago, when on the way up, and we were making Alex.

Another convoy of five ships arrived this morning and are making port.

Got up anchor at 12.30pm, and proceeded in finally and anchored at 1.00pm, patients were alongside almost at once and by 5.00pm we were away, having taken on four hundred and fifty patients including German and Italian POW's

Sunday 9th May   -   **777th Day Out**

After capturing Tunis and Bizerta, the Allied Forces are pushing on and have advanced another fourteen miles. The Axis forces are now being chased into the Bon peninsula, their last footing in Tunisia, here they will either evacuate or fight it out, or possibly surrender, and so the much vaunted Afrika Korps is at last rounded up.

Good news coming in from Russia particularly in the Cuban.

On the home front, things are much the same. Eased down today and should make Alex Monday morning.

Plenty of activity amongst the crew in their spare moments, as this is their last trip and are busy packing up. As far as I am concerned a few heavy days lie ahead.

Monday 10th May   -   **778th Day Out**

Allied planes, four hundred in number, attacked Palermo in daylight yesterday causing widespread havoc. Von Arnim, German C-in-C North Africa, is reported to be in Italy. An Italian General is now in charge, so to him will go the honour of surrendering. A typical German move, an Italian to give in, not a German!

All armed resistances finish in Tunis and Bizerta, mopping up having been completed.

Tuesday 11th May   -   **779th Day Out**

Allies continuing their all out blitz on the Axis forces in Tunisia by land, sea, and air, a few days, or maybe less, should see the end.

Wednesday 12th May   -   **780th Day Out**

Arrived Alex from Tripoli 7th Time

Picked up the pilot at 9.00am, and proceed into port and alongside. Some of the new crew (officers) were waiting for us including our chief steward. I have met him before whilst on the staff in Southampton. It appears they took sixty five days to get here.

Mr Churchill is in Washington again.

Left the quay at 2.00pm, and came to the buoys, where we are likely to stay for a couple of weeks.

Later

11.45pm;   In the late news we heard that Von Arnim had been captured and was a prisoner in Allied hands.

Thursday 13th May   -   **781st Day Out**

War! Even events in Tunisia take second place today, what a shambles, men coming, men going, paying off, signing on, to crown it all I have to change my office, and right in the midst of all this uproar, I can't find a damn thing!

Tomorrow the old crew leave and new arrive, work is the watch word!

Chapter Nine

New Articles - Same Old Ship

Friday 14th May   -   **1st Day Out**

Signed on New Articles.

At 10.00am, the new crew arrived complete with baggage, as soon as all were aboard, old hands made ready to leave - by noon all was in order - New men on and getting on with business, the old away for a rest.

After a day of hell more or less, retired at 11.00pm and very much satisfied with the day's work and progress.

Whilst the ship is being fumigated etc. quite a few of the RAMC are on leave including the matron and sisters.

The last batch of Axis Forces in Tunisia gave up this morning, so another chapter closes.

Allied aircraft bomb several German cities including Berlin.

Saturday 15th May   -   **2nd Day Out**

War news today much the same, with the Blitz in full force on Germany and Southern Italy.

On the home front things are taking shape after the upheaval of yesterday.

Axis prisoners in Tunisia now number over 175,000.

Sunday 16th May   -   **3rd Day Out**

War news and events generally take second place as far as I'm concerned. (At the moment.) After two hectic days I take a few hours off, although nothing particularly happened, the change and rest was appreciated.

After the Americans landed on Attu Islands in the Aleutians, they are on the point of dislodging the Japs, another stepping stone to Japan and the bombing of the same!

Berlin bombed again last night.

Monday 17th May   -   **4th Day Out**

War news much the same.

Still very busy with the ship, getting stores on board.

Tuesday 18th May   -   **5th Day Out**

Much the same as for yesterday. A British tanker which ran aground just last week outside the entrance caught fire this morning and set fire to a small tanker and tug which were alongside. Sixteen men lost their lives and there are rumours of sabotage.

Went ashore to say cheerio to my old boss, and had a very enjoyable evening.

RAF berated the Mohne and Eder dams in the Ruhr Valley causing widespread damage and serious loss of life, acclaimed as a master stroke by the RAF.

Wednesday 19th May   -   **6th Day Out**

Fighting on all fronts very much the same with the Yanks doing very well in the Aleutians.

Thursday 20th May   -   **7th Day Out**

American forces making good progress on Attu Island, and it looks as though the Japs will have to yield.

Allied aircraft in the Med destroyed sixty six Axis planes yesterday.

Mosquito bombers raid Berlin again.

Slight enemy activity in and around London.

On the home front things are beginning to take shape, all work has finished, storing completed, and we are more or less ready for sea again.

Friday 21st May   -   **8th Day Out**

News generally much the same.

Saturday 22nd May   -   **9th Day Out**

Allies destroy one hundred and thirteen planes in attacks on enemy bases in the Med.

Mosquitoes again raid Berlin, also Essen.

Had another run ashore and went to the YMCA for lunch and dinner. Went to the park in the afternoon which was a very pleasant interlude.

Hired a Felucca at 10.00pm, and was back on board at 10.45pm.

Heard today that another hospital unit joins us for the voyage to Tripoli - fifty six sisters and six medical officers.

Our old "Ships Crew" are still awaiting news as regards to going home, at the moment they are housed ashore and get more fed up every day.

Sunday 23rd May   -   **10th Day Out**

Pretty busy on the home front, fifty four sisters joined the voyage for Tripoli, unfortunately we have been delayed and possibly will not leave until Thursday, what a blow, and with a double sitting too.

Allies continue to batter Axis ports and aerodromes in the Med.

Fighting on Attu Island reaching it's climax.

Monday 24th May   -   **11th Day Out**

Goering's boast completely exploded. To date 100,000 tons of bombs have been dropped on Germany.

The heaviest raid of the War was carried out by the RAF on Monday night, 2,000 tons of bombs were dropped on the mining centre of Dortmund.

Tuesday 25th May   -   **12th Day Out**

Had a few more hours off and went to the Royal to see "Blossoms in the Dust", very good and I enjoyed it very much.

On board by 12.30am.

Allies still maintaining their air blitz in the Med.

Japs on point of being pushed out of Attu Island.

Wednesday 26th May   -   **13th Day Out**

Several large transports arrived today, probably with troops for the 8th Army coming back for a spell.

Saw one or two of the old crew and they appear very fed up with no news of moving yet.

Thursday 27th May   -   **14th Day Out**

Dusseldorf blasted by giant RAF bombers.

Italian armies in the Med. get another heavy raid.

Hope to be away by tomorrow with luck.

Friday 28th May   -   **15th Day Out**

Should have gone this morning, but owing to more engine room trouble we were delayed, we are now all ready and have a full ship regarding extra ratings etc. and awaiting events.

'HS Somersetshire' pulled out today for Tripoli.

Allied blitz continues on the Med. Axis ports.

Italy has been made to realise the folly of her ways and is being bombed day and night.

Later

More delay, probably away in the morning.

Saturday 29th May - **16th Day Out**

Left Axis for Tripoli 8th Time

Should have been away at 7.00am, but still have minor trouble down below.

'HS Maine' came in this morning with more wounded from a Tripoli based hospital.

We finally pull out at 10.00am, through the boom and away to sea, this after a delay of almost a week.

At the moment we are doing about 8 knots, probably the engineers as well as the stewards take time to settle down!

Sunday 30th May - **17th Day Out**

Heard tonight that the Yanks had taken over Attu Island, another step nearer to the bombing of Japan.

According to Swedish reports, casualties in the German dam disasters are estimated to be over 20,000.

Things on the home front are much the same but we are making slower headway than usual and will no doubt arrive Wednesday, instead of Tuesday, bordering on the 5th day instead of the usual 4th.

Monday 31st May - **18th Day Out**

Much the same as yesterday.

Tuesday 1st June - **19th Day Out**

The French fleet at Alex consisting of a Battleship, four Cruisers, three Destroyers, and a Sub have now come over on the side of the Allies.

At the moment the ship is doing about 6 knots,. having to ease down to enable us to arrive first thing in the morning.

The sisters travelling to Tripoli gave a farewell concert this evening. A minor affair, but quite good, if rumour is to be believed, never saw it myself unfortunately, I happened to be busy at the time.

Wednesday 2nd June - **20th Day Out**

Arrived Tripoli from Alex 8th Time

Entered the channel this morning at 6.00am, paravanes put out.

At 9.30am we dropped anchor, this time on the seaward side of the breakwater. On all other occasions we have gone inside to anchor and take on patients, but there were today too many MN ships off loading in the bay, so elbow room was denied us.

We started to load at 10.00am, and once the first barge was cleared, the travelling sisters disembarked. In spite of one steam winch out of action we were loaded and away by 4.00pm, having taken on are usual five hundred or thereabouts.

Owing to our being a day late, the patients had a nasty time, as they were brought down from the base hospital to the waiting barges and after being kept waiting for several hours they were taken back to the hospital and brought down again this morning.

At 6.00pm, two hours after leaving Tripoli, the main Dynamo went wrong and all lights went out, owing to our having to be lit up at sea we had no alternative but to return to port, to effect repairs, this continued through the night and we will possibly get away tomorrow and I hope for good this time.

No news tonight - no juice - no radio!

It's been terribly hot today, our hottest so far.

Thursday 3rd June - **21st Day Out**

Early this morning, Naval men came on and got busy with repairs (Dynamo), so for another day we are without light or water. This last fortnight has been one long continual run of misfortune, just one damn thing after another.

Last night and again tonight we have been completely blacked out, and for the patients in the various wards the heat was almost unbearable.

During both nights, two motor patrol vehicles were doing guard duties against possible submarine attack and at about twenty minute intervals they dropped depth charges, explosives of which could be heard quite distinctly on board here, and from time to time actually gave us a shaking.

Friday 4th June - **22nd Day Out**

Left Tripoli for Alex 8th Time

Pulled out this morning at 5.00am all our thoughts are on what will happen next. Passed the 'Dorsetshire' going into Tripoli. The 'Somersetshire' is also due today, having made the trip to Malta first.

War news much the same.

Saturday 5th June - **23rd Day Out**

Pantelleria again shelled by the Navy, this island has now been shelled four times in as many days.

News Flash - Mr Churchill back home.

On the home front, things are much the same, engine room in a state of chaos, without light and water from time to time, and doing about 8 knots, and doing our best to make port Tuesday.

Sunday 6th June - **24th Day Out**

American aircraft based in North Africa raid the Italian naval base of Spetzia and score direct hit's on two of Musso's battleships.

On the Russian Front the main news is of continued air battles, and mass raids on each others supply lines.

Monday 7th June - **25th Day Out**

War news much the same, but Allied subs in the Med. are keeping up their good work, eight ships were sunk or damaged last week in sweeps ranging from the French Med. coast to the toe of Italy.

On the home front things have improved considerably, all light and water now available, but we are only doing a steady 8 knots, should make Alex tomorrow morning.

The 'HS Somersetshire' passed us this afternoon and no doubt will unload before us; Saw her again about 10.00pm away off our port beam.

Tuesday 8th June - **26th Day Out**

Arrived Alex from Tripoli 8th Time

Picked up the pilot at 8.00am, through the boom and to anchor. The 'Somersetshire' has gone alongside and we should be there at noon.

The oil tanker which caught fire on the 18th May is still burning, unfortunately she is on a sand bank and can only be left to burn out.

Widespread raids continue on Italian bases, and Musso is getting the wind up.

Stayed anchored until 4.00pm, then came in alongside to discharge passengers and patients. So ends the worst voyage of the whole two years. During the past fortnight everything possible has gone wrong. The old crew is still here, saw some of them this evening, three weeks they've been there (Ye Gods thank goodness I'm not amongst them).

Stayed alongside for the night, possibly away to anchorage tomorrow.

Wednesday 9th June - **27th Day Out**

Had a particularly busy morning, storing ship non stop from 9.00am to 2.00pm.

Just after 2.00pm we went out to the outer anchorage; At 7.00pm the powers that be came to the conclusion we were in the wrong place, so away once again and back to our mooring buoys of earlier days, we are now thank goodness quite near to the shore.

Plenty of activity here at the moment many ships beings loaded with War stores and several others embarking troops.

The French navy is very active, painting ship, doing trial runs (small craft) and taking stores and ammunition on board.

Thursday 10th June - **28th Day Out**

Had a few hours off again today and went ashore, amongst other things, intended to have swim but could not get a cabin so sunbathed instead. After a couple of hours on the beach, I came back to town and had a sundowner then went to the Globe Theatre to see an E.N.S.A. show, "French for Love", quite good, and very amusing, unfortunately halfway through the show the lights failed, eventually they were got going after about half an hour, and the show continued.   At about 10.00pm, I took a cab to the docks and a Felucca to the ship, and so ended another pleasant day.

Italian island bases still coming in for a hammering with Pantelleria as the main target. This I imagine will soon be in Allied hands.

Russians still doing very well; Other War news much the same.

Friday 11th June - 29th Day Out

Heard the good news today that Pantelleria has fallen to the Allies, so much for Musso's boast; An Italian bastion against democracy, the Italian Malta (the twerp), Whereas Malta held out for three years and never gave up, Pantelleria after thirty days surrendered.

On the home front all is topsy turvy, all sorts of repairs going on, sometimes we are without light, sometimes water, at times both. We are here indefinitely I should imagine!

Saturday 12th June - 30th Day Out

Lampedusa Island eighty miles South of Pantelleria has been battered into submission by the Allies.

Official communiqué; After twenty four hours of Naval bombardment, Lampedusa today surrendered and is now occupied by Allied Forces.

The Royal Airforce attacked Dusseldorf and Munster and it was the heaviest raid of the War so far, more than 2,000 tons of bombs were dropped on these two cities.

Sunday 13th June - 31st Day Out

Another Italian Island, Linosa, fell to the Allies yesterday, this gives the Allies all the islands dominating the central Mediterranean.

War news generally very good on all fronts, United Nations are making steady headway.

Went on shore and had a wonderful day, saw Mr Bee, my old Boss, and then went to the beach. In this we were very lucky, for no sooner had we got on the front when we met Mr. Nicoli our agent, who put his cabin at our disposal. After changing we had a marvellous swim and an equally good lunch. We sunbathed for the next hour or so, met more people, friends of Mr. N, and after a chinwag, we had tea, finally leaving the beach at about 6.00pm. Mr N. took us to his home to see his garden, this was very pleasant indeed and we finally finished up taking it easy in a garden chair enjoying a Turkish Coffee.   Having expressed a desire to be moving, Mr. N. put us in his car and drove us back to town by way of the sea front, dropping us as requested in the centre of the town. Saying cheerio to Mr. N. we went and had dinner, it was very nice and I thoroughly enjoyed it. Took a taxi back to number six gate, Felucca to the ship, and so ended one of the most pleasant days spent in Alex.

Monday 14th June - 32nd Day Out

Had a busy day storing ship.

Tuesday 15th June - 33rd Day Out

An even busier day today, started storing at 10.00am, and finished at 5.00pm.

War news much the same, with Italy getting a lot of attention from the Allied Forces.

In view of things to come here in Alex, there is a lot of activity in the harbour and there are well over one hundred ships, cruisers and destroyers, invasion craft of all types, and Merchant Navy ships. Something or other arrives every day.

The French navy is showing good promise, one already having gone into the floating dock.

Heard a first class buzz today, after repairs and storing we are going South - I wonder?

Wednesday 16th June - 34th Day Out

King George is now in North Africa, other news much the same.

Thursday 17th June - 35th Day Out

The ship is still in a state of chaos, workmen everywhere and we are trying to carry out usual routine. Storing again today, we finished but after getting in the usual amount we were suddenly ordered to store for three months, so all over the same ground again when once could and should have been sufficient!

King George inspecting a Guard of Honour of Marines on board a Battleship

According to rumour, we are going to be based further West, personally I think either Tripoli or Malta, with an occasional run back to Alex for stores and repairs etc.

American troops win great air battle over the Solomons, seventy seven Japs shot down, with a loss of six planes to the Yanks.

Home based bombers over Germany again, this time Cologne was objective, fourteen bombers missing.

Hospital Ship 'Aba' arrived today possibly from the South, the stage is gradually being set for the next performance. More MN ships arrived, also several invasion barges.

So many ships are here now that they have to anchor outside the breakwater.

Friday 18th June - **36th Day Out**

Sicily now the main target for the Allied bombers.
Storing again today.

Saturday 19th June - **37th Day Out**

War news much the same.
Air blitz on Sardinia and Sicily resumed.

Sunday 20th June - **38th Day Out**

After waiting all day for stores, not a thing arrived, so it was in more ways than one, a day wasted.
More and more ships arrived, one continual movement.

Monday 21st June - **39th Day Out**

Things on board not too comfortable, so we decided to go ashore; Went after lunch, had a swim and back to town for the usual sundowner and had a good rest. Back on board again by, 10.00pm.

Tuesday 22nd June - **40th Day Out**

All the French fleet with one exception, put to sea this evening, the Heavy Cruiser 'Duguesne' still at her moorings.

Heavy raid by the RAF on the Ruhr - forty four bombers lost, but over seven hundred took part.

American aircraft bomb Germany in daylight.

Wednesday 23rd June - **41st Day Out**

Germany again heavily raided, we lose thirty five bombers.

USA coal strike settled.

French generals in North Africa reach agreement.

Axis forces gathering in South of Italy in view of possible Allied invasion, this will come by way of Sicily in my personal opinion.

On the home front things are fairly quiet had an easy day today for a change!

Thursday 24th June - **42nd Day Out**

Great activity here in port today, ships of all types leaving, and one gathers the impression that things are on the move. Landing craft large and small, made for sea later in the day.

Very busy for a couple of hours.

Friday 25th June - **43rd Day Out**

King George VI arrived safely at home this morning.

British subs still very active in the Med.

RAF start shuttle raids on the Axis forces.

Bombers from home bombed Germany on the way out then went on and landed in North Africa. They refuelled, bombed up, and then went on to Italy, and after dropping their bombs on Spezia, returned.

This is the first double bomb trip of the War.

In Russia things seem to be fairly quiet, and if rumour is to be believed, troops are massing on both sides as a prelude to another fierce battle.

Heard today that we may be here another fortnight, what a blow, thought it was only a matter of days!

On the home front, the chief gripe is mosquitoes there must be thousands of them on board, unless those that are here all make a rendezvous in my cabin, all devices for the extermination has failed so far, a 14lb hammer would be about the only weapon. No sleep since 4.20am this morning, what a life!

Saturday 26th June - **44th Day Out**

War news very much the same from all quarters, air blitz by the Allies continue, their targets being the Ruhr and Italy.

Sunday 27th June - **45th Day Out**

Another beach day, and very pleasant it was too, finishing up with a show.

Increased activity here, and everything points to a clash of arms in the very near future, and I think we are destined to play our part.

Monday 28th June - **46th Day Out**

Things generally much the same.

Tuesday 29th June - **47th Day Out**

Allies resume high pressure air attacks on the Axis.

RAF heavies over Cologne, with Fortresses doing a blitz on Leghorn.

On the Eastern Front air battles seem to be the order of the day.

On the home front we are still awaiting repairs, with no idea as to when we may move.

Wednesday 30th June - **48th Day Out**

Had another run ashore, this time to a cabaret; Not too bad, made a change.

Thursday 1st July - **49th Day Out**

US forces land in the Solomons, other War news much the same.

Friday 2nd July - **50th Day Out**

Allied Pacific drive makes headway, sixty five Jap planes shot down in one day, and their land forces wiped out on the Island of Rendova. Aussies going ahead, they are now only two miles from Salamaua.
The French Island of Martinique in the West Indies has come over to the Allies.
Another convoy left here this morning, things generally nearing the climax.
The general tone of things is that we are here for at least another week.

Saturday 3rd July - **51st Day Out**

Things in the Pacific warming up, and our land forces have made good progress.
Powerful American Naval squadron is speeding at full speed to the Pacific battle area, a clash between two Navies expected any moment.
Mediterranean blitz continues.
U-boat kills and Merchant Navy losses, are the most favourable for any month during the whole War.
The old crew leave Alex for England tomorrow by way of Suez and the Med. I think.

Sunday 4th July - **52nd Day Out**

A big convoy came in this morning, about twenty ships I should imagine, majority of which were loaded with troops.
Still more freighters arrive during the afternoon.
The old crew finally left today by train to Port Tewfik.

Monday 5th July - **53rd Day Out**

This morning a British Naval squadron arrived.
Two Battleships, one Aircraft Carrier and six Destroyers.
The hour of attack is gradually approaching.

Tuesday 6th July - **54th Day Out**

Today we get in the last of the stores and are now ready for sea.
Oilers and water barges are alongside, and it looks as if things will happen any day now.
We have just heard, that we leave tomorrow.
Went ashore for the last time to say cheerio to some of my friends and to see a movie "Twin Beds", not too bad at all! Good news from the South Pacific and also from Russia.

Wednesday 7th July - **55th Day Out**

Left Alex for Tripoli 9th Time

At long last we get under way (after a stay of four weeks) and I think everyone is glad to be on the move again.
I imagine Tripoli to be our objective, with Malta a good runner up. According to news now released, we should have left on Monday, but not being quite ready, the 'Dorsetshire' left in our place, now it may be interesting to see a turn of events.
Every Hospital Ship now attached to the North East is at sea or in a North African port waiting events.
We have all been asked to volunteer to help generally in the rescue of troops in the water and on the beaches. Those who volunteer will have to wear tin hats and gas masks and I can see myself being tucked up any moment!
All cameras have been taken away, and private wireless sets are not to be used as from today.
Alex harbour is almost void of any ships, a few that were there when we left, are under orders to move, so the line up I imagine is almost complete.

Returning to ship after a day off

Thursday 8th July - **56th Day Out**

Although to date our destination is still a secret, a call for volunteers was made today to assist in getting the wounded aboard and to do any other additional work for the comfort of the wounded. ALL VOLUNTEERED. This afternoon we were all issued with tin hats, a gentle reminder, so the day draws gradually nearer.

Terrific battle raging on the Eastern Front.

Allied Forces in the Pacific going steadily ahead.

Friday 9th July - **57th Day Out**

Bitter fighting taking place on the Eastern Front.

Allied aircraft make over twenty sorties in one day over Sicily.

Heard today our destination is Tripoli.

The situation in the South Pacific is very satisfactory.

Saturday 10th July - **58th Day Out**

ALLIES BEGAN LANDING OPERATIONS ON SICILY THIS MORNING.

Good news from all other War Fronts.

On the home front things are much the same, we are now eased down, and should make Tripoli tomorrow at about 10.00am.

Saw the 'Maine' this evening catching up on us and presumably making for the same destination.

The weather has changed considerably with a fairly strong wind blowing and a moderate sea running, it is rather on the cool side considering our position.

Sunday 11th July - **59th Day Out**

Arrived Tripoli from Alex 9th Time

It is now revealed that the Allied landing was made on the Western side of Sicily, and at seven different places. In less than an hour they had established themselves on the beaches and were moving forward. The opposition was very fierce but with superior air cover, the issue was never in doubt.

The landing was backed up by the Royal Navy and unit's of the Allied Navies.

The Merchant Navy played a great part in the transport of troops and stores, and so far no ship has been lost in the initial landing.

The absence of Axis fighter aircraft was very noticeable, probably busy on the Eastern Front.

In summing up so far, the landing has been a great success.

Later 10.00am

On arriving off the harbour entrance, the usual happened, pilot, billet etc, we come in through the boom past our old anchorage, and eventually tie up alongside an old hulk. This hulk was a sea going freighter until a few months ago, but she is now lying on her side in fifty feet of water and the Navy has turned her into a jetty come wharf, come pier, sort of thing. The first occasion we have actually tied up here.

There are about six Merchantmen here and as many Hospital Ships, the latter being the 'Llandovery Castle,' 'Somersetshire,' 'Maine,' 'Vasna,' 'Veta' and the Dutch ship 'Aphir.'

We have quite a lot of hospital equipment to off load, and we are then ready for any eventuality.

Hope to get my wireless going later on, and so get the latest news, everyone is wondering what is happening, so far the news has been very brief.

Monday 12th July - 60th Day Out

Heard today that the 'HS Talamba' had been sunk off Sicily, whilst at anchor and with over four hundred wounded on board.

According to the last report received, all crew and wounded are safe having been taken on board the 'Tairea' a sister Hospital Ship.

Pulled away from our berth (so called) and made for an anchorage outside the main entrance.

Good news from Sicily, everything going according to plan.

Tuesday 13th July - 61st Day Out

Still the right type of news, the British 8th Army has made good progress and has advanced well inland from Syracuse.

The Americans and Canadians also have done a good job and are pushing forward.

Suddenly get news that we are on the move, and at 8.00pm we up anchor, and are away towards our destination, somewhere in Sicily.

The 'Tairea' came in this evening from Sicily and on her were the 'Talamba's' crew, wounded and personnel.

Wednesday 14th July - 62nd Day Out

At sea and we get very little news, apart from the early morning news sheet.

We ease down about midday, so as to make our destination early in the morning.

Everything very quiet, and anything may happen tomorrow.

Thursday 15th July - 63rd Day Out

Arrived Syracuse from Tripoli

First saw the island this morning at 5.00am, presumably Passero, and at 10.00am we finally dropped anchor about ten miles South of Syracuse.

We anchored in the bay with good sandy beaches in places, and the dozen freighters that are here are making good headway off loading, with the help of the Navy of course.

After taking on less than a dozen patients it was decided to send us to Syracuse, to see what was happening there. We were away about noon and pulled up about 2.00pm, anchored off but finally came inside the boom at 4.00pm, as with the previous place quite a number of M.N. are here with a good show from the RN with ships of all kinds.

It is particularly quiet here with no guns or bombs flying about, saw one plane first thing this morning, otherwise it's hard to believe War is so close. Patients keep coming in, being brought alongside by invasion barges.

Had to leave port at sundown and proceeded to sea to steam around all night with lights on, and to make port again in the morning. Raid on the town during the night directed mostly on transport and roads leading from the town.

Friday 16th July - **64th Day Out**

Came in again this morning to finish loading and carried on steadily getting the wounded aboard until 6.00pm, when we made to the sea and Tripoli, with our customary good luck we should be there Sunday.

Not a plane seen again today (enemy) but a formation of about twenty bombers (ours) went Northwards this morning and flying very low.

Quite a lot of activity with reference to ships, Naval as well as Merchant Naval have been on the move all day.

From the harbour where we anchor, we can see well out to sea, from time to time one can see the Royal Navy on patrol.

Ships ranging from battleships to motor boats. What of the Italian navy that we heard so much about? For their insults during the Abyssinia crisis we are ready to pay interest!

About 7.30pm this evening we saw a wonderful sight, 'HMS Nelson' and 'Rodney,' two cruisers and six destroyers cruising off the Sicilian coast.

The sea along this coast is just full of every type of ship, sheer proof of our having the situation well in hand.

According to the patients things are going very well, but from time to time the Axis makes severe counter attacks, which proves very costly in men, as well as material. Most of the wounded are in rather a bad state as most of them come straight from the scene of action.

Patients on board number thirty eight officers, and six hundred and six other ranks.

Saturday 17th July - **65th Day Out**

Underway from Sicily to Tripoli with patients.

War news from the Island is still very good, but our hardest task still lies ahead; The taking of Catania, and it's adjacent airfields. German tanks are taking up positions on the Catanian Plains to try to stop our breakthrough.

More Allied paratroops have been dropped behind the Axis lines.

Good news from Russia.

Sunday 18th July - **66th Day Out**

Arrive Tripoli from Syracuse 1st Time

Off the channel at 6.00am but owing to various setbacks we are not able to go alongside until nearly noon.

Started to off load as soon as possible and was finished by 5.00pm, quite a good effort under the conditions in which one had to work, and also the many stretcher cases.

Rather surprised to see so many Hospital Ships here, there are eight altogether. They are the 'Tairea,' 'Veta,' 'Vasna,' 'Dinard,' 'Dorsetshire,' 'Maine,' 'Aphir,' 'Amra' and now us. There are also twenty Merchant Navy ships here, all outside the boom and apparently ready to move off.

Had my radio on this evening, first time since leaving Alex, I may only use it in harbour now.

Had a walk along the famous "Spanish Mall" this evening,, not a thing left, whole or standing, found two brass shell cases and a little more for my collection.

Monday 19th July - **67th Day Out**

Stayed alongside all night, and apart from being very hot, it was quite peaceful in fact there has been no raid here since the end of April .

First batch of prisoners arrive today from Sicily.

Tuesday 20th July - **68th Day Out**

Things on the home front much the same, once again playing the waiting game.

Heard that the Yanks had bombed Rome, or at least the factories there (about four years too late!)

Jolly good news from Sicily and also from Russia.

Wednesday 21st July - **69th Day out**

According to the news of this morning the British 8th Army is now only three miles from Catania and massing for the final assault.

Yanks and Canadians well into the heart of the islands.

Russians advancing in the Orel sector.

Allied bombers in the South Pacific have sunk three more Jap ships, one cruiser and two destroyers.

Pulled out this morning at 7.30am, and we are now at anchor in the bay.

Went ashore in the afternoon.

Thursday 22nd July   -   70th Day Out

Took on hospital stores today, so it looks as though we will soon be on the move again.

Another new Hospital Ship came in today 'St Julian', a GWR channel boat.

Friday 23rd July   -   71st Day Out

Left Tripoli for Syracuse 2nd Time

At 6.00am this morning we got up anchor and moved to an outer billet, in readiness for leaving.   At 2.00pm, up anchor once more and away. It has been very hot this last day or two but I think today has been the worst so far. War news much the same from all quarters, the 8th Army is still battling for possession of Catania but the Nazis seem bent on keeping it. The Yanks and Canadians have made further gains in the North of the island.

Saturday 24th July   -   72nd Day Out

Heard this morning that the Yanks had entered Palermo and were still advancing.

The British 8th Army were still encountering strong resistance before Catania.

Passed the 'Tairea' this morning on the way back from Sicily to Tripoli with wounded.

It has been particularly hot today, thank goodness there has been little breeze to cool one down a bit.

Sunday 25th July   -   73rd Day Out

Arrived Syracuse from Tripoli 2nd Time

After an uneventful trip we arrive once more in Syracuse.

Apparently there was a blitz here last night, an oil tanker is partially sunk and on fire, whilst another freighter has been sunk and is on an even keel, the crew is still aboard. This one probably received an aerial torpedo.

Other Merchant Navy ships are busy off loading.

Came in through the boom at 8.00am, and anchored in the harbour.

The War news is very good in Sicily. Here everything is going fine, the only hold up being Catania where our 8th Army is fighting to gain mastery over the Jerry's.

The Yanks and the Canadians are doing fine on the North West sector, there are mostly Iti's here and they are offering very little resistance.

Wonderful news from Russia, even the Jerrys admit they have had a setback and that the Russians have broken through their lines.

Later

(Mussolini resigns, Bagdolio in charge)

Started to load at 10.00am, and by 5.00pm had taken on nearly six hundred patients.

Through the boom by 7.30pm, and away to sea.

During the day over one hundred fighter bombers passed over us on the way North, to Catania I should imagine.

Monday 26th July   -   74th Day Out

It was confirmed this morning that Mussolini has resigned and Marshall Bagdolio has been given the post. Much speculation as to what might happen now.

Other news much the same.

RAF carry out big raid on Hamburg.

On the home front things are going very well and with a bit of luck we should make Tripoli tomorrow.

Tuesday 27th July   -   75th Day Out

Arrive Tripoli from Syracuse 2nd Time

Owing to wind and poor visibility we were much later in getting alongside, still making fast at 1.00pm. Once we were finally tied up the job of off loading was soon under way and by 5.00pm all patients were gone.

We heard the news this afternoon that the ship is going home. To Alexandria first then leaving there for England on the 10th August, in which case we should be there about the 26th August. Now to see what happens!

Stayed alongside all night and are to pull out in the morning.

War news much the same from all fronts.

Wednesday 28th July - 76th Day Out

Pulled out this morning at 7.00am, and away to our outer anchorage.

After all our excitement of yesterday we may not go home after all, at the moment the orders are cancelled and we are just waiting for something else to happen, probably back to Syracuse now, trust the Army to mess one about, or maybe it's the Navy, anyway, someone or somebody has slipped up.

I think today has been the hottest day ever with a warm, nay, damned hot wind, it is almost unbearable.

Heard this afternoon that the 'Dorsetshire' was going home in our place!

Thursday 29th July - 77th Day Out

And so we still swing around the buoy.

The 'Somersetshire' came in this morning, having been recalled on the way to Syracuse, no one seems to know why.

There are no orders for us, we will just have to wait.

It's terribly hot here, I wish to goodness we would go somewhere out of it.

Peace Terms Offered

To the Italian Nation by the United Nations - awaiting results.

General Smuts has a sweeping majority in the South African election; A very good omen.

Friday 30th July - 78th Day Out

'Dorsetshire' pulled out this morning for Alex then England, so once again we miss the bus.

Russians going ahead in their main drive on Orel.

Yanks and Canadians going ahead in North Sicily.

Australians and Yanks going ahead in the Pacific.

The British 8th Army are at grips with the Jerrys before Catania.

According to the German radio, the Italians are to continue waging war against the Allied Nations.

Hamburg has seventh raid in six days.

Allied heavy cruisers and destroyers shell the Italian mainland.

Saturday 31st July - 79th Day Out

Russians still advancing on Orel.

General Smuts has a huge majority in the South African election one hundred and seven for, and seventy three against.

Our air offensive against Germany still continues.

Very heavy fighting before Catania, the Yanks and Canadians have made slight advances on our left.

Much speculation regards Italy, as to what she may or may not do.

Sunday 1st August - 80th Day Out

War news much the same, Allies have made slight advances in Sicily.

Heard at 11.00pm that we are to sail tomorrow and I think to Syracuse.

Monday 2nd August - 81st Day Out

Left Tripoli for Syracuse 3rd Time

News of sailing confirmed this morning and we are to load eighty tons of cargo and I think thirty officers and one hundred and fourteen other ranks are embarking.

Came in alongside to water and should be away this evening.

Officers and ratings joined Naval medical unit.

Pulled out at 5.00pm, through the boom and to sea.

There is a lovely breeze blowing, quite cool and it's really a treat to be underway again.

The going home "bogey" is aboard again, this is our last voyage to Syracuse back to Tripoli, Alex, then home. Only time will tell!

Tuesday 3rd August - 82nd Day Out

At sea, very little news, with luck we arrive tomorrow and I hope it's the last time, this is the most uninteresting work, outside of actually carrying the wounded, stuck in a GFH, days on end, hot as hell, and nowhere to go, nor anywhere to see, bathing seems about the only pastime.

Wednesday 4th August - 83rd Day Out

Arrived Syracuse 3rd Time

After a quiet trip and a fairly cool one, fortunately we arrive at Syracuse, we were right on time dropping anchor at 8.00am.

Still a lot of activity here in the way of ships and shipping.

Have not been able to get to the town but had a run ashore this afternoon landing on an open beach, and open countryside. Tramped for a couple of hours but found very little, apart from lemons and almonds and a few grapes, which we brought back to ship.

On getting back aboard, loading of patients had been completed and we were ready to sail, which we did at 5.30pm.

Have been going full speed all night possibly with a view to arriving in Tripoli tonight. Normally we do a fair speed and get to our base in the morning.

If rumour is to be believed this is our last trip to Syracuse and we are billed for home, we are all, I may say, working and planning for that end in view, hope there won't be too many disappointments.

Thursday 5th August - 84th Day Out

Heard the good news this morning that Catania had been taken by the 8th Army, also that the Russians had retaken Orel, two very big events favouring future operations.

After speeding all day we anchored at the channel entrance and will I presume follow the coast, when getting underway at daybreak.

Friday 6th August - 85th Day Out

Arrived Tripoli 3rd Time from Syracuse

Up anchor at 6.00am, entered the channel and so to Tripoli.

Came alongside at 9.30am, and were discharging patients by 10.00am.

The news is through and we are going to Alex and we start to take on patients for home.

It appears we are taking wounded from here who could be no further use to the War, through either serious wounds, amputations etc., or organic disease. We proceed to Alex where we finish loading with more wounded, store, then home?

This afternoon we took on thirteen Officers and Sisters of the New Zealand Hospital Unit, with eighty other ranks for passage to Alex, tomorrow we take on the wounded for home.

Stayed alongside all night ready to take on the wounded at 7.00am.

Saturday 7th August - 86th Day Out

Left Tripoli for Alex (and for home)

The wounded came on board at 7.00am, nearly three hundred for the voyage to Alex.

Took on quite a lot of hospital equipment and finally away at 5.00pm.

War news from all fronts particularly good.

At the moment the 'Somersetshire' is just a head of us Sicily bound.

Sunday 8th August - 87th Day Out

On the home front all is going along nicely and all is quiet.

On the Russian Front things are going extremely well, and the Soviet Forces are making good strides in all sectors.

The Allied Forces in Sicily are making good progress beyond Catania and the Axis forces are being gradually pushed back to Messina and the sea.

It would appear that the Jerrys are making plans for evacuation, but as yet only on a small scale.

The French liner 'Normandie' which sank in the Hudson River last year is now being re floated.

In the Pacific, an American Warship sunk a Jap cruiser and two destroyers without loss to themselves.

The Allied Forces in the same area have also captured the air base at Munda, one of the chief bases for Jap activity in the South Pacific.

Monday 9th August - **88th Day Out**

All quiet on the home front, War news much the same.

Tuesday 10th August - **89th Day Out**

Russians doing very well.

Things nearing a climax in Sicily.

Mr. Churchill with his wife and daughter are in Canada (news flash at 10.00pm).

Wednesday 11th August - **90th Day Out**

Arrived Alex from Tripoli 9th Time

Having been engaged in the Sicilian campaign five weeks.

Picked up the pilot at 8.00am, so through the boom to our usual berth at number 22 gate.

The harbour is absolutely packed with ships, and mostly Merchantmen, a few Naval craft but nothing big.

One Hospital Ship is here, the 'Vasna,' having made the journey from Tripoli a few days ahead of us.

We are all on tenterhooks wondering what the news will be; England, possibly on Sunday, is my shot!

Staying alongside all night, possibly pull out in the morning to allow the 'Amra' to come in.

Heard this evening that we pick up forty five officers and four hundred patients for England on Saturday.

Thursday 12th August - **91st Day Out**

Fairly busy getting in stores etc in readiness for our leaving on Sunday at the latest.

Heard the good news that the Axis forces had started mass evacuation from Sicily to Italian mainland.

'Amra' came in alongside this morning.

Friday 13th August - **92nd Day Out**

One of the busiest days ever, storing. Thank goodness it is the last time for a while, can't even get ashore, might possibly make it tomorrow.

War news still good, Berlin and Rome bombed.

Saturday 14th August - **93rd Day Out**

A few more stores on today, and then we go alongside to pick up patients for home, which are due to embark 6.00am Sunday.

Should have moved in at noon today but we were delayed so we did not get alongside until after 5.00pm. This may be the last chance of getting on shore as we should sail tomorrow.

Went at 9.00pm, and back at midnight, not very exciting but a very welcome change.

Sunday 15th August - **94th Day Out**

All the patients started to embark at 8.00am, and by noon all were settled in. Faint rumours are going round the ship as to our not being able to sail owing to engine trouble (words fail me).

Went to sea stations at 2.15pm, but did not get away from the quay until 4.30pm, and then it was to anchor in the bay to have minor repairs done.

War news particularly good, Russians and the Allied Forces in all parts of the world are steadily advancing and the past seven days has been the best week of the War for the United Nations.

Although the land news is significant, the greatest feat in the past few weeks has been the sinking of 90 U-boats. (Mr. Churchill's own words) this is actual sinkings not probables, add to this the terrific bombing of Hamburg, which is the chief U-boat base, the situation is well in hand and we have just cause to be grateful for everything. After our last heavy raid on Rome, it has been declared an open city.

The Soviets have entered Kharkov, and bitter fighting is going on in the streets.

Stayed at anchor all night whilst repairs were being carried out, and so we still wait to see what tomorrow will bring forth.

Monday 16th August   -   95th Day Out

Left Alex for England

Engine room is now in a state of preparedness so we are pulling out today sometime.

We got underway at 4.00pm, and according to latest rumour our first stop is Gibraltar, the next and last is Avonmouth. I wish it was Southampton, but I think that is too much to expect.

The War in Sicily is reaching it's climax, any day now may see the end. All Allied Forces those North and South are only fifteen miles from Messina, the town it'self is already within range of our big guns.

Italy is getting a good pounding from the Allied Air Forces, Milan being the chief objective.

It is still very hot but I hope within a week or so we shall be in cooler weather.

Tuesday 17th August   -   96th Day out

Heard the good news that all the enemy resistance in Sicily has ended. American troops entered Messina it'self at 8.00am this morning, a little later the British 8th Army entered the town from the South.

Other War news very good. On the home front things are going to plan and we are all looking forward to our arrival in England and wondering what will happen when we do get there.

Very busy at the moment trying to get my house ship shape.

Wednesday 18th August   -   97th Day Out

Very heavy raids on Germany by the RAF and the Yanks.

Russians still going ahead.

On the home front, things are much the same, going along nicely and it is actually a little cooler.

Thursday 19th August   -   98th Day Out

War news much the same.

Russians still doing extremely well on all fronts.

Very little news from the Pacific area.

Mr. Churchill and President Roosevelt are to meet in Ottawa, great things are expected in the near future. With the continued bombing of all airfields in Nazi occupied Europe, particularly France and Belgium, a long looked for invasion is imminent.

Saw search lights away to starboard at 8.30am, presumably we were passing Malta to the South.

Friday 20th August   -   99th Day Out

So far I think today has been the hottest day ever.

At 10.00am, we saw an Aircraft Carrier with an escort of four Destroyers moving across our starboard bow and in the direction of Malta. At noon we were opposite Pantelleria, but were rather a long way away, the island was visible but not in any detail.

Whilst at boat stations, four heavy bombers passed across our port bow, and in the direction of Tunis; Presumably looking for subs as there was no fighter escort.

At 9.00am, we are steering practically due West and I should imagine at the moment off Cape Bon.

With our continued good luck and weather we could make Gib Tuesday morning.

Saturday 21st August   -   100th Day Out

Allied Airforces are now pounding airways of Southern Italy, presumably to stop the South bound traffic.

Kiska in the Aleutians have been retaken by the American and Canadian forces.

We have passed Bizerta and are now steaming almost due West.

Sunday 22nd August - **101st Day Out**

What a welcome change this morning, quite cool, the sun being hidden by cloud. It looks as though it may even rain, a typical English sky.

Making very good headway and we should be at Gib on time.

Passed Algiers at 2.00pm, rather a long way off unfortunately, but it gave one an idea of the place; Quite a number of ships at anchor in the bay, and a convoy of six ships with escort vessels about ten miles off the coast and heading North East.

The coolest evening for many a long day.

Monday 23rd August - **102nd Day Out**

News flash this morning, Kharkov has been evacuated by the Germans.

Saw the Spanish coast at 10.00am, Almeria.

Very heavy raids on Southern Italy

German troops reporting to be entering Northern Italy in great strength.

Tuesday 24th August - **103rd Day Out**

Arrived Gibraltar from Alex

Saw the "Rock" this morning at 6.00am, and by 9.00am we were at anchor well inside the bay and near to the Spanish coast.

Quite a lot of Merchantmen here, and smaller Naval craft. Five Aircraft Carriers are alongside.

We have to take on over 1,000 tons of water and it looks as if we might spend the night here. The first water barge came out with about 50 tons.

We were to receive our mail here, that which we missed at Alex, but so far nothing doing.

We should get the lowdown today as to our next port of call (England) we are all on tenterhooks as to where it might be. (Southampton I wonder?)

Very heavy raid on Berlin and we lose fifty eight bombers in the heaviest raid of the War.

Heard we may be here a couple of days, usual trouble, engine room.

The 'HS Dorsetshire' called here on the way home to Avonmouth, that is probably where we shall go.

Wednesday 25th August - **104th Day Out**

Got up hook at 7.00am, and moved in nearer to shore probably to save time and distance for the water barges, and general storing facilities.

Russians still forging ahead.

RAF again bomb Berlin, but on a smaller scale.

Still no definite news as to when we may leave.

Thursday 26th August - **105th Day Out**

Went on shore this morning to do business and get a few necessary items.

It was quite a change to see a shop with real British goods for sale, and no badgering as to price etc., as was the case at Alex.

Most things were plentiful including beer and cigs and no restrictions on either items, tried a beer, 2/8d a large bottle, fairly expensive, but very good!

Returned to ship at noon and found stores alongside, those which I had ordered a couple of hours previously, so down to work.

I hear that we sail tomorrow, and this time I really think it's true.

War news much the same, heavy bombing in Southern Italy continues, and Berlin has had another taste of falling metal. The place is still burning, from Monday and Tuesday's heavy raids I should think. In spite of all the Germans can do, the Russians are gradually pushing them back. According to reports, 12,000 people were killed in Berlin during the RAF Blitz.

Friday 27th August - **106th Day Out**

Left Gibraltar for England

Pulled out at 7.30am, through the boom, turned North and to England. Have no idea as to our destination, but the general conclusion arrived at, is Avonmouth, for my part, any place bar Glasgow or Liverpool!

Cooled down considerably, and if this rate continues it looks as if we shall soon discard our shorts.

War news much the same.

Italy getting it in the neck, probably the other extremity could be more correct!

Saturday 28th August - **107th Day Out**

King Boris of Bulgaria died today, one of Hitler's play things out of the picture!

New Georgia Islands in the Pacific have now been occupied by the Allies, one more island wrested from Japan.

British Naval losses in the Sicilian campaign were, two subs, three torpedo boats, and one motor gun boat.

On the home front things are going very well, and with luck should be off Barry Roads on Thursday night.

Back in Blues today, a sure sign of cooler weather. My clothes seem all bunched up somehow, but I suppose we shall get used to it once again.

Saw several bombers this lunchtime on patrol, Americans I believe.

Sunday 29th August - **108th Day Out**

In spite of it being cool, almost cold, on deck that is, it is still damn hot down below and a busy morning too. Generally things aren't going too well at the moment.

Still doing a steady 10 knots, and I should imagine we are possibly off Lisbon or thereabouts.

The weather as far as I remember is typically English, sun completely clouded over and likely to rain at any moment!

War news good from all fronts.

Nazis have declared Martial law in Denmark, and according to rumour Naval craft have escaped capture by the Nazis by sailing to a Swedish port, forty five other ships were scuttled by their crews in Danish ports. Eight Warships amongst their number.

Monday 30th August - **109th Day Out**

This morning at 9.00am six aircraft, Germans this time, after making quite sure of our markings, dived in formation level with the ship and very close. Their aircraft markings were plainly visible as were the pilots for that matter, after flying around the ship a couple of times they finally made off to the North West.

Several hours later a Yankee bomber gave us a look up.

In the early afternoon we picked up a message to look for a machine that had been downed, made for the spot but found nothing. Russians still doing very well and have re-taken Taranvog a town in the Don Bas area that has been in German hands for over two years. Danes still resisting the Nazis where and whenever possible.

Tuesday 31st August - **110th Day Out**

Still on top and going ahead. The weather, although a mixed bag, fog and rain etc., is tolerable.

I don't think we have sighted a ship of any description since leaving Gib.

A Catalina gave us the once over this morning and promptly reported our position, no further happenings.

War news very good particularly from Russia. It is good too from the South Pacific.

Wednesday 1st September - **111th Day Out**

Made the Fastnet light Southern Ireland this morning 5.00am. I imagine we have about 300 - 350 miles to do, as we should be off Barry Roads early evening tomorrow.

Followed the Irish coast until 6.00pm and when off the Barrels Lightship we changed course for the channel. We should see the Welsh coast 6.00am tomorrow morning; My reckoning!

Thursday 2nd September - **112th Day Out**

Arrived Avonmouth from Gibraltar

Picked up the coast at 5.30am, and if all goes well should make our anchorage tonight.

Arrived off Avonmouth at 6.00pm, and had to wait for the tide; Came in through the locks at 7.00pm, and tied up. No one allowed on shore, I hear that we discharge patients tomorrow morning and then proceed to Liverpool - what a blow!

No letters and very little news really.

Friday 3rd September   -   1st Day Home

Allied landing by British and Canadian forces on Italian mainland opposite Messina.

Started to Disembark this morning at 9.00am, and we were finished by 3.00pm, took on a few stores enough to take us round to Liverpool. It now transpires we are remaining here until further notice, we may go anywhere.

Saturday 4th September   -   2nd Day Home

Ye Gods, don't know whether we're coming or going, first one thing then another, going here going there, crazy is not the word for it.

Fifty percent of the lads are ashore now, the order has just gone through to cancel all leave, sailing tonight for Swansea, goodness only knows what will happen there.

Got away at 7.15pm, and into the lock, had to drop about six feet to tide level. Finally made down stream anchoring at midnight.

Weather on the cold side and not a bit like September, slight rain coming from time to time; Lousy in a few words. Heavy raid on Berlin by the RAF. Allied Forces in Southern Italy have made good progress, capturing Reggio and San Giovanni. Resistance had been fairly light as the fighting force were mainly Iti's.

Sunday 5th September

Arrived Swansea

Came alongside at 10.00am, all sorts of rumours as to what we may do.

Thursday 9th September

Proceeded on leave for six days!

Sunday 12th September

Left Swansea for Glasgow

Tuesday 14th September

Arrived Glasgow

Thursday 16th September

After a long tiring journey arrived back on board.

Friday 17th September

Doing more stocktaking and settling down.

Saturday 18th September

Had to leave the ship today for forty eight hours as it is being fumigated, I got digs at the YMCA and they weren't too bad taking everything into account.

Went to a football match in the afternoon and saw the Rangers beat Lanark 6 - 0, and a very good match too. Went to the pictures in the evening.

Sunday 19th September

Had little to do, so I wrote a few letters. In the afternoon, I had a look around Glasgow.

Went to the ship in the early evening, on the opening up from fumigation, and closed all store rooms and offices etc.

Went to the Merchant Navy Club in the evening and saw a travel film!

Monday 20th September

Heard today that I am to get some more leave, probably a fortnight.
Busy most of the day trying to get straight and preparing for leave.

Tuesday 21st September

Left the ship at 2.30pm, and proceeded to the office for instruction; I am to get seventeen days, returning on 10th October.
I finally left Glasgow at 8.30am, over one hour late.
Caught the 11.30am train from Waterloo for Southampton, arriving at 1.30pm.

Wednesday 22nd September

Moved around all day visiting relatives and friends.

Thursday 23rd September

Much the same again today.

Friday 24th September

Went to Southampton and BOT (board of trade)
Met Mavis in the evening.

Saturday 25th September

Day at home.

Sunday 26th September

Usual routine in the morning and then took Mavis to the station.

Monday 27th September

Went to Southampton again, saw the "Sea Folk" on the train to Weymouth

Tuesday 28th September

Just messing about. Good news from all the battle fronts.

Wednesday 29th September - Saturday 9th October

Still on leave,

Sunday 10th October

Returned from leave.

Monday 11th October

Joined the ship at Glasgow.

Tuesday 12th October

Busy today getting around the ship and taking over.
Portugal gives the Allies the use of the Azores.

Wednesday 13th October

Still Busy.
Italy has gone over to the Allies and has declared War on Germany.

Germans start a Balkan drive.

Russians doing well before Kiev and Gomel, both these cities are likely to fall at any moment.

Thursday 14th October

Heard today that I am to leave the ship, possibly to go on the shore staff for a while.

Friday 15th October

Much the same today, tried to do a little work, but the thought of leaving, somewhat damps my enthusiasm.

Good news from all battle fronts.

Saturday 16th October

Only worked this morning, and spent this afternoon getting correspondence up to date.

More good news from the battle fronts, Russians still going ahead, with the 8th and 5th Armies doing very well in Italy.

Sunday 17th October

Our worst day ever, everything at a standstill, no water or light and virtually little to eat, even the canteen has closed down.

Rained all day, in a few words, a typical Sunday.

Monday 18th October

A little better today, fine and fairly warm.

Still have to go to the canteen for meals.

Tuesday 19th October

Thank goodness, we started messing today, no more trudging through the mud and rain to get something to eat.

Wednesday 20th October

Went into dry dock and should be out again by Friday afternoon.

Heard today that the Officers and Sisters join on Friday.

Thursday 21st October

Finally gave over the job to my relief, so know I am beached once more, although I may remain working on board for a day or so.

Friday 22nd October

Paid off this afternoon (final plunge) but stayed on board to pack, I shall leave the ship tomorrow.

Saturday 23rd October

Got all my gear together and left the ship at 12.30pm, and so to the YMCA for a spell, although it may be only a short one.

Sunday 24th October

I hear that I am to sign on Tuesday and go or at least be prepared to go to join a new Liberty Ship which is at present in the States.

Monday 25th October

Usual procedure, date of signing on has been put back for a week, and now it is next Tuesday, but fortunately I can get leave (six days I think).

Later

Can get away tonight by 9.10pm train for London.

Tuesday 26th October

What a journey, arrived at Euston three hours late owing to fog, finally arrived home at 3.00pm tired, dirty, and fed up.....

Wednesday 27th October

Enjoying a few days break.

Thursday 28th October

Went to Bridgwater

Friday 29th October

Arrived home.

Saturday 30th October

A few odd jobs, and got ready for tomorrow.

Sunday 31st October

Left home for Glasgow - and the unknown!

Chapter Ten

S.S. Samtrent

Thursday 4th November

This morning at 8.00am, all members of the crew of the Liberty Ship mustered at number 4 York Street Glasgow, then boarded a bus and proceeded to Greenock where we passed customs and immigration officials, all baggage was marked and we were to join the vessel M53 for passage to New York. Once on the tender we made down stream, finally pulling up alongside the 'Aquitania,' which proved to be the M53, and our home for the next seven days.

A cabin was allotted to me number 117 B deck. After settling in I had a look around and came across some lads I had met on previous ships.

Got underway at 10.00pm and so into the unknown in more ways that one!

Friday 5th November

Had a minor scare this morning, a plane flew in, but very high, nothing happened so possibly it was one of ours. Boat stations at 10.00am, this will be a daily routine.

Rolling a little and very warm inside the ship otherwise all is ok.

Saturday 6th November

Passed most of the day in going around the ship. In the evening played cards until 11.00pm.

Sunday 7th November

Heard we were doing about 20knots and with luck should be at our destination, which is believed to be New York, about Friday.

Went to the Church service and found it very enjoyable, first time for many moons. The service was taken by an American Padre´.

Sea much calmer today and a trifle warmer.

Monday 8th November

Much the same as yesterday (no service) but boat stations instead.

Tuesday 9th November

Not too pleasant today, heavy sea running and we are rolling somewhat. Although everything is very nice, it's getting a bit boring, nothing to do but eat and sleep, with an occasional game of cards as a diversion.

Wednesday 10th November

Weather has improved and one is able to get a much needed walk.

Thursday 11th November

As for yesterday.

Friday 12th November

Up and about this morning getting a view of everything possible.

Entered the Hudson at 10.00am, and from then on everything was of a particular interest. We passed the famous Coney island to starboard, and made for upstream, where the sky scrapers came into view, really a grand sight.

We then came abreast of the Statue of Liberty, another impressive sight, and so to our berth, number 86.

Once tied up we were soon going, and in quite a short while we were passing customs, down the gangway and into the receiving shed.

Here were the Red Cross awaiting us with coffee and doughnuts. Busses for baggage and cars for the lads, we were soon on the spot and we were taken away, myself and all others to "Times Square Hotel" right in the heart of the city. Finally got a nice two berth bedroom sharing with the third officer Mr. Drummond, what a room! Phone, shower, lav, and all other necessities.

After getting tidied up, I had dinner and phoned my uncle, we finally made contact and had a very pleasant evening.

Saturday 13th November

In view of our being here a few days and having to get security vouchers, I took the opportunity in getting the job done. A rest in the afternoon and took a walk along Broadway in the evening.

Sunday 14th November

Went to Jersey city to see my uncle and stayed till 11.00pm, lost my way coming back, finding myself down town instead of up town!

I asked the way of an American who not only took me home, but stopped in a night-club en route (Havana Madrid) it was all very gay, floor show then dancing. Left at 1.30am, home by 2.00am.

Monday 15th November

Owing to several reasons, particularly financial, I decided to get a job and went to a departmental store for an interview; Mr. Greerys on 43rd Street, got going and was sent to the basement department to help despatch packing materials to the various floors, made good progress in the job and incidentally with the staff, interesting from many points of view!

Tuesday 16th November

Away at work again and here I am to receive five dollars a day, not a great deal but nevertheless very handy.

Wednesday 17th November

Owing to pressure of work stayed until 11.00pm; Five hours overtime.

Thursday 18th November

Much the same today but had a change this evening went to Radio City which is a place I had heard so much about. It's a wonderful building in it'self and the show was extremely good, more so the picture "Claudia", both items took over four hours.

Friday 19th November

As for yesterday (no show)

Saturday 20th November

Change of work today, instead of issuing stores, received new consignments, Christmas boxes and wrappings.

Sunday 21st November

With the Chief and Third Officer I toured the town and went to the Empire State Building, where we went to the top and had a grand view of the city and also the docks and the Hudson River. Went back to the hotel for lunch in the afternoon, then we went to Jersey City to see my uncle, had a very nice time and got home by 10.00pm.

Monday 22nd November

Worked during the morning, but at lunch time received orders to pack and to be away to Portland Maine by 7.00am the next morning. Got paid at the store said a hurried goodbye and was away.

I got packed during the balance of the afternoon and early evening.

A few more cheerios and away to the Grand Central station for the 9.00pm train. A sleeper had been booked and all very nice, bed by 9.30pm and awakened as the train was pulling into Portland.

Tuesday 23rd November

Train arrived at 7.00am, I secured a porter and finally a taxi so away to the Falmouth Hotel and breakfast.
Bitterly cold here and snow falling. I thought of the Middle East and wished I was back there again!
Saw the Captain, and at 10.00pm received details for tomorrow, and then I was finished for the day.

Wednesday 24th November

Not so very much to do after all, got the stores ordered, and then back to the hotel again.
Having nothing at all to do in the evening, I went to the Merchant Navy Club and was fortunate enough to meet a young lady who asked me to spend thanksgiving day at her peoples, I accepted, and now await events!

Thursday 25th November

The hostess of yesterday came and picked me up this morning, so away to the party, which by the way was being held at a house many miles from town, the drive out was very enjoyable and most interesting.
Introduced all round, cocktails, then dinner.
In the late afternoon went sightseeing, finally returning at about 10.00pm, so ended a very nice day.

Friday 26th November

Went to the ship to check stores, and to have a general look around, first impression very nice.

Saturday 27th November

In the morning to the ship again and after a couple of hours I had finished all that I could, so came back to the hotel, and spent the rest of the day getting a few letters off.

Sunday 28th November

Checking stores again in the morning and then had the afternoon off.
Went to the pictures in the evening with my hostess, quite a nice show, saw "Rosey O' Grady" and really enjoyed it.

Monday 29th November

Nothing much happening.

Tuesday 30th November   -   1st Day Out

All is a hurry and busy this morning for we leave the Falmouth Hotel to join the 'Percy H Haughton' as it was known until yesterday. Now it is the 'SS Samtrent.'
Left the hotel at about 9.00am, and by noon we were almost settled on board.
Got busy with the stores getting them on board and prepared for our first meal which was tea.
Later
What a day and by the looks of things many more of the same type are in store.
Sailed from the fitting out berth and cruised around testing gear etc. then finally left for New York.
Still bitterly cold, with a little snow falling, and freezing hard.

Wednesday 1st December   -   2nd Day Out

Underway and still testing gear, compasses, steering gear, etc., then anchored for the night.

Thursday 2nd December   -   3rd Day Out

Proceeding through Cape Cod Canal, what little I saw was very interesting, even pretty in some places.

S.S. 'Samtrent' 30th November 1943   *Roland Jacques*

Friday 3rd December   -   **4th Day Out**

Anchored most of the day owing to fog and did more testing.

Saturday 4th December   -   **5th Day Out**

Fog cleared this morning so away once more and for New York, finally arrived at Brooklyn and tied up at 29th Street Pier at 5.00pm.
A crowd was soon on board rigging out torpedo nets.

Sunday 5th December   -   **6th Day Out**

Got into the loading berth and started to load immediately, also having a few minor repairs done in the meantime .

Monday 6th December   -   **7th Day Out**

Ordered stores for six months, Ye Gods, what a headache, to the agents for this and that, what a journey, underground to here, to there, everywhere in fact. At least that's what it seemed like.

Tuesday 7th December   -   **8th Day Out**

Everything and everybody working at full pressure, personally I have hardly had time to breathe, got to bed by midnight.

Wednesday 8th December   -   **9th Day Out**

Going all out as usual, far too much to give detail. Each day is simply full of work and more work.

Thursday 9th December   -   **10th Day Out**

Even worse today, our stores are arriving, what a mess, what a game, oh for the LC and a little peace a little comfort!

Friday 10th December   -   **11th Day Out**

Still storing.

Saturday 11th December   -   **12th Day Out**

My Birthday; What a day, one of the worst I've ever spent I think, just one mad rush from morning till night. I shall be extremely glad to get to sea, and then try and get a bit ship shape.
Possibly leave tomorrow, thank God, this I say in all sincerity.

Sunday 12th December   -   **13th Day Out**

Pulled out at 5.00pm and down stream, fully loaded with cargo, even some on deck, shall we ever get tidied up?
I hear we are proceeding to Norfolk in Virginia to pick up the next outward convoy.

Monday 13th December   -   **14th Day Out**

Whilst coming down, we run on a mud bank and get stuck for about seven hours, had to wait for the tide to take us off!

Tuesday 14th December   -   **15th Day Out**

Set off this morning at 1.00am for our journey which is believed to be Bombay, and possibly without a stop until we reach Port Said.
It's about the foulest weather imaginable, rough, snow, and damn cold and a new ship into the bargain which is taking some getting used to, this particularly from a working point of view. The ship it'self is doing splendidly and I think it is a good sea boat, we are loaded to the hatch tops, even on top, so she should be steady.
Our convoy is a large one, mostly Liberty Ships, some Yanks, some ours. I have seen a few escort vessels, but the weather has been so dreadful, it is impossible to see all the ships at once. Very strict blackout being observed and I am the blackout officer, come doctor, come chief steward, and every other job that anyone else doesn't want seemingly to do. I look upon this job from now on as my War Effort, and when the War is over I shall not be wanted!

Wednesday 15th December   -   **16th Day Out**

The weather is as foul as ever, I have only seen two more ships besides ours, lost somewhere I suppose, all pull up again later, I presume and hope.
Everybody still working at full pressure. So far I have managed to get at least six hours sleep during twenty four hours and I shall be very thankful when all is straightened out and things are more or less normal, if that is ever possible.

Thursday 16th December   -   **17th Day Out**

It's true this may not be the worst day I have ever spent in my life, but it's awfully near it. Awakened during the night by nearly being thrown out of my bunk, and from then on it has been hell, ship rolled and rolled and did everything I imagine bar turn over. Smashed gear here and there, and threw my stores all over the place, and one could not do a thing about it, it was bad enough in New York what with one thing and another and we prayed to get away, now we almost wish we were back, what a life!

Friday 17th December   -   **18th Day Out**

Possibly a little better today, almost as rough, but distinctly warmer, I imagine this ship will be the last thing in heat once we get where it is warm. Saw some of our escort vessels today, about half our size, some not that, they certainly have my sympathy.
War news has paled, in the light of recent local events, but according to today's news, the first I have seen since leaving, the War still goes on, and I think we are more than holding our own.

Saturday 18th December   -   **19th Day Out**

Heard the bad news that Mr. Churchill was ill again, same complaint pneumonia, he is still in Cairo and his wife has flown out to be with him, to my mind a bad sign, I only hope and pray he will pull through and live at least long enough to see some of the results of his hard labours.

The weather is a little better today and much warmer.

Sunday 19th December - 20th Day Out

Into some more bad weather, it is blowing like hell, mountainous seas rolling and pitching. We are rationed with water, what more could one wish for, I am now going to go to bed and the clock goes back one hour, another great help. I get little sleep enough as it is. If I had only known that the 'Samtrent' was going to be here but without me in it, once I touched England I wouldn't have come again for all the tea in China or India or both for that matter. I have never been so fed up or disgusted in my life and that's saying something.

Monday 20th December - 21st Day Out

This morning at 6.00am when called, although I was awake, I felt like nothing on earth. What a night, I thought the ship would roll it'self inside out, and myself with it. It tossed and turned all night and it was just hell and I had a splitting headache. Liberty Ship? I can't see where the liberty comes in, not at the moment anyway.

Hope to get going and make a show, I think we all had a rough time, and all looked washed out and felt it.

During the day things eased considerably and during the afternoon one or two doors were opened, even a few ports, and life seemed more bearable, then we actually saw the sun for the first time in a week. Had it been shining I still shouldn't have seen it for I was far too busy, and just to think a few months ago I hadn't enough work to keep me out of mischief, what I mean is to keep me occupied!

Aircraft gave us the once over today so we are somewhere within reach of civilisation.

It is now 10.00pm, so I am away to see what sort of a night I can get.

Tuesday 21st December - 22nd Day Out

Strange as it may seem and did seem, I had my best night so far.

The wind has dropped and the sea is comparatively smooth with a moderate swell which gives us an occasional roll at times.

We are now getting things sorted out and some of my work is well in hand, the result of fifteen hours a day non stop for the last fortnight.

My usual afternoon is a thing of the past, no doubt I shall get back to the usual routine at a later date, at about Port Said I should imagine!

Made our Christmas cakes today and hope all will have the chance to enjoy them.

Wednesday 22nd December - 23rd Day Out

Things generally much better, but I am still waiting for the time when I should be looking for a job, this certainly is a full time one so far, as I am never finished, I just leave off.

It's getting quite warm, particularly down below, I can see myself losing weight once we really get where it's warm, anywhere beyond Port Said.

Thursday 23rd December - 24th Day Out

Things really quite nice today, particularly with reference to the weather, ship steady and with only just an occasional roll, what a difference from last week.

Friday 24th December - 25th Day Out

Made a few preparations for Christmas, but I'm afraid it won't make much difference. Personally I shall be glad when it's all over, because really at sea Christmas is only a farce.

Were I still on the 'Llandovery Castle' I have reason to believe I would be home, just my luck, still this may be my last Christmas away from home if the War is over, and hopefully it will be soon.

Christmas Day at Sea
December 25th 1943 - **26th Day Out**
Christmas Message from H.M.
The following is a gracious message from His Majesty the King, addressed to the British Merchant Navy and Fishing Fleets.

Buckingham Palace.

On behalf of my peoples throughout the world, I send Christmas Greetings to all the seamen of the Merchant Navy and the Fishing Fleets, and especially to those who must spend Christmas away from home.

On this 5th Christmas Day of the War, we can listen with an ever growing hope to it's message of peace on earth, even though we cannot forget that there is much to be accomplished, much to be endured, before that message can be fulfilled.

Meanwhile, the thoughts of all of us turn with gratitude to the men who stood steadfast through the darkest days; Who never faltered even when the enemy's attacks on our ships were at their fiercest, and who have played so great a part in the success achieved by our fighting forces in all their overseas theatres of War. Without your devoted service there could be no victory for our arms. From the master in command to the boy on his first voyage you have worked together with the steady discipline of free men who know what is at stake. Your reward is the consciousness of duty done and the affection and respect of all your countrymen.

I send you every good wish for a safe voyage and a happy landfall.

George R.I.

It is 9.00pm, and my Christmas Day is over, all went off very well as far as the job was concerned but the social side was nil!

I had an invitation to see the Captain at 11.00am for the usual, but just couldn't make it. Had another invitation with the Second Engineer at 9.00pm, but turned it down, just well and truly fed up and I don't mean maybe.

Last year we were in Alex and had quite a nice time, plenty to eat and drink etc., perhaps one shouldn't make comparisons. Anyway it's bedtime and time to read and finally forget - what a life!

Sunday 26th December - 27th Day Out

Not quite as much work today, outside of the usual preparation for meals.

I got all my office work up together and was away to my room by 8.00pm, the earliest yet.

Later

The clock goes on one hour so I'm not very early after all!

Monday 27th December - 28th Day Out

Heard the good news this morning that the German ship 'Scharnhorst' had been sunk by our Naval Forces off Norway at North Cape, that's one less to annoy us, no details yet.

Also heard my old ship 'Llandovery Castle' was to make Avonmouth, wish I was on her!

Slightly colder today with a heavy swell at times.

Hope to make Gib by, or possibly on, New Years Day, then there is still another 3,000 miles to go before we finally pull up.

Tuesday 28th December - 29th Day Out

Heard some good news today, Mr. Churchill is now off the danger list.

On board much is the same.

Wednesday 29th December - 30th Day Out

Much the same on board - the home front. Settling down now to a daily routine after about three weeks, but what an ordeal it has been.

Thursday 30th December - 31st Day Out

Still very good weather and still on top.
Big raid on Berlin.

Friday 31st December - 32nd Day Out

Changed positions and course today, some of the convoy carried on and presumably are making Casablanca, whilst the balance of us veered North East and are now heading for Gib, should be there early morning. We will then go on for another fortnight at sea before we pull up. Unless something unusual happens Port Said is our next stop or at least our first one.

Saturday 1st January 1944 - 33rd Day Out

A Happy New Year to all relatives and friends may this New Year see the end of the War then home.
Been messing around all day but still don't know what's been going on, we were to have made Gibraltar today, but perhaps we will slip past during the night and be well inside the Med. before the neutrals realise the fact, or are able to give it out over the radio.

Sunday 2nd January - 34th Day Out

Passed Gib this morning at 9.00am, and saw the "Rock" quite plainly, some of the convoy pulled up there.
We were hoping it would have been possible to get letters away but no such luck, so it looks as if it will have to be either Port Said or Suez.
We are bound for Bombay and then Karachi, from there we have no idea. I hope it's Cape ports, and then home, in which case we should pull up somewhere about the end of April, but it maybe the States again, in which case I will be horribly disappointed.

Monday 3rd January - 35th Day Out

So far we are going along nicely, but seem to be on the top line for any event.
Put our torpedo nets out today for the first time and dropped smoke flares to screen the stern view of the convoy, then got away at good speed at about 10 knots. For a few days this area is apparently the danger area as far as convoys are concerned going through the med. Roll on a couple of weeks and let's get to Port Said and beyond. I hear we may get a few days there, I wonder how far it's true.

Tuesday 4th January - 36th Day Out

Still on top and doing very well, passed Algiers this morning at 10 o'clock.
Went to action stations this evening but nothing actually happened thank the Lord. Another day, and we shall be in a safe zone, from South of Sardinia to well beyond the island of Malta.
What a lovely night, beautiful moonlight, it is like day almost. Other ships of the convoy look like black gems set in a sea of silver, apart from the War Effort what a waste of good time.

Wednesday 5th January - 37th Day Out

The weather of yesterday was but a passing fancy, for at about midnight it started to blow and before morning had reached gale force, I was very glad when the time came to get up, as a matter of fact I was up before time. The weather grew steadily worse as the sun grew, so did the wind, and by noon we were shipping huge green seas and rolling gunwale under, a real nightmare or should I say daymare! Towards 5.00pm it gradually eased off and now at 9.00pm although I can hear the wind howling through the shrouds, life is more tolerable not rolling quite so badly and heaters (steam) are turned on in our cabins, so I am hoping for a better night.
Quite a strange sight tonight, the ships had their steaming lights on, also the side lights, this I am led to believe is because of the position we are in which is between Sicily and Tunis and in the direct shipping route, to and from those mentioned places.

We are now about a third of the way to Port Said, our first port of call and with luck we should be there at about the 12th, which is another eight days.

Rather hope that we stay there for a day or so. In the first place to get a few stores, secondly to stretch the legs and possibly wet the whistle to say nothing of being amongst some other people.

This sameness has a tendency to drive one to distraction, who said variety was the spice of life?

Found some aerographs today, so if I can cadge the typewriter I will try and get a few off in the next day or so.

Thursday 6th January - 38th Day Out

What a night, absolute purgatory, it's true I did go to bed at about 10.00pm and I don't think I got two hours sleep in the whole night. The ship just rolled and rolled at times I was on my back and the next minute or the next second I was on my tummy, sleep was impossible. It is certainly a little better now, so I hope there is rest tonight, I sincerely hope it doesn't blow up, the weather that is!

Passed Cape Bon late last night and Pantelleria this midday, we will possibly see Malta tomorrow morning. I've also heard that we may make Port Said with luck on Tuesday. We have yet to pass within about 300 miles of Crete, so I guess Jerry will have a go sooner or later, we are keeping well in to the coast as we near Tobruk to get all air cover possible, so we may yet be alright. Saw some floating mines this afternoon which passed quite harmlessly, we let go at them with the Horlikons, but they still floated on so we warned the ship astern of us. I don't know whether they had better luck than us.

Too lively to get my aerographs typed, but I hope to be able to do it tomorrow.

Friday 7th January - 39th Day Out

Things on the home front not too bad, still doing a little rolling on and off, I think she has rolled herself from New York!

War news very good; Russians at the old Polish frontier.

Saturday 8th January - 40th Day Out

Still rolling and with a following sea.

Off the coast tonight, almost opposite Benghazi, should be off Derna tomorrow and possibly Tobruk, it seems like old days again in some respects.

Outside of the ships in the convoy we have not seen another vessel.

We now number thirty six of the original ninety vessels, and they keep disappearing some to each port as we move from West to East by the time we get to Port Said I gather we shall be but a few, but not going through the canal I believe.

Sunday 9th January - 41st Day Out

It came at last, at about 12.30pm; The air alarm went and into action stations, got into my clothes somehow and was soon on the job.

'Twas a mild attack really as I think the Jerrys paid more attention to the Westward bound convoy, anyway, all the ships, all thirty six of us, did our stuff and must have kept them off, because the all clear went at about 1.30am so to bed again and I might say I was expecting to get up again at any moment, but luck was with us this time and we slept it out.

Passed Tobruk at noon so are getting well on the way.

Had plenty of air cover today, I hope they will be about tonight, any way I hope Jerry isn't come to that.

This evening we had official news to say that we shot down one bomber last night and neither convoy received either loss or damage; Nice work eh!

Now to bed and let's hope I sleep through this one, but I've got my bluey ready just in case.

Monday 10th January - 42nd Day Out

Had another alert last night, stood by for quite a while but nothing happened.

Passed Alex today at 4.00pm and fairly close, could see all the old land marks and some of the old haunts, almost wished we would make it but let's get to the end of this trip outward, then let's see what happens, possibly South Africa who knows?

A few more of the ships left us today so we are now numbered about twenty seven out of an original ninety.

Tuesday 11th January - **43rd Day Out**

Arrived Port Said

This is the 29th day out from Norfolk Virginia USA, a trip I shall never forget in more ways than one!

On arrival at the port we took up a single line ahead and passed through the boom and so into the canal, no stop and so to Ismalia where we stayed for the night, no blackout, what a God send, and had a real good nights rest.

Wednesday 12th January - **44th Day Out**

Up anchor and away at 7.00am, finally reaching Suez at 11.00am.

Anchored in the Roads and took on water and a few stores then stayed the night, no blackout and another good nights rest.

There are only a few of us proceeding beyond here, I think only seven.

I had one hell of a time with my mail, it had to be all unsealed and only a few minutes to do it in. Whether they will ever reach their destination or not I don't know, I think it is most unlikely.

Couldn't get a wire or anything away.

I guessed mails would be a problem but not to this extent!

Thursday 13th January - **45th Day Out**

We've been out for forty five days and I have not been ashore. I shall soon forget what it is like.

On the way again, our next stop being Aden, or at least it should be.

Hope to get on shore, if only to send a cable and letter maybe.

Weather warming up, we are still in blues, perhaps after Port Sudan it may be warm enough for us to get down to shorts, thank God, if only to save some washing, this damn washing is enough to drive me to drink.

Up to yesterday the fresh water had only been turned on for three hours a day, it's now on all the time, a real treat, no saving a drop in buckets and having a bath in the same amount.

Friday 14th January - **46th Day Out**

Quite nice today, had a couple of hours in the sun.

Saturday 15th January - **47th Day Out**

Still warmer today so we all donned shorts. I hear we get to Aden on Tuesday morning and I think we will possibly get oil and water and be away again.

Sunday 16th January - **48th Day Out**

Much the same today, weather, routine, etc. did a little sunbathing.

Through "Hells Gate" early this morning so we are well towards our destination.

Monday 17th January - **49th Day Out**

Eased down a little today so as to make port in the morning, at 8.00am.

Still plenty of sun, and a strong wind blowing.

Tuesday 18th January - **50th Day Out**

Arrived Aden at 8.00am, and to the outer anchorage, where we dropped hook, all letters were got away, no other means of connecting with the shore.

Took on water and was away by 4.30pm, next stop Karachi in about a week's time, then to Bombay to finish discharging cargo, where then I wonder?

Wednesday 19th January -
51st Day Out

On our own now or at least there is not another ship within fifteen miles either way.

During the day we zig zag and during the night keep a straight course, zig zagging effects a loss of about 10% of the days run, so it will take us a week to make Karachi.

So far I have only heard two men who want to go back to the States, we all want to go to South Africa to load and then home, but I'm very much afraid the two will get their wish, if so a thousand curses!

Hottest day so far, too hot by a long way. I take a little sun daily, but it is too fierce to stay out for very long.

Thursday 20th January   -   **52nd Day Out**

Saw a couple of ships, both Liberty Ships and homeward bound, or at least going West.

War news from Russia still very good.

Friday 21st January   -   **53rd Day Out**

Nothing to report.

Saturday 22nd January   -   **54th Day Out**

According to the latest buzz we arrive at Karachi Tuesday morning but it will be only for a day or two, for nearly all the cargo is for Bombay, which is where I presume we will be for almost a fortnight.

Thank goodness one will be able to stretch ones legs once again.

Sunday 23rd January   -   **55th Day Out**

Just another day.

Monday 24th January   -   **56th Day Out**

Caught up on our old friend 'Samrick' so presume we are nearing our goal, tomorrow I think.

Tuesday 25th January   -   **57th Day Out**

Sighted land this morning at 7.00am, and made for the clear channel.

Saw the dock and lighthouse dead ahead at 10.00am.

Came to anchor until noon then proceeded alongside.

We start to discharge tomorrow.

Wednesday 26th January   -   **58th Day Out**

Very busy discharging cargo.

Have not been able to go ashore, according to those who have, it's a pretty awful dump, so I'm aboard until Bombay.

It's the cool season here by all accounts, but still pretty hot during the day.

No mail here for us, and I think it's difficult to get mail away, well, easy to get away but a devil of a long time to get home, so again Bombay.

No news as to where we may go, but the previous two ships have gone home. I only hope we can complete the trio.

Thursday 27th January   -   **59th Day Out**

Very little news, but plenty of activity.

Friday 28th January   -   **60th Day Out**

As for Thursday.

Saturday 29th January   -   **61st Day Out**

Sunday 30th January   -   **62nd Day Out**

Got all my mail away, even the cables.

'Llanstephan Castle'

Monday 31st January - **63rd Day Out**

Heard no news as to where we are to go or what we are to do apart from going to Bombay to load, I mean discharge then load.

We shall certainly know this week sometime, and we are all more or less on tenterhooks as to what the outcome may be.

Pulling out tomorrow.

Tuesday 1st February - **64th Day Out**

Left Karachi for Bombay, and thank goodness, I never want to see the place again.

We are now at sea doing the usual, about 10 knots and more blackouts.

Wednesday 2nd February - **65th Day Out**

Everything going nicely and we shall make port tomorrow early afternoon.

Thursday 3rd February - **66th Day Out**

Arrived Bombay and anchored in the roads at 2.30pm. Quite a good number of ships here, amongst them the 'Llanstephan Castle.'

Although it's early spring it's very warm, and any rig is order of the day.

So far no mail, I will give up on it I think.

Friday 4th February - **67th Day Out**

Busy discharging cargo, about all one can say apart from the fact I am still waiting for mail.

Saturday 5th February - **68th Day Out**

Mail at last, and although very welcome, it is all November correspondence.

Had six letters altogether, and two aerographs. I haven't been ashore so far and I don't feel a bit like it, browned off in other words.

Shall be glad when we get to sea again, as this is a filthy hole, at least as far as I'm concerned.

Sunday 6th February - **69th Day Out**

Just one of those days.

Monday 7th February - **70th Day Out**

Heard the very good news that we are to go to Durban, thank goodness for that.

Should be pulling out on Thursday if all goes well.

Tuesday 8th February - **71st Day Out**

All is bustle and go to get away on time, very busy myself stocktaking etc.

War news is still good with the Russians well to the front.

Wednesday 9th February - **72nd Day Out**

Almost a week behind with my diary, so a week as far as events go is about to pass quickly. Still very warm, still very busy, still to go ashore.

Thursday 10th February - **73rd Day Out**

About the last day on cargo and we should be ready for sea once again by tomorrow.

Heard we are to make Durban and this is from the powers that be, so we can't be away too quickly as far as I am concerned!

Waiting daily for more mail, but nothing ever arrives, we have had our first and our last by the look of things.

Friday 11th February - **74th Day Out**

All is now ready and it is only minor repairs holding us up.

Saturday 12th February - **75th Day Out**

Battening down and making ready for sea tomorrow, no cargo, we are travelling light.

I hear from good authority that we are going on our own, so it's a case of running the gauntlet, or waiting another ten days for a convoy and who wants to wait ten days with Durban in the offing, lets go says I, fortunately the Captain has interests there to!

Sunday 13th February - **76th Day Out**

The 13th but who cares about that, we pull out and we are on our own, we make for the down channel stream, so out to sea and full speed ahead, 11 knots with Durban our first stop, so we should be there in fourteen days time which will be about the 29th, if we don't ever get there, then I have been wasting my time, but somehow I don't think it's wasted.

Monday 14th February - **77th Day Out**

All is well and we are knocking off the miles, I've put out the torpedo nets this morning as a precaution, possibly only out for a few days while we are near the Indian coast.

Tuesday 15th February - **78th Day Out**

What a day, hot as hell, and more in store I presume, not a wag of air, the sun is enough to burn one.

Did some practice firing at 4.00pm.

Wednesday 16th February - **79th Day Out**

Presumably we are in a fairly safe area, as the torpedo nets were taken in this morning.

Still very hot with the temperature in some parts of the ship as high as 110^0 degrees. The engine room is 130^0 degrees and my room is nearly 100^0 degrees.

Thursday 17th February - **80th Day Out**

Things much the same today, still as hot, still on top, still doing a comfortable 12 knots.

Heard we may arrive Durban 26th February.

Friday 18th February - **81st Day Out**

Did the best run ever today, 350 miles, if we could only keep this up, still we are doing very well, let's hope the good luck continues, making Durban by Sunday week.

Saturday 19th February - **82nd Day Out**

I think we crossed the line today, or was it yesterday? Anyway it's pleasing to know we are gradually running out of the very hot weather, but I presume it will be fairly warm the whole time, even in Durban.

Sunday 20th February - **83rd Day Out**

One more week and then perhaps a diversion of sorts, it will be my first time ashore since leaving Portland Maine. (Pleasure bent) the 30th November '43.

I really believe it's a little cooler today, anyway there is a little more breeze.

Monday 21st February - **84th Day Out**

Hotter than ever today, as a matter of fact it's been the hottest day of the whole voyage (97^0 in the shade).

Very little other news on the home front, apart from the fact we are steaming well, and should make Durban by Saturday.

Tuesday 22nd February - **85th Day Out**

Just another day, just as damn hot.

Wednesday 23rd February - **86th Day Out**

After an extremely hot day, it gradually cooled with quite a breeze during the evening. A heavy thunderstorm during the night, helping to cool things a bit more, but driving the sleepers out to shelter.

Heard we make Durban daybreak Saturday so we should get a decent weekend. What of mail I wonder? I hope there is some waiting for us.

Thursday 24th February - **87th Day Out**

Going along nicely and all is well and possibly a little cooler.

Friday 25th February - **88th Day Out**

Situation well in hand, and if all goes well we should make the Bluff at 7.00am tomorrow. Saw Cape St Lucia at 5.30pm, the first land sighted since Bombay.

I saw an Albatross too, a clear indication we are well South.

Busy getting things a bit ship shape in readiness for tomorrow, we are the first Union Castle Liberty Ship to arrive here, so I presume they will have a prowl around.

Saturday 26th February - **89th Day Out**

Arrived Durban

On going on deck this morning at 6.00am I saw Durban in the distance.

We were in quite close by 8.00am. The pilot came aboard, and before going in we are to test the degaussing gear.
Went in eventually at noon and anchored in the bay alongside the coaling plant at 1.00pm to take a cargo of coal.
We came in quite clean and tidy, goodness only knows what we shall look like going out.
Went on shore for the first time for pleasure since leaving Portland Maine in November.

Sunday 27th February - 90th Day Out

Getting ready to coal and doing a few repairs. .
Got in touch with Freda, possibly go along this evening.
Later
Called at Halvozby Court only to find Freda out, so I went to the Beach hotel to see Mrs. Pace, stayed a while then returned to HC and found her ladyship had returned. Usual introductions and settled down for an hour or so, back on board at midnight.

Monday 28th February - 91st Day Out

Stayed on board and did a few jobs but hope to get away tomorrow.

Tuesday 29th February - 92nd Day Out

Went on shore in the evening, after a quick drink came back on board.

Wednesday 1st March - 93rd Day Out

Made arrangements to meet Mr. Chamberlain and get things settled. Took Freda and Ann along whilst waiting at the office, or at least whilst waiting for Tim. I then went out and did some shopping.
Got down to business at 2.00pm and by 4.00pm all was finished or nearly so.
Went back to Freda's for tea, and then back on board quite early.

Thursday 2nd March - 94th Day Out

On shore quite early, 10.00am and went to the bank, then back to the office and finally settled up. On the way back to Freda's called into see Miss N. Arrived at 2.00pm and after a light lunch had a sleep.
In the evening took Freda to the playhouse to see "The Talk of the Town" a really good show, and enjoyed every minute of it, back by 10.30pm, on board by midnight. Coaling is in full swing and we look a sorry sight!
Heard we are going to Alex, don't quite know whether I am glad or sorry, if this is true and I think it is, we shall arrive at the beginning of the summer. Ye Gods, we are certainly getting our share of hot weather in this joint.

Friday 3rd March - 95th Day Out

Whilst ashore yesterday the ship moved to the oiling site to discharge oil.
We were to leave, but we are now being kept back until tomorrow, took on more coal after moving to the coaling plant again.

Saturday 4th March - 96th Day Out

Pulled out at noon and away to sea and for Alex, with a possible stop or two en route, weather not too good.

Sunday 5th March - 97th Day Out

Weather even worse today, and we are taking on board huge seas at times, and things are far from pleasant, but no doubt in a day or so we shall be in the tropics again. Apart from the heat we should have settled down.
Heard that our first port of call is Mombassa.

Monday 6th March - 98th Day Out

What a day, what a night, had very little rest during the day and very little sleep during the night, just been rolling and shipping tons of water.
After our rough passage of the last two days, very little coal dust remains, an ill wind etc!

Thought of getting some letters typed, but it's rolling so much the machine simply refuses to work, better luck tomorrow may be.

Tuesday 7th March - 99th Day Out

Still as bad as ever, and we are rolling ship side under, what a life, should run into better weather soon. Still no letters written, see what tomorrow has in store.

Wednesday 8th March - 100th Day Out

Got down to business this afternoon, and typed five letters, good going I think.
Weather has eased, hardly any wind and a flat sea, it is supposed to be warm tomorrow.

Thursday 9th March - 101st Day Out

Just as I expected, today has been a real teaser and now what with blackout, it is hot enough to kill one, shall we ever strike the happy medium?
Very heavy raid on Berlin with losses fairly light.
Russians still forging ahead.
In Italy things seem to be at a standstill.
I hear that we will make Mombassa on Monday.

Friday 10th March - 102nd Day Out

Still very very hot, haven't been comfortable all day.
Put out the torpedo nets this morning, a clear indication we are in the danger zone but thank goodness that doesn't mean aircraft, we will get more than our share of that later on no doubt.

Saturday 11th March - 103rd Day Out

Still every bit as warm, and hardly any breeze at all, still hoping it will eventually cool down a little.
It's definitely Mombassa and we should make it on Monday if all goes well, what of our mail I wonder?
War news much the same, with Russians going ahead, and the Armies in Italy probing for positions.
Heavy raid on Marseilles by home based bombers, very effective, with no losses.

Sunday 12th March - 104th Day Out

A little more breeze today thank goodness.
Saw a plane this morning, came around and gave us the once over.
War news much the same.

Monday 13th March - 105th Day Out

Arrived Mombassa

Saw the land at about 6.00am, entered the swept channel and made for the harbour. We came to anchor inside at about 10.00am, and proceeded to take on water.
Left at 2.30pm, linking up with the convoy, consisting at the moment of fourteen vessels including another Castle boat the 'Sandown.'
Very much cooler during the afternoon, and quite a strong wind blowing, I only hope it lasts.
Very good news from the Russian Front in the South. German troops seem to be falling back all along the front of over 1,000 miles.
Red Army now only 120 miles from the Czech frontier.

Tuesday 14th March - 106th Day Out

The convoy is formed up and we are steaming along at a steady 8 knots, this means Aden sometime next week.
Put out the torpedo nets this morning, so we feel a little safer, although I've got an outside billet!
Russians still doing extremely well and continuing their advance on the extreme Southern Front.
In view of Mr. Churchill's comment in the press, the Second Front is not so very far off, possibly this month.

Wednesday 15th March   -   **107th Day Out**

All out air offensive on Germany, a prelude to the opening of the Second Front.
Other War news very good, with things beginning to move on the Italian Front.

Thursday 16th March   -   **108th Day Out**

News generally much the same.

Friday 17th March   -   **109th Day Out**

Things generally much the same.

Saturday 18th March   -   **110th Day Out**

Very little news on the home front, still jogging along at a steady 8 knots, maybe it's safer in convoy, but it's very slow, we make Aden on Tuesday sometime. Still a nice breeze with us and in comparison to other days it's quite cool.

Sunday 19th March   -   **111th Day Out**

Eased down today so as to make Aden Wednesday morning, we are doing about 6 knots. Trouble in the offing last night, but it never came our way.

Monday 20th March   -   **112th Day Out**

Passed Cape Guardajui and so around the corner into the Gulf of Aden, it is very much warmer and no breeze either. Looking forward to some mail!
One of our convoy left us yesterday, so now we are fifteen altogether, and all on top!
A plane has been around these last two mornings at daybreak to give us the once over.

Tuesday 21st March   -   **113th Day Out**

A little cooler today, possibly because it's cloudy and the sun is hidden.
Another ship left us this evening at 5.00pm and carried straight on, we did a big sweep to starboard and are now heading direct for Aden.
It's pitch black at the moment (8.00pm) but I heard a plane go over. One of ours I presume, they know we are about, so at least that's something.
I heard the 'Llandovery Castle' giving out her position and she must be somewhere off Tunis towards Algiers, possibly going home.
Arriving tomorrow at 9.00am, and have just heard that all our sea mail is at Alex, Ye Gods, shall we ever get it!

Wednesday 22nd March   -   **114th Day Out**

Arrived Aden going North

Saw the land first thing this morning, and after a reshuffle we take up a position astern, and make for the anchorage arriving at 10.00am. About a dozen other ships here, making about thirty in total.
Very little happened during the balance of the day. No mail, all at Alex! I've heard that one before. Took on a little water during late afternoon. At 6.00pm we pulled out on our own, and with a little luck should make Suez next Tuesday.
It has been very warm at anchor but every indication of it being cooler once we get well out to sea.
I've got my usual weekly additions away, living in hopes that I'll receive something in return at our next port (still hoping).

Thursday 23rd March   -   **115th Day Out**

Well underway this morning with a strong following wind and it is fairly cool at the moment.
Later
"Ot as 'ell" but still we are in a fairly safe quarter, something to be thankful for.

War news still good from Russia, whilst at home the Airforce are battering at Germany day and night.

In Italy conditions are pretty grim and very little headway is being made.

Friday 24th March — 116th Day Out

Just another day just as hot and just as boring.

Saturday 25th March — 117th Day Out

Same again.

Sunday 26th March — 118th Day Out

At the moment it is very much cooler with a lovely breeze blowing from the North, I hope to goodness it continues for a while.

A massive raid by the RAF on Berlin and over 2,500 tons of bombs dropped, a fire in the centre of the city is reported to be six miles long.

Russian troops have captured more towns in the Southern sector and are still going ahead.

Bitter fighting still raging in what was the town of Cassino, with no material gain on either side.

Mr. Churchill speaks tonight, maybe we will get the low down.

Monday 27th March — 119th Day Out

I think this has been one of the best days of the voyage with regard to weather, cool with a nice wind and no sea running, we've had it cooler, damn cold in fact, then the sea was rough and rather spoilt things.

Gun practice this afternoon.

Arriving at Suez tomorrow morning - letters, I wonder?

Tuesday 28th March — 120th Day Out

Arrived Suez

On turning to this morning a sand storm was blowing and land marks were blotted out, at 7.00am it became so bad, that we dropped anchor. It cleared at about 10.30am sufficiently to allow us to get under way again, we now make Port Tewfik.

Came to anchor in the Roads at about 11.00am, and stayed for the night. Mail arrived during the evening, had three from home, but there is still a lot in the offing somewhere though.

Wednesday 29th March — 121st Day Out

Arrived Port Said

We were away this morning at 6.00am and through the canal to Port Said. There was quite a lot of shipping in the canal and we docked at about 4.30pm, then tied up for the night, if rumour is to be believed we leave again tomorrow at 11.00am - no leave!

Thursday 30th March — 122nd Day Out

Pulled out this morning just after 11.00am, and once outside waited for the convoy to form up, there are now fourteen ships altogether with a Naval escort, doing a steady 8 knots and with luck should be tied up in Alex by this time tomorrow (6.00pm).

The weather has changed considerably, and most of us have discarded shorts for the usual rig, which at the moment is blues.

We were all hoping our mail would be here tomorrow, now owing to our being a bit on the late side, we shall possibly have to wait until Saturday .

Friday 31st March — 123rd Day Out

Arrived Alex from Port Said

Left the convoy at 3.00pm and left for Alex, where we arrived at 5.00pm. Had a good look for the 'Llandovery Castle,' but no luck.

Imperial Airways Caledonia flying boat delivering mail

One of the first dozen people I saw was Hassen who informed me that the 'Llandovery Castle' had left over a fortnight ago homeward bound!

We anchored in the bay for the night and will go alongside at 8,00am in the morning.

No mail!

Saturday 1st April   -   124th Day Out

Came in alongside this morning to discharge our cargo, 10,000 tons of coal and I hear it's going to take ten days, Ye Gods what a mess!

Went to Raz el Din for the mail and sure enough some letters were there, although I received fifteen altogether, it should have been many more, they've gone to Bombay I dare say, or gone for good.

One of my letters was dated January, so much for those poor souls who continue to go down to the sea in ships.

Sunday 2nd April   -   125th Day Out

What an awful day, coal dust everywhere, and we have nine days of this to endure, one can't see the difference between the outside of the ship or the inside, coal dust in the food even!

Got a few letters written and getting things generally up to date.

All sorts of yarns going around, States, South Africa, Home, even Italy, but only time will tell.

Monday 3rd April   -   126th Day Out

Things are just as black as ever, and in more ways than one.

Went to the bank this morning to see if transfers had been effected, all was ok.

Went to Hasseram and also went to get my watch glass put back in. I did a little shopping and back by noon, so much for my first jaunt ashore. I may go to the pictures one evening.

Sidi Gabir Alexandria 11th April 1944

Tuesday 4th April - **127th Day Out**

Just a huge black spot, never in all my life have I seen such a bally mess, coal dust everywhere, thank God when Saturday comes, and this business is finished and we can all get clean once again.

No news as to what we may do, but plenty of rumours.

Wednesday 5th April - **128th Day Out**

Living in one huge cloud of dust.

Thursday 6th April - **129th Day Out**

Living for the day when we finish discharging coal.

Friday 7th April - **130th Day Out**

Hope to finish discharging coal tomorrow other news much the same.

Saturday 8th April - **131st Day Out**

Have just heard we are going to USA. Ye Gods, another long commission.

Sunday 9th April - **132nd Day Out**

Pulled out this morning and tied up in the bay, leaving sometime this week for Port Said to load ballast and then Norfolk Virginia for orders, I hope it's load for home even if it is the Second Front.

Monday 10th April - **133rd Day Out**

Trying to get the ship cleaned up, but what a hopeless task, I don't think it can ever be the same again.

Saw a ship with a split personality !

Other half

'Winchester Castle'

Tuesday 11th April - **134th Day Out**

Pulled away from the old moorings and are now tied to a buoy waiting to move off. No convoy this time thank goodness, but I suppose we shall be in one, once we leave Port Said. At the moment there are just two of us.

Passed through the boom at 5.00pm, and we are on our own after all. We shall be there quicker anyway we hope. Passed the 'Samsteel' on the way out, another of our Liberty Ships on the run from Alex to Taranto and they are welcome to it, The 'Samflora' is also here. I guess she had already gone to port for ballast, and we shall I assume, be in the same USA convoy.

We are both going to Port Said to load ballast (sand) none here I suppose.

Our old friend of other days, the 'Samrick', came in this morning with coal, we wish her luck!

Had our balloon fitted today, sold out of windmills maybe!

Hope to be there in the morning and leave for the long trek on Thursday.

Wednesday 12th April - **135th Day Out**

Arrived Port Said from Alex

After a peaceful journey, we arrived off Port Said 9.00am but had to wait until a convoy (ten ships) went in first. The 'Winchester Castle' was amongst them, all are now tied up here as we are. Heard we may leave Friday, let's get to sea and get straight again.

Thursday 13th April - **136th Day Out**

Dashed ashore this morning to get a few essentials before finally pushing off. It will be at least another month before I set foot on land again.

Went to the 'Winchester Castle' to see a few old ship mates and what a mess, not a bit like a Union Castle Liner.

Busy during the evening getting some letters off, a final cheerio.

Friday 14th April - **137th Day Out**

'Sandown Castle'   *Roland Jacques*

Left Port Said for USA

Pulled out at about 1.30pm, and made for the Roads, we are to be in a convoy, and shall remain so I suppose until Norfolk, or some place. We now have about 6,000 miles in front of us, and I guess it will take us well over three weeks, possibly a month if it's a slow convoy.

Took up stations and we are the centre ship of the line of five ships, all balloons up so away to Alex where more ships will join us.

Saturday 15th April   -   138th Day Out

Doing a steady 6 knots, and losing time for the other ships to get ready.

They join us at about 4.00pm, off to Alex, there are now about thirty of us.

Sunday 16th April   -   139th Day Out

All very peaceful at the moment, weather quite good too, not so very hot and a moderate sea. Had a little gun practice though just in case.

Monday 17th April   -   140th Day Out

Put our torpedo nets out this morning as another precaution. We are now off Sollum and can see the land quite easily, we shall soon be about three hundred miles off Crete and to the nearest based enemy aircraft, so if we don't get a visit tonight I shall be very surprised but not disappointed!

So far things have been very quiet, let's hope it continues.

Tuesday 18th April   -   141st Day Out

The expected never happened; But I heard this morning that a convoy had been attacked during the night off Sicily, still that's their funeral I suppose.

Yesterday at 4.00pm the convoy that passed us going into Port Said passed us again going Westwards. Within three hours they were in sight and out of sight! Had to look over the side to see if we had stopped but no, we are still doing a steady 6 knots, they were doing sixteen I should imagine, we get planes for all that!

Passed Benghazi during the night, so every hour takes us further away from the danger area, but still further would suit us all very much better.

Wednesday 19th April -   142nd Day Out

We are now doing 5 knots and if this continues it will now take us five months to get to New York! What the idea is goodness only knows, but I hope someone does.

Saw several mines today, and all passed harmlessly, but we tried to explode some with gunfire.

Nearing Malta and there are plenty of planes about.

Weather changed a good deal, it's quite cold today but very little wind and a calm sea.

Thursday 20th April   -   143rd Day Out

Passed Malta this afternoon away to starboard and another convoy has joined up with ours, there are now just over sixty ships and it is quite an impressive sight. Out of the whole bunch I should imagine that there are over fifty Liberty Ships.

A smoke and a pint at Bar 20
Sunday 16th April 1944

Even colder today thank goodness, a real change, have got the woollies out!

War news much the same, Russians on the point of taking Sebastopol.

In Italy apart from the air assaults things are fairly quiet.

Friday 21st April   -   144th Day Out

Passed the island of Pantelleria this morning, so we must have put on more speed doing about 8 knots I think.

At the moment we are opposite Bizerta and I can see the town quite easily; More ships have joined the convoy, we now number over one hundred.

Changed our escorts this evening we now have Yankee destroyers with us, this I presume will be our escort all the way across.

Passed a convoy this afternoon Eastward bound, well over one hundred ships, we're beginning to wonder if there are any ships outside the Med.

Every day we expect to hear that the Second Front has opened up, thought it might have been yesterday which was Hitler's birthday, particularly as there is no moon, it will come I suppose!

Saturday 22nd April   -   145th Day Out

Off Bizerta

Nothing very much happened, a few ships left the convoy today and several more joined. Saw the 'Llandovery' this morning Eastward bound, for Malta I think.

Sunday 23rd April   -   146th Day Out

Off Algiers

Just another day.

The Harbour Malta

Monday 24th April - **147th Day Out**

Passed Oman, more Warships joined us and a few left.
War news much the same, we are all waiting to hear whether or not the Second Front has opened up.
Russians are on the point of taking Sebastopol.

Tuesday 25th April - **148th Day Out**

Passed Gib at 8.00pm, and a few more ships left us, so we are now on the long run to Norfolk, about sixty ships now altogether, with an American Destroyer escort.
Feeling a bit browned off, just the same thing day after day with not a change of any description we all hope it's the UK from the States.

Wednesday 26th April - **149th Day Out**

Doing very nicely, and very little to report.

Thursday 27th April - **150th Day Out**

Still on top and weather improving daily.

Friday 28th April - **151st Day Out**

Had an idea that once near the Azores some more ships would leave us and strike North for home but that's not so. We are now a convoy of nearly ninety ships and all for the States, one in every ten being a Liberty Ship a good proof of the USA war effort.
A plane from the Azores gave us the once over this evening so all is well.

Saturday 29th April - **152nd Day Out**

Even warmer today and doing about 9 knots.

Sunday 30th April - **153rd Day Out**

A day of rest?

Monday 1st May - **154th Day Out**

General and War news much the same; A little diversion on the home front, a man from the ship ahead of us fell overboard and we of course passed close to him. We tossed a life jacket to him and sent word by Morse lamp to the destroyer escort to try and get him, this they did and he was got safely aboard, although it was getting fairly dark.

Tuesday 2nd May - **155th Day Out**

The man who fell overboard last night was returned to his ship this morning, a line was fired from the destroyer on to the ship, he was then hauled across on a breeches buoy.

Heard that we had made a small raid on the island of Crete, gathered useful information, and captured a few prisoners including a Panzer General.

Wednesday 3rd May - **156th Day Out**

Weather not too good at the moment otherwise things are tolerable.

Thursday 4th May - **157th Day Out**

She started her nonsense again, one hell of a time last night; At times the rolling was so bad that people were thrown out of their bunks - I got out!

Friday 5th May - **158th Day Out**

A slight improvement today, gradually running out of it, (maybe).

Very little news on the home front, as I have said many times before, one day is much the same as another.

Saturday 6th May - **159th Day Out**

Heard this morning that we may get there on Thursday next. I can't say I'm very excited about it, as far as I'm concerned it just spells more work.

Sunday 7th May - **160th Day Out**

Another day of rest.

Reorganised the convoy this afternoon and we are detailed for New York, what next I wonder? Load for home, or Alex I guess.

Monday 8th May - **161st Day Out**

Very much warmer today, some have even donned shorts!

Still going along nicely and should make New York by Thursday morning.

We are all wondering if it is to be home or back to Alex again.

Tuesday 9th May - **162nd Day Out**

Convoy separated today, with a larger portion of them making for Norfolk Virginia. About thirty of us are making for New York.

Other news much the same.

War news still the same, possibly Russia is waiting for the Second Front to open, and one big general offensive will then begin, from Russia, from Italy and from the West.

Whatever happens I hope to goodness we soon finish Germany off, then the Japs then peace.

Later

Just heard that Sebastopol has fallen to the Russians, one more good stroke!

Wednesday 10th May   -   **163rd Day Out**

On the last lap, and may probably rest at anchor tonight.

Thursday 11th May   -   **164th Day Out**

Arrived New York

Had to anchor off the Ambrose Light owing to fog, and what a time we had, about thirty to forty ships all blowing sirens at the same time, no sleep for me. Stayed at anchor until 1.00pm and then made for the Hudson River and so to our berth which I believe to be number thirty five.

Later

Owing to the many ships that had to anchor in the river, we will not move in until 8.00am tomorrow morning. Had a quiet night and no blackout.

Five months ago today we left New York for the Middle and Far East, Durban, Alex, and so back here again.

Lots of speculation as to what we may or may not do, only a matter of hours before we know the worst - or best!

Friday 12th May   -   **165th Day Out**

Up anchor this morning and way up stream to 35 berth, this being almost opposite Manhattan Island.

Once alongside we start to discharge cargo i.e. sand ballast.

Heard officially that we go to India again, this time Calcutta, not so healthy.

Also heard the good news that the Allies in Italy had started their great offensive which, if successful, should culminate in the fall of Rome (the first phase).

The 5th and 8th Armies meet bitter resistance in the mountains thrust.

In some places we have advanced up to three miles. Air assault in Nazi held Europe has continued now for twenty eight days without respite.

Had some mail today four letters, three of which are from home and one from Miss H.

Saturday 13th May   -   **166th Day Out**

News from Italy still very good, Allies still advancing in spite of stiff resistance.

Russians on the move again.

Waiting now for the Second Front.

By the looks of things we shall be here for about a fortnight to three weeks.

Sunday 14th May   -   **167th Day Out**

Had a few hours off today went over to New Jersey to see my uncle.

Quite a nice change really, but things weren't too pleasant, his wife having passed on the previous week.

Monday 15th May   -   **168th Day Out**

Plenty of activity on board, but we haven't started to load yet; So far no cargo for us. It would appear we are bound for the Indian run again, but it's not quite settled yet. Who knows, we may go home?

Good news is still coming in from Russia, and Italy, there it looks as if we really intend to do something this time; According to today's news we have advanced in some places as much as seven miles.

Tuesday 16th May   -   **169th Day Out**

Still good news coming in from Italy and it looks as if we mean business this time.

Very busy getting in stores etc., thank goodness there was not as much as last time.

Wednesday 17th May   -   **170th Day Out**

Generally much the same all round, and we are all ready to start loading.

Allies still going ahead in Italy, and according to the papers here, the Second Front is liable to open at any time.

Thursday 18th May - **171st Day Out**

Went ashore today for a few hours and combined business with pleasure buying stores for the canteen and seeing places.
British 8th Army have captured Cassino, and are driving on towards the Hitler line.
I have heard that we leave here a week on Monday.

Friday 19th May - **172nd Day Out**

Fairly steady day, and trying to get a bit square.
Received letters from home also a cablegram.

Saturday 20th May - **173rd Day Out**

Pretty busy on cargo, and by the looks of things we should be away by the end of the week.
Good news coming in from Italy.

Sunday 21st May - **174th Day Out**

One lovely day off, I toured Long Island.

Monday 22nd May - **175th Day Out**

Good news from all War Fronts, particularly from Italy.
Very busy on board getting cargo stowed etc.
Change in the weather, it has been raining most of the day.

Tuesday 23rd May - **176th Day Out**

Things much the same.

Wednesday 24th May - **177th Day Out**

Had my last evening ashore, and went to the pictures with my American lady friend and saw "See Here Private Hargrove" it was very funny, I've never laughed so much for many a long time.

Thursday 25th May - **178th Day Out**

Went over to New Jersey to say cheerio to my Uncle, and got back at 5.00pm.
Heard the good news that the Allied Forces in Italy have connected with troops at the Anzio bridgehead, they have gone sixty miles in fourteen days. What of Rome?

Friday 26th May - **179th Day Out**

Beginning to rush things a bit to get us away over the weekend.
Good news from all War Fronts, there has been a 6,000 bomber raid on occupied Europe.

Saturday 27th May - **180th Day Out**

Practically finished cargo apart from that which will go on deck.
Hoping to get mail before we leave.

Sunday 28th May - **181st Day Out**

All is squared up and we are ready for sea, seven weeks in front of us, Ye Gods! We leave dock first thing in the morning, possibly go to anchor in the river to await orders.

Monday 29th May - **182nd Day Out**

Pulled away from the quay this morning and so out into the river, did a turn, up and down and then came to anchor. The river is simply full of ships of every description. At a rough guess we should be near our destination about 22nd July, and home by the end of October.

Chapter Eleven

Back to India

Tuesday 30th May - **183rd Day Out**

Left New York

Started on our long voyage this morning at 2.00am, to Calcutta.

Left the anchorage in Hudson River and are now making Norfolk to pick up a convoy for Gibraltar.

Wednesday 31st May - **184th Day Out**

Arrived off Norfolk at 2.00pm after being in convoy from New York.

Came to anchor in the Roads with at least another fifty or more vessels, we will be here till Friday.

Thursday 1st June - **185th Day Out**

Lying at anchor all day, and it's as hot as hell.

Friday 2nd June - **186th Day Out**

Convoy started to get underway at daybreak, we pulled anchor at 7.30pm, and so away to sea and Calcutta. I've been all day trying to catch up and form up, it's now 6.30pm and we still mess about.

All this has been taking place under the watchful eye of the Navy and the US Airforce.

Very warm again today so much so that I have got into shorts, now I presume that's my rig for next four months, what an outlook!

Saturday 3rd June - **187th Day Out**

Settling down to the long voyage lying ahead, things not too bad generally.

Weather is still particularly hot, but a very nice breeze is with us at the moment.

The convoy comprises of one hundred ships mostly Liberty Ships and tankers.

We have an American Destroyer escort, also an American flat top (aircraft carrier) so we should be alright.

Sunday 4th June - **188th Day Out**

Into our stride and settled down to a steady 9 knots, much better than our previous trip.

Weather seems to be on the change, more wind and not so hot.

Allies Capture Rome

Monday 5th June - **189th Day Out**

D-Day; Allied Forces land on the Normandy coast with Navy well to the front.

Tuesday 6th June - **190th Day Out**

The invasion still making headway, but the position as yet still has to be clarified, to get a true vision of what's actually happened.

Italy is still very good, with the Allies past Rome and they have crossed the Tibor in many places.

Possibly a general offensive is imminent on the Eastern Front.

Wednesday 7th June - **191st Day Out**

War news from the Western Front is still a bit confused, and I only wish we were where we could get a paper.

Things generally seem pretty good, our losses to date have not been as heavy as expected.
Weather here much cooler today.

Thursday 8th June - 192nd Day Out

British and Canadians have further consolidated their positions in the Caen Bayeaux area.
Arms and supplies of all kinds are being landed without respite.
In the air it is estimated that the Allies have a two hundred to one superiority, this should convince the Nazis that we intend to stay put.

Friday 9th June - 193rd Day Out

Good news from all War Fronts.
I hear we may get to Gibraltar a week today.

Saturday 10th June - 194th Day Out

All news much the same.

Sunday 11th June - 195th Day Out

Allied troops are making good progress in the Cherbourg peninsular with the Yanks only seventeen miles from the actual town it'self.
The 21st German Panzer division under Irwin Rommel is counter attacking many places but without result.
Mosquitoes again raided Berlin using four-ton block busters dropping one hundred and twenty in three minutes.
From Algiers came the news that the Allies there are advancing on all fronts.
In Italy the Americans are to the North of Viterbo. The 8th Army have captured Avezzano, whilst the Indians of the 8th Army have captured Biscara on the Adriatic coast.
The Russians have opened up a new offensive in the Karelin Isthmus against the Finns and have advanced twenty two miles in two days.
Germany has now three fronts on which she is engaged , an impossible task to say the least.
Americans in the Pacific have attacked the Isles of Guam and Saipan, getting nearer each week to the vital ports of Japan proper.

Monday 12th June - 196th Day Out

Allies still doing very well in Normandy.
Mr. Churchill, and General Smuts have visited the beaches travelling in 'HMS Calvin,' One thousand four hundred American bombers attacked targets in the area of the beaches and Paris.
German prisoners taken to date, number over 10,000.
On the Italian Front things are even better, all the Allied Front is moving forward.
Russians within forty miles of Vipuri.
I hear we make Gib possibly on Saturday.

Tuesday 13th June - 197th Day Out

Allied bombers still blasting German oil and industrial centres, and are advancing slowly but surely, but nevertheless on all sectors of the Normandy front.
Still going ahead in Italy too.
Here on the home front the expected hot weather is long delayed, and today it's even cooler, cold in fact.
So far we have had a much quicker voyage than last time, reducing the time by several days, but we still have a long way to go and perhaps the worst part of the voyage from a danger point of view anyway.

Wednesday 14th June - 198th Day Out

Fierce fighting is raging in all the Normandy sectors, and Rommel has flung in another Panzer division.   British and Canadians have made further small gains, whilst the Yanks have yielded a little ground.
Allied Airforces continue to batter German airfields in Northern France, and also troop concentration behind the battle area.

Both armies advancing steadily on the Italian Front.

Weather here has taken a turn for the worse, and has turned quite cold, and we have been forced into semi winter clothing again, there is a fairly high sea running and the ship is heaving slightly.

Thursday 15th June - 199th Day Out

Good progress by the Allies is reported from some sectors in the Normandy battle zone.

Allied Airforces still going all out and giving wonderful support to our ground forces.

There are advances reported also in Italy and Russia.

American super Flying Fortresses based somewhere in China have carried out a daylight raid on Tokyo.

Weather improving gradually.

Friday 16th June - 200th Day Out

News much the same from all fronts.

Pilotless aircraft have been used against Britain for the first time.

For reasons unknown we are not making Gibraltar until Sunday, it was originally supposed to be Friday.

Saturday 17th June - 201st Day Out

News still good from all fronts.

Sunday 18th June - 202nd Day Out

Passed Gibraltar this morning at 9.00am, and so into the Med. once again. I heard the good news today that the Yanks had cut the Cherbourg peninsular and had now bottled up about 30,000 Germans who can now only surrender or fight to a finish.

Allies in Italy advancing on all fronts and have reached Berugia, so we have now about half of Italy freed of the Germans.

Russians still going ahead.

Good news from the Balkans too, General Tito forces have killed 8,000 Jerrys in two weeks.

We put out torpedo nets at noon, not that we want to catch anything, just don't want to be caught!

Pilotless Nazi planes over the South Coast.

Monday 19th June - 203rd Day Out

All balloons up today, getting nearer to the War maybe.

Passed Oman at 4.00pm.

American troops have launched a general offensive and the going is good.

Good news also from Italy and Russia.

Mr. Churchill stated unofficially that the War may be over by the end of the summer, he gave no reason for saying so but he has without doubt something up his sleeve, if only it is true.

Several more Destroyers joined us yesterday.

A quiet night, although we expected the worse.

Tuesday 20th June - 204th Day Out

All sorts of funny things have joined us today; Aircraft Carriers, and more Destroyers some say a rescue ship is with us, I can't make up my mind as to whether I like that or not!

Passed Algiers at 5.00pm

In the hot weather again now, there to remain for many weeks I dare say.

Wednesday 21st June - 205th Day Out

American troops are now on the outskirts of Cherbourg.

Robot planes coming in for quite a lot of attention, the planes themselves being attacked from all angles, whilst the ramps from where they take off were heavily bombed yesterday.

Good news from all other theatres of War.

On the home front we had a blue warning but nothing more developed.

Yanks shoot down 300 Jap planes in and around Saipan, their greatest bag!

Thursday 22nd June - 206th Day Out

Passed Cape Bon at 2.00pm.

Several more ships join us, so far none have left.

British escort vessels take over as from today.

Weather quite good considering where we are really, but it is quite cool

Still good news coming in from all quarters, we now await the result of the Naval battle which is raging in the Pacific between American and Jap fleets.

Hope the latter get a damn good tousing!

Friday 23rd June - 207th Day Out

The encirclement of Cherbourg is now almost complete, but the Germans so far have refused to surrender, other War news is much the same.

German forces reported a Russian offensive from White Russia.

Two thirds of the convoy left us today for Italy, we now number about thirty ships.

Saturday 24th June - 208th Day Out

All War news much the same.

Sunday 25th June - 209th Day Out

American bombers attack Rumanian oil wells for the second day running.

We are now opposite Benghazi, but of course well to the North.

Tomorrow we will pass Derna.

Monday 26th June - 210th Day Out

War news good from all fronts.

Passed Tobruk.

Battle for Cherbourg practically over.

Tuesday 27th June - 211th Day Out

Germans being pushed back on all fronts.

Enemy resistance is practically finished in Cherbourg.

Heavy fighting in and around Vileosk and it looks as if the Germans will be surrounded if they don't soon pull out.

Wednesday 28th June - 212th Day Out

Arrived Port Said

Cherbourg has fallen to the Allies.

Vileosk also has been taken by the Russians.

Advances in Italy and also in Burma.

On all fronts, and in every theatre of war the Allies are going forward .

Entered the canal at 8.00am, and then to the Bitter Lakes where we anchored for the night.

Particularly warm, a forerunner of what we have to come.

Thursday 29th June - 213th Day Out

Still good news from all battle fronts.

After staying in the lakes all night, we up anchor and are away by 5.00am.

No mail so far, I wonder what await's us at Suez, what the soldier shot at I guess!

Had a wonderful surprise on arrival at Suez, mail arrived, and there were twenty two for me, everything and everybody is OK.

We are now waiting for water.

Friday 30th June - **214th Day Out**

After waiting all night for water, it finally arrived at 9.00am, we were away again by noon.
Heard good news from all fronts, the Russians are doing particularly well.

Saturday 1st July - **215th Day Out**

In the Red sea, and it's as hot as hell, my cabin of all places is a 100_ degrees.
Heard the good news that Minsk has been bypassed by the Russians, this means they are only 200 miles from Germany proper (Prussia). The Allies being 270 miles, the net is slowly but surely closing in and I am patiently waiting for the squeal.
I hope and pray the War in Europe at least will be over this year I for one want to get back and start a new life. That is what I intend to do.

Sunday 2nd July - **216th Day Out**

All is well on the battle fronts, Russians driving on the Northern frontier of Poland.
The Allies in Italy are making for Florence.
In France the battle is about to begin.
Here it is even hotter than yesterday, even the little breeze that there is seems hot, or at least warm, we are now passing Port Sudan.

Monday 3rd July - **217th Day Out**

Hottest day ever.

Tuesday 4th July - **218th Day Out**

Russians doing extremely well and now converging on Minsk, the last big German strong hold in White Russia.
More flying bombs dropped on Southern England, I imagine Southampton to be well in the area, I sincerely hope everything is OK.
Thunder, rain, and lightning last night, seems as if we may have reached the tail of a monsoon already, anyway it is a trifle cooler.

Wednesday 5th July - **219th Day Out**

Arrived Aden 8.00am.
Quite a large number of ships here, so we are hoping to get an escort to our next destination.

Thursday 6th July - **220th Day Out**

Pulled out this morning at 6.00am, and so away to Colombo, where we oil before proceeding to Madras.
Heat almost unbearable.

Friday 7th July - **221st Day Out**

Just as hot as ever but there is more breeze and it looks as if we may be running into bad weather.

Saturday 8th July - **222nd Day Out**

Ran into terrible bad weather, we are just steadily breaking up everything from crockery to boats.
The hot weather is awful it's true, but this is even worse, apart from it being dangerous these ships are not too good at the best of times, roll on the UK and let's leave this curse behind.

Sunday 9th July - **223rd Day Out**

One of our worst days on this ship, struck a monsoon, to soon for me, and the ship just rolled herself silly, sleep is almost impossible and with any kind of work out of the question, what a life!

War news pretty good, favourable reports coming in from all battle fronts.

Monday 10th July - 224th Day Out

A little better on the home front, still heavy seas running, and it is possible we shall have this weather for many days yet, roll on "Mavidene!" *

"Monty" opened an offensive in Normandy and Allied troops have taken Caen.

Russians still forging ahead and have taken Vilna, and are within one hundred miles of the Prussian border, by next week this time I hope they are attacking Prussia proper.

Possibly the War will be over this year after all.

According to the news flying bombs are still being fired at Southern England.

Tuesday 11th July - 225th Day Out

Much of the same sort of news from the various battle fronts.

Still fairly rough on the home front.

Wednesday 12th July - 226th Day Out

Things seem to be going very well in Normandy, with the Allies advancing, although very slowly.

Much the same sort of thing prevails in Italy but we are steadily gaining ground.

Over 1,100 American Fortresses and Liberators from Britain escorted by hundreds of long range fighters made the heaviest daylight raid yet on the Nazi Party's home at Munich.

Berlin was also attack by Mosquitoes.

The Germans sent more of their flying bombs over Southern England during Monday and Tuesday, but for the first time none were directed at London.

The Russian offensive in White Russia is making sweeping progress.

On the home front things are not too bad, the weather having abated somewhat.

Hope to make Colombo on Saturday sometime, with luck.

Thursday 13th July - 227th Day Out

Very much better today and it's quite a treat to be more or less steady. It's true it is very much warmer, but that's by far the lesser of the two evils.

War news very much the same.

Friday 14th July - 228th Day Out

Still on top and doing 11 knots, hope to make Colombo tomorrow at noon.

Torpedo nets are out, which is a clear indication we are nearing a shipping route where subs may be operating. Let's hope we make it safely now after battling along for about seven weeks.

Heard that Vilna has been finally taken by the Russians, this means they are well on the way to East Prussia, around fifty miles by my guess.

Saturday 15th July - 229th Day Out

Arrive Colombo

Sighted the island at about 9.30am, finally anchored at noon.

Quite a few ships here, Merchant and Navy.

We have to go from here in a convoy, and may have to wait several days there's no other news and no mail.

Sunday 16th July - 230th Day Out

We are here until Wednesday, when we go in convoy to Madras, should be there on Sunday.

War news much the same, going out on all fronts.

Russians getting nearer to German Frontier, what then I wonder?

'Samflora' came in this morning, hoped to be able to go on board whilst in Madras.

* "Mavidene" was the name of his house on Sarisbury Hill near Southampton

Monday 17th July - **231st Day Out**

Things beginning to move in Normandy.

Tuesday 18th July - **232nd Day Out**

Just another day of waiting.

Wednesday 19th July - **233rd Day Out**

Left Colombo

Pulled out this morning at 9.00am, and so away to Calcutta, originally we were calling at Madras but being in charge of the convoy we have to go straight on, which is rather a good thing in a way, let us soon know the worst or the best!

Thursday 20th July - **234th Day Out**

Only eighteen ships in the convoy and at the moment everything is going according to plan.
Good news from all the battle fronts.

Friday 21st July - **235th Day Out**

Even better news from the War fronts today, in Normandy, the British and Canadian troops are now well South of Caen, and armoured unit's have entered a town six miles to the South.
Russian troops are at the gates of Lwow, whilst to the North the Russians are shelling the railway connecting Brest Litovsk with Bialystok. Leghorn and Ancona in Italy has also been taken.
Still quiet on the home front, doing a steady 8 knots and we may be in Calcutta next Wednesday.

Saturday 22nd July - **236th Day Out**

Off Madras at 4.00pm and several ships leave us, including the 'Samflora'. We are to go on.
Weather still good, but very hot, the much dreaded monsoon has so far missed us, let's hope our luck continues.

Sunday 23rd July - **237th Day Out**

A day of rest?

Monday 24th July - **238th Day Out**

Good news from all the battle fronts.
On the home front things are much the same, weather fairly cool and still on top.

Tuesday 25th July - **239th Day Out**

Arrived off the pilot ship at the entrance to the Hugli River, but owing to the very rough weather, pilots could not come out so we had to turn about and wait until morning. Steaming South all night we returned in the morning to make another attempt.

Wednesday 26th July - **240th Day Out**

Turned around this morning at 7.00am, and are now making the river entrance once again, sincerely hope we make it this time as we have been at sea two months, and a few days in port would be very much appreciated.

Thursday 27th July - **241st Day Out**

Didn't make it; Stayed at anchor all night.
This morning the pilot came on board and we were away by 7.00am at the moment we are going up river, but it's very doubtful we shall make Calcutta, possibly anchor again, and then proceed to the docks in the morning, I wonder what awaits us. Personally I think it will be Durban.

Friday 28th July   -   **242nd Day Out**

Arrived Calcutta

Got up hook this morning and away by 6.00am.
After a somewhat difficult task we were tied up, and now await our fate.
Usual swarms of Indians on board but no one seems bent on any particular job.
Received our mail and the usual good news.

Saturday 29th July   -   **243rd Day Out**

Started off loading cargo, by the speed of things we are here at least a fortnight possibly three weeks.
The usual yarns going around and home seems to be the most popular one, personally I will wait and see. I would much rather say we may go back to the States, but we may possibly know this next week sometime.

Sunday 30th July   -   **244th Day Out**

Usual routine, busy on cargo, or their idea of busy anyway.

Monday 31st July   -   **245th Day Out**

It's now cargo everyday, working day and night when weather permit's.
Killing hot here, plenty of rain, flies and mosquitoes, if we weren't fed up before arrival here we certainly are now!

Tuesday 1st August   -   **246th Day Out**

Heard the good news that we are going home.

Wednesday 2nd August   -   **247th Day Out**

Everybody a little happier; Now the question is what port, any port I say as long as it's home.
Good news from all the War Fronts.

Thursday 3rd August   -   **248th Day Out**

Much the same today.

Friday 4th August   -   **249th Day Out**

Still busy with cargo, still hot and still raining and it's rained for every half of the day since we have been here.

Saturday 5th August   -   **250th Day Out**

The only bright feature is the War news, and it looks as though the War might be over this year, as far as Europe is concerned.

Sunday 6th August   -   **251st Day Out**

Just another day.

Monday 7th August   -   **252nd Day Out**

Still battling with cargo, and once empty we load for home, that's all that matters as far as I'm concerned.

Tuesday 8th August   -   **253rd Day Out**

Wednesday 9th August   -   **254th Day Out**

Thursday 10th August   -   **255th Day Out**

Dry docked.

Friday 11th August   -   **256th Day Out**

Finished dry docking.

Saturday 12th August   -   **257th Day Out**

Waiting for orders.

Sunday 13th August   -   **258th Day Out**

Same as yesterday.

Monday 21st August   -   **266th Day Out**

Just waiting.

Tuesday 22nd August   -   **267th Day Out**

The long awaited day at last! We pull away from the quay for the stream, and so away to sea.
Not a man is sorry; Everybody absolutely fed up to the teeth.
We have started to count the days when we shall be home, it maybe the middle of October or even before, that's at least seven weeks.

Wednesday 23rd August   -   **268th Day Out**

Owing to the low tide we can only get to the sea by hops sort of thing, so we are going down river in stages; A few miles then anchor, a few more then anchor again.
Still as hot and as miserable as ever.

Thursday 24th August   -   **269th Day Out**

Still making down stream, reached the open sea at 4.00pm, anchored and stayed the night.

Friday 25th August   -   **270th Day Out**

Still resting at anchor, several Warships joined us here and I think we are away in convoy this evening sometime.
This is the first stage of the journey and already we have wasted two days.
Good news from all the battle fronts.

Friday 1st September   -   **278th Day Out**

One week gone and we arrive at Colombo, let's hope our stay is short and soon away again.
Very good news still coming in from all the battle fronts.

Later

Our stay was short, arrived at noon and away at 5.00pm, should have taken in fuel but we were told to make the next port and oil there, which is about 350 miles away.
We are now on our own once again, let's hope that luck is still with us, particularly as we are going home.

Saturday 2nd September   -   **279th Day Out**

Very good news from France and Russian.
The 8th Army has opened up a full scale offensive against the Gothic line.

Sunday 3rd September   -   **280th Day Out**

Arrived Cochin to take on fuel.

Went in alongside the oil tanker 'Empire Thain' which serves as a storage tank unable to go to sea, having been torpedoed off Crete, she made the canal and got to Suez, only to be bumped again and finally towed to Cochin.
This is quite a nice place, and particularly clean in comparison to Calcutta.
Good news coming in from all the battle fronts.

Monday 4th September - **281st Day Out**

Pulled out this afternoon at 2.00pm and away for Aden, where we are to take on the maximum fuel, about 3,000 tons.

We hope to make it by the 12th October and with good luck maybe we shall.

Not quite so hot and a fairly good wind, we are all hoping the monsoon has passed, we had our share outward bound.

Tuesday 5th September - **282nd Day Out**

Still on top and doing a steady 10 knots, every day being one day nearer home.

Wednesday 6th September - **283rd Day Out**

Going along nicely, doing a steady 10 knots, moderate sea, with a fairly strong wind at times.

Wonderful news from all the War Fronts, particularly Northern France.

Thursday 7th September - **284th Day Out**

Doing the usual, and all is well.

Friday 8th September - **285th Day Out**

A little cooler.

Saturday 9th September - **286th Day Out**

Still very cool and much appreciated.

War news still very good.

Sunday 10th September - **287th Day Out**

Much the same as far as weather and news is concerned.

Monday 11th September - **288th Day Out**

Entered the Gulf of Aden, so we shall make port tomorrow.

Struck a hot patch, and is it hot?

Tuesday 12th September - **289th Day Out**

Arrived Aden

Arrived and left Aden after a stay of only four hours.

Wednesday 13th September - **290th Day Out**

Entered the Red sea, and ran into very hot weather.

Thursday 14th September - **291st Day Out**

One of our hottest days.

Going along at about 11 knots, and we should make Suez on Sunday sometime.

Friday 15th September - **292nd Day Out**

A little cooler today, and long may it continue.

War news very good.

Saturday 16th September - **293rd Day Out**

Allied Forces now fighting on a 500 mile front, from Belgium to the Swiss frontier.

Red Army forces have crossed Bulgaria and entered Yugoslavia, joining up with the Tito forces.
Doing well , and should arrive midday tomorrow.

Sunday 17th September - 294th Day Out

Arrived Suez Homeward Bound

Dropped anchor at noon and now await orders and mail.
Mail arrived at 6.00pm, (all is well) orders at 8.00pm. Taking on fuel here, so by tomorrow night we should be ready for the final lap - thank God.

Monday 18th September - 295th Day Out

Doing engine repairs - that's delay.

Tuesday 19th September - 296th Day Out

Wednesday 20th September - 297th Day Out

Thursday 21st September - 298th Day Out

Engine repairs.

Friday 22nd September - 299th Day Out

Still here, and to me just wasting good time, I presume we are awaiting a convoy as the engines are now repaired and all stores aboard. We will possibly move tomorrow as far as Port Said, then more waiting. We all had hoped to be home by the 15th October but I doubt it now, goodness only knows what course we shall take from Gib, not too far out I hope, now that the French coast is clear.

Saturday 23rd September - 300th Day Out

Moved away from Suez at 6.30am, and to the Bitter Lakes arriving at 11.00am where we remained all night, and shall be away in the morning.

Sunday 24th September - 301st Day Out

Arrived Port Said Homeward Bound

Arrived at Port Said 11.00am, and tied up near the oiling site.
Apparently we are here to remain until Tuesday.
Went on shore in the evening with Mr. Hopper and had quite a nice time, it made a real change anyway.

Monday 25th September - 302nd Day Out

Usual routine, took on a few stores.
War news still good, it is quite nice to be able to get a paper.

Tuesday 26th September - 303rd Day Out

Left Port Said for Home - Three Weeks Run?

Made a very good start, almost running down a small coaster!
We were convoyed up by 6.00pm.

Wednesday 27th September - 304th Day Out

Passed Alex at noon, could pick out all the old land marks, Raz-el-Tin, Cecil Hotel etc.
Should get a quiet voyage this time, Jerry being too busy in other places.

Thursday 28th September - **305th Day Out**

Doing the usual convoy run about 8 knots, still I guess they know best.
Still as warm as ever; Had been hoping it would cool down.

Friday 29th September - **306th Day Out**

Ambling along at 7 knots, Ye Gods, I could walk faster.
Good War news.

Saturday 30th September - **307th Day Out**

Getting cooler, at least we have a nice cool breeze with us, we will possibly pull up at Malta sometime tomorrow night.
Heard that the big guns at Calais had been silenced for good.

Sunday 1st October - **308th Day Out**

Getting towards the Malta Channel, when we received news to turnabout. The area is mined I guess, so now at the moment we are making Port Said at least in that direction, more hours lost. Nearer than ever now to my date of arrival at home 20th October!
Later
Turned again, and this time going South West of the island; Actually about six hours have been lost.

Monday 2nd October - **309th Day Out**

Getting much cooler and with the strong wind the sea is getting up.
Towards evening, the wind is semi gale force and we are beginning to pitch and we are taking on board heavy seas.
Our forces in Holland are meeting with heavy resistance but we still gain a little ground.
Guns at Calais silenced for good, all the enemy giving up the ghost.

Tuesday 3rd October - **310th Day Out**

Very heavy sea today, and a lovely wind, the ship is much cooler but unfortunately we have to keep most of the ports closed, so we really benefit very little.
Passed Pantelleria this midday, so we should get round the corner sometime tomorrow (Cape Bon) then a straight run to Gib.

Wednesday 4th October - **311th Day Out**

Passed Bizerta at noon.
Once round the corner we lost the heavy seas, we are now once more, more or less on an even keel, we hope to make Gib on Saturday or the very latest Sunday.

Thursday 5th October - **312th Day Out**

Apart from the heavy swell, things are quite comfortable, lovely cool weather and only a fortnight to go!

Friday 6th October - **313th Day Out**

Passed Algiers.

Saturday 7th October - **314th Day Out**

Going along nicely and should make Gib tomorrow.

Sunday 8th October - **315th Day Out**

Passed Gib at noon, so we are now on the last lap.
No idea as to where we may go, possibly London but I think possibly Swansea.

Monday 9th October   -   **316th Day Out**

Slowed down for a little to allow more ships to join us from Casablanca.

Underway once again with ten ships having joined us, so there are now twenty two of us with the 'St. Clare' as a rescue ship, let's hope she won't be wanted.

Tuesday 10th October   -   **317th Day Out**

Doing nicely, weather quite cool with a calm sea.

Off Lisbon at noon.

Wednesday 11th October   -   **318th Day Out**

Heard we go to Falmouth for orders, so it looks as if we may be going to London after all.

For my part any port in the South will do.

Weather not quite so good today, heavy sea swell, typical bay weather and the ship is rolling somewhat, but we are homeward bound, that's the main thing.

Thursday 12th October   -   **319th Day Out**

Ran into a bad storm today (in the bay) and she is doing everything but roll over. It is impossible to get any sleep during the night.

Saw a plane this morning (one of ours) so I presume we have been reported.

Friday 13th October   -   **320th Day Out**

Weather is bad today, and had another awful night, roll on tomorrow when we shall be stationery for a while.

Tons of bookwork to do, and with this rolling it's a very hard job.

Saturday 14th October   -   **321st Day Out**

Arrived off Falmouth at 8.00pm, we came to anchor, what a wonderful sight and change.

Hope to get in a good nights sleep.

Heard that we are going to Hull.

Sunday 15th October   -   **322nd Day Out**

Got away this morning at 9.00am, in a very calm sea, we are making progress at a rate of 7 knots. Convoys, Ye Gods!

May possibly stop at Cowes Roads for a while, I can't see myself getting home this next week, but oh for that months holiday, it's getting near to Christmas anyway.

Monday 16th October   -   **323rd Day Out**

Arrived off Pompey at 9.00am, and anchored in the Cowes Roads, so near and yet so far. One mass of ships here of all kinds and sizes, seeing all familiar spots, makes one quite homesick, next week maybe.

Awaiting orders at the moment.

We have all the cold weather we need now. The many months that we have looked forward to such a time as this, if only there were no delays.

Tuesday 17th October   -   **324th Day Out**

Away again and this time as far as Chatham.

Arrived and now await orders.

The channel just seems full of ships and both ports we touched are full to capacity, what a contrast to this time last year.

Heard this evening that we leave tomorrow morning for Hull, definitely our last stage!

Only hope the weather holds good, no fogs etc and lets get tied up for a while, not forgetting of course the months leave!

Wednesday 18th October   -   325th Day Out

Underway at 8.00am, and so to hell, sorry I mean Hull!

Saw hundreds of planes this morning making their way to France, with fighter escort. What a lovely sight, and going the right way too. By what I gather we should with all luck be tied up by tomorrow night and paid off on Friday sometime.

All sorts of orders for me I guess, but I have the last say this time, it's leave first, work after!

Thursday 19th October   -   326th Day Out

Arrived Hull

Friday 20th October

Off loading cases of tea.

Sunday 29th October

Leave for Dundee.

Tuesday 31st October

Arrive Dundee

Paid off and RESIGNED.

I Finally left the 'Samtrent' on 14th November 1944 and then proceeded to Glasgow office for leave. I started my leave on the 15th November for twenty six days.

11th December 1944

My Birthday

Left home to travel to Glasgow to join 'Winchester Castle' as Second Steward.

12th December 1944

Arrived Glasgow

Taking stock of my new surroundings I was not too impressed. I hear we are to remain here until the end of February. The ship is undergoing an extensive refit for some special mission but I've no idea as to what it may be. At the moment the crew just carry on the usual ship's routine whilst repair work is going on around us.

Whilst I was in Calcutta on the 'Samtrent' wearing shorts I became the target for many mosquitoes, sitting at my knee hole desk writing and typing in the dark almost, the mosquitoes seemed to congregate and I realised that I may suffer for it later on, so much so now, that I have become too ill to work. So I am remaining in my cabin and I have asked one of the lads to ask the ship's doctor to come and see me.

He came and saw me and gave me the once over and a few pills, but in spite of that I have got steadily worse and another doctor has been sent for. I am now shaking like an aspen leaf. An ambulance has been sent for and I am to be taken to hospital.

30th December 1944

I have just woken up in hospital. I remember nothing since leaving the ship. I have been told I have a severe attack of Malaria and I shall be in hospital for at least a couple more weeks.

January 1945

I gradually started to get better at the end of the second week, and now I feel quite good again, I have received a lot of parcels from home, which cheered me up no end. As I was feeling better I decided to start to give the nurses

'Stirling Castle'

a hand with meals and cleaning medical instruments etc. All the nurses were quite good and one nurse gave me undivided attention whenever possible. In turn, I told her that towards the end of the week I would take her to town to have a drink and perhaps go to a show. So the evening before I left we did just that and had a lovely time and enjoyed every minute of it!

I was almost sorry I had to leave, but all good things come to an end.

The following morning I was discharged and made my way to the Union Castle office in Glasgow, where they made arrangements for me to go on leave (convalescent) and when I felt fit enough I was to inform them. This I did in due course and once again I found myself on the shore staff where I remained working until the end of the War in August.

Eventually on 1st September 1945 I was allowed to go back to sea and I joined the 'Stirling Castle' at Liverpool as Second Steward and sailed for Australia taking as passengers over two hundred females who had married Australians during the War, there were no men on board apart from the crew, but that's another story!

Sailed from Southampton the 24th March for the Middle East, Western Route, via Cape Town, calling at Freetown en route.

Total number of Crew :- 142.

Pace W.	Master.	Ferris D.	Chief Engineer.
Lloyd G.	Chf Officer.	Parker N.	2nd Engineer.
Bainbridge E.	2nd Officer.	Sparkes F.	Inter 2nd "
Anson W.	Extra -do-	Aldred C.	Jun 2nd "
Davies T.	3rd Officer.	Hilliard A.	3rd "
Evans W.	4th Officer.	Lockhead G.	4th "
Owen H.	Purser.	Hunt A.	5th "
Townshend W.	1st Radio.	Williamson R.	Electrician.
Phillips D.	2nd Radio.	Balmforth G.	Dnkyman.
Mc/Lennon K.	3rd Radio.	Norris A.	Storekeeper.
Haxton R.	Carpenter.	Childs H.	Greaser.
Wood M.	Carpenters Mate.	Paul W.	-do-
Johnson V.	Bos'un.	Hurst G.	-do-
Hall H.	Bos'uns Mate.	Tudor E.	-do-
Watson A.	-do-	Curtis G.	-do-
Roberts H.	Lamps.	Foreman A.	Fireman.
Spencer R.	Q.M.	Houghton G.	-do-
Pearce J.	Q.M.	Banks W.	-do-
Jarrold J.	Q.M.	Harnett E.	-do-
Whittaker A.	Q.M.	Tall T.	-do-
Mason J.	Q.M.	Hosey A.	-do-
Bruce W.	Q.M.	Tutton K.	-do-
Mathews J.	Storekeeper.	Venton C.	-do-
Hughes J.	A.B.	Churchill A.	-do-
Stone F.	A.B.	Rew G.	Cleaner.
Bendell W.	A.B.	Calloway F.	-do-
Slade D.	A.B.	Saunders P.	5th Engineer.
Hague S.	A.B.	O'Connor R.	Firemens Stwd.
Smith A.	A.B.	Lacey R.	Fireman.
Butcher E.	A.B.		
Hill F.	Sailor.		
Mailing C.	A.B.	Bazeley T.	Chief Steward.
Young W.	Sailor.	Penny L.F.	2nd Stwd.
Coulson E.	-do-	Birkenshaw A.	Barman.
Mackenzie M.	-do-	Holloway E.	Canteen Stwd.
Boyd G.	-do-	Weston A.	Storekeeper.
Hall L.	A.B.	Cheal E.C.	Asst "
Gillespie E.	O.S.	Nason E	Asst "
Bray E.	O.S.	Hay A.	Linen Stwd.
Vine G.	O.S.	Voller B.	Hairdresser.
Richmond J.	O.S.	Mc/Nair J.	Printer.
Miller J.	Dk Boy.	Bloomfield E.	Librarian.
Lansley J.	-do-	Palmer W.	Smokeroom Stwd.
Floyd G.	-do-	Robinson J.	Nightwatchman.
Amor J.	-do-	Grundy B.	Officers Stwd.
Gamble F.	-do-	Mc/Hugh F.	Engineers Stwd.
Robinson E.	-do-	Pye G.	Asst "
Westley E.	Sailor.	Wood P.	Captains Stwd.
		Butt L.	Head Waiter.
		Green A.	Asst Stwd.
		Mason R.	-do-
		Ames J.	-do-
		Stinton E.	-do-
		Mc/Farlane W.	Ward Stwd.
		Curtis C.	-do-
		Rogers H.	-do-
		Longman J.	-do-
		Thatcher L.	-do-
		Parry W.	B.R.Stwd.
		Davis W.	-do-
		Ward E.	Pantryman.
		Hill J.	Asst Pants.
		Day H.	Asst Pants.
		Pestifield W.	Boots.
		Clark D.	Peak Stwd.
		Clarke Miss.	Stewardess.
		Bugden H.	Laundryman.
		Grant W.	Asst "

Inventory of crew "Llandovery Castle" 1941

INDEX OF PHOTOGRAPHS AND ILLUSTRATIONS

Acknowledgements

My special thanks to the following people for helping me to realise Leslie's dream and making the publication of these journals a reality.

To:- Paul Cave, my publisher, and Editor of 'Hampshire - The County Magazine.' Kim my wife for typing the manuscript and for all her other valuable input. Roland Jacques and the Southern African Postcard Research Group, for the use of photographs and postcards, also A. Duncan and B & A Fielden and any other copyright holders, whose pictures I have used, but have been unable to trace and make contact with. Leslie Ruecroft and Union Castle Mail Steamship Company Ltd., for help, encouragement and contact names. Barry and the team at Graphic Direct for the mammoth typesetting and printing job that they undertook to complete in such a short space of time. To the enduring memory of Miriam Harris, and finally to my mother Mrs Penny for entrusting the journals to me.